SBAC

S0-AXT-053

JUL - - 2022

The Baseball Talmud

The Definitive Position-by-Position Ranking of Baseball's Chosen Players

HOWARD MEGDAL

TRIUMPH
B O O K S

Copyright © 2009, 2022 by Howard Megdal

No part of this publication may be reproduced, stored in a retrieval system, or transmitted in any form by any means, electronic, mechanical, photocopying, or otherwise, without the prior written permission of the publisher, Triumph Books LLC, 814 North Franklin Street, Chicago, Illinois 60610.

The Library of Congress has catalogued the previous edition as follows:

Megdal, Howard
    The baseball Talmud: The definitive position-by-position ranking of baseball's chosen players / Howard Megdal with illustrations by George Brace.—1st ed.
    p. cm.
ISBN-13: 978-0-06-155843-6
    1. Jewish baseball players—United States—Biography. 2. Jewish baseball players—United States—History. 3. Baseball—United States—Statistics. 4. Baseball—Records—United States. I. Title.
    GV865.A1M44   2009
    796.357092'2—dc22
    [B]   2008040534
    09 10 11 12 13   OV/RED   10 9 8 7 6 5 4 3 2 1

This book is available in quantity at special discounts for your group or organization. For further information, contact:
    Triumph Books LLC
    814 North Franklin Street
    Chicago, Illinois 60610
    (312) 337-0747
    www.triumphbooks.com

Printed in U.S.A.
ISBN: 978-1-63727-001-1
Design by Patricia Frey
Photos courtesy of AP Images

Mirabelle and Juliet, this book is for you, leaders of the Jewish people in the century to come. Thank you for telling me, every time I returned to my home office, "You've got this!" Someday, they'll write books about you both.

Thank you to Rachel. Everything, everything is for you, my love.

Contents

Foreword

On the morning after the final game of the 2021 World Series, I got a text from my friend Brian about a moment in that game, which the rest of the planet had barely noticed but one that was basically the highlight of his night.

I'll paraphrase it here, if only to perform the valuable service of translating it from text-ese to English: "In the second inning, Max Fried pitched to Alex Bregman, who flew out to Joc Pederson..."

This was not a play that changed the World Series. Of the 14.3 million people who watched this game, it's a good guess that it never even registered on the radar screens of 14.299 million of them. But for people like my friend, this was a moment that rocked their universe. Here's why: never before in baseball history had three Jewish players taken the field in the same World Series game at the same time. And then, somehow or other, the stars lined up, and all three were involved in the same World Series play. "Amazing," Brian wrote in that text.

And for folks like him, Jews with an appreciation for the nuances of baseball and the greatest Jewish ballplayers debate that has long been a mean-ingful baseball subplot in their world, it truly was. Long after they'll forget the

Jorge Soler home run that gave the Atlanta Braves the lead for good that night, they'll remember this moment in time, when three Jewish baseball players got mixed up in one magical play.

And now, the more I think about that, the more I think it sums up why Howard Megdal had to write this book—because it matters. Not for everyone walking around Planet Earth but for people like my friend Brian, who need to know all there is to know about the history of Jews in baseball.

My mother-in-law, Norma, is one of those people. Every once in a while, a letter will arrive in my mailbox from her. And inside is a story she found somewhere on all the Jews currently playing Major League Baseball, or the 10 greatest Jewish players in history, or the day Sandy Koufax chose Yom Kippur observance over the World Series, or about some new book or film on Hank Greenberg and what it meant to be a Jewish athlete in the 1930s and 1940s. She's sure I know about all those things. She just wants to make sure I don't forget about any of those things. And thanks to books like this, none of us will ever forget.

Because I've turned into that quirky writer who is supposed to know all the trivia there is to know in baseball, people love to spring questions on me—in my travels, on social media, via email—that they expect the answers to. It's a fun niche but not always.

Ask me how many times the 2011 St. Louis Cardinals were one strike away from losing the World Series to the Texas Rangers, I can answer that. And it feels good to know the stuff I know, even if I have no idea why it's still rattling around my brain. But ask me how many Jewish shortstops there have been in history, and...*ummm...ehhh...hmmm...hey—can I get back to you on that one?* What I've often struggled with, though, is where would you find something like that? I can't ask the Elias Sports Bureau. I can't ask FanGraphs, Baseball-Reference.com, or STATS Perform. Their databases aren't programmed that way. So boy, am I grateful that Howard Megdal came along to write *The Baseball Talmud.*

You know how cool and helpful it is to have the rankings in this book—all of them exhaustively researched and explained in meticulous detail? You know how huge it is that someone as sharp, eloquent, and thoughtful as Howard has done his best to settle stuff like the *Who's the greatest Jewish third baseman ever—Al Rosen or Alex Bregman* debate, coming soon to a Bar Mitzvah reception near you?

For the people who never even noticed that Fried pitched to Bregman, who flied out to Pederson, it may not matter. But for those of us who notice, who care, or are alerted by our helpful friends that we *should* notice and care, this is one of the most important baseball books ever written. And it's one I'll keep handy on a shelf near me every day of the year—so that the next time I'm asked One of Those Questions, I'll be ready. Thank you, Howard!

—Jayson Stark, senior baseball writer, The Athletic

Introduction

Back when I wrote the first edition of *The Baseball Talmud* in 2007 and 2008, I celebrated the accomplishments, large and small, of the greatest Jewish players in the American game. On my subsequent book tour, and in the years since, I engaged with fans young and old who cared about this the way I did.

But I'm not sure until recently I understood why.

I grew up in Cherry Hill, New Jersey, an oasis of a Jewish community. Yes, it's true, we had Fred Neulander, a murdering rabbi, but even that didn't disrupt our Jewish enclave all that much beyond a significant number of sensational headlines and casting a retroactive pall on the Bar Mitzvahs of some of my friends.

After all, we had four other reform congregations to choose from. And the worst thing my rabbi ever did was let the liturgy linger a bit too long at the concluding service on Yom Kippur even as the bagels and cream cheese and lox sat on the counter at home, calling me.

So sure, I held an appreciation, a love for the strikeouts of Sandy Koufax, the home runs of Hank Greenberg, and, as I grew up, the stardom of Shawn Green and Mike Lieberthal, who lived 10 minutes from my home. But I didn't truly see high stakes in reveling in those stories, let alone telling them. But there has always been an imperative behind those older than I in the current chronological sampling of American Jews, something that moved well beyond delight into what felt like need. People on my book tour didn't just engage—they'd beseech me about a favored player.

And the America we all live in now helps explain why. Because I feel it, too. We live in an America now where hate crimes against Jews have been steadily climbing. The Anti-Defamation League reported a 56 percent rise in assaults in 2019 and an overall all-time high since the ADL began tracking hate crimes against Jews in 1979. We live in the America of 2017 Charlottesville, Virginia, an America where my local Jewish Community Center received bomb threats. It is an America of Marjorie Taylor Greene looking into the camera, comparing masks to the Holocaust, apologizing for it a few weeks later, and then comparing COVID-19 vaccines to the Holocaust. It is an America where some figures on the left, preaching intersectionality, always manage to leave Jews out of the equation.

This is not an accident. We hear those comparisons. We hear that silence. These people mean to write us out of the American story. This is the American Jewish conversation in the summer of 2021 at socially distanced barbecues and family dinners.

The childhood me in Cherry Hill would not have believed it, though our parents' generation born just after the Holocaust knew it implicitly from their own life experiences, as did my grandfather, who escaped from a concentration camp. Societies have moments of peace for Jews, not monuments to them.

This is most definitely not the book that grapples with such disturbing, sinister trends. This is where we go to escape from it, to revel in what the Jewish people have accomplished, and to celebrate what achievements lay ahead. What makes baseball such a perfect emotional haven for us all is the sheer size and complexity of it. That we could engage with the game, even as we all navigated the early unknowns of COVID-19, speaks to the ways baseball can fill our lives even during periods when most other aspects of life are shut down.

But the reason it matters so much to us as Jews is the extent to which baseball itself is an extension of America writ large. We've even seen this in the emerging figures in the game since my last edition. There are people like Justine Siegal, the creator of Baseball For All, a Jewish leader who is creating a pipeline for women across the country to play the game, not just get shunted into softball—a great sport, but a distinctly different one from baseball. A trailblazer herself, now for others, Siegal was a coach for the Oakland Athletics, then for Team Israel. Make no mistake: Siegal will be a Jewish Hall of Famer someday.

A surging Orthodox Jewish population is a reflection of American life as demonstrated during the 2021 MLB Draft, when both Jacob Steinmetz and Elie Kligman were selected by the Arizona Diamondbacks and Washington Nationals, respectively. Steinmetz signed with the Diamondbacks, receiving a $500,000 bonus, and becomes a key Jewish baseball prospect to watch, high on my list alongside people like Hunter Bishop, an outfielder in the San Francisco Giants' organization, and Zack Gelof, a third baseman beginning his career in Oakland's system. See my top 18 at the end of the book.

And let's not forget the rise of Team Israel, which made its first appearance in the Olympics during the summer of 2021 in Tokyo and was powered by American Jews like Ian Kinsler, the new standard-bearer for second basemen in this book.

Celebrating Jewish excellence in baseball is not a difficult thing to do despite all the jokes through the years. It is, at its heart, a supremely Jewish thing to do, too: finding joy in the argument, in the discussion of statistical evidence and sense memory and arcane topics, in cultural pride. It's a recognition that one of us did something that made our group proud and a larger group, us among them, collectively cheer.

But we must take to it with a renewed sense of purpose to make sure those who would separate us out from the American story cannot do so. Just as Hank

Greenberg once hit home runs against Hitler, as he put it before serving in World War II, and Sandy Koufax refused to pitch in the World Series on Yom Kippur, elevating Jewish concerns at the climax of the baseball season, we will continue to weave our 21ˢᵗ century Jewish experience into the greatest game.

The great Major League Baseball historian John Thorn declared this back in 2014: "It is today routine, rather than remarkable, for Jews to be baseball players—stars and supernumeraries just like every nationality or creed. Is that a triumph? Yes, but it is also a challenge. What are those things that make Jews special—chosen, even—if not their outsider status? What will drive us to prove our people's individual excellence by ourselves or through our heroes? As a people forged in adversity, America's Jews will have to find something else to supply the tie that binds. As in the past, baseball will be a help."

I fear Thorn was premature, as I was, in declaring the time of Jews as outsiders in America to be over, even as we saw a record four Jewish players in the 2021 World Series. But on his latter point, I could not agree more: whatever lies ahead for the Jewish people in America, baseball will be our refuge.

1

Catcher

For a people who pride themselves on intelligence and education, donning the so-called "Tools of Ignorance" would seem to be a fool's errand. Indeed, I was forbidden to play catcher in Little League by my mother, and it is hard to imagine a Jewish matriarch willingly agreeing to let her precious Morris or Sol repeatedly sit in front of blazing fastballs; sly, deceitful curveballs; or even deceptively dangerous knuckleballs.

Nevertheless, the position has provided the Jews with some of our greatest players. Although other positions are littered with obscurity, many of our catchers have been both productive and well-known.

The best at this position is essentially a toss-up between Harry Danning and Mike Lieberthal, two gifted offensive players at a position where hitting is at a premium. Defensive stalwarts like Steve Yeager, Brad Ausmus, Jeff Newman, and Joe Ginsberg also provided their teams with quality service behind the plate. Moe Berg, linguist and spy, is in a class all his own.

Harry Danning

1. Harry Danning

Bats Right, Throws Right
New York Giants, 1933–1942

Danning gets the nod despite very similar production to Mike Lieberthal. They were also both California products, though Lieberthal grew up in upscale Glendale, and Danning grew in a working-class Mexican American neighborhood in Los Angeles, watching Pacific Coast League games and Negro League teams with his father. Danning's first team was a semipro outfit sponsored by a Mexican grocery, and 95 percent of his teammates reportedly spoke little to no English.

He debuted in 1933 for a New York Giants team that was desperate for a Jewish star and box office attraction. (Back then, New York City had a lot of Jews.) Both he and fellow Semite Phil Weintraub were spare parts for the pennant-winning Giants, who were managed by first-year skipper Bill Terry (who had taken over after John McGraw's 30-year run).

Danning had the misfortune of being stuck behind All-Star Gus Mancuso until 1937, playing sporadically on Giants teams that won two pennants and at least 90 games each year. The press took it as an article of faith that Terry preferred Mancuso. George Kirksey of UPI wrote in his World Series preview on September 25, 1936: "Jewish boy from Los Angeles. Never been in Terry's good graces since he was a holdout in 1935. Will see World Series from the bench unless Mancuso is hurt." Kirksey was correct—Danning got just two at-bats as the New York Yankees won in six games.

Danning finally broke through on the 1937 Giants team that...also lost to the Yankees in the World Series, hitting .288 with a .438 slugging percentage in 292 at-bats. That performance was enough to earn him a 14th-place finish in MVP voting and Mancuso a permanent seat on the bench (he was traded after the 1938 season). Though the Giants slipped to third in 1938, Danning improved his batting average to .306 while slugging an identical .438, placing

16th in MVP voting despite the Giants' finish. Even so, Danning and his manager often fought. Once again, Danning held out before returning to the Giants for a $3,000 raise. But in July, suffering from a kidney ailment, he asked Terry for time off. Terry responded by refusing, then suspending him without pay for a week. Danning didn't return to the lineup until July 27, and for a Giants team that lost the National League race by just five games, it is fair to wonder whether a healthy and fully utilized Danning in July could have put them over the top.

Even so, give Terry credit: as Danning told *The Baltimore Sun* in 2004, when a Florida hotel tried to keep Danning and Weintraub out, Terry insisted his Giants would only stay there if all were welcome. By the spring of 1939, Kirksey wrote that Danning was "rated by many as the league's top catcher." Danning got better and better, though his teammates—best among them an aging Carl Hubbell (who was an early supporter of Danning) and unprotected Mel Ott—did not provide enough support to keep the Giants from sliding to fifth place in 1939–40.

Despite the poor team records, Danning finished in the top 10 of National League MVP voting both years, a clear indicator that his outstanding play was not lost on observers. Danning got off to a particularly scalding start in 1940 and was hitting .364 as late as July 1 before the toll of playing behind the plate nearly every day—Terry might not have liked him, but he knew what he had, and Danning played 140 games in 1940 alone—ultimately dropped his season average to .300 by season's end.

Although Danning did not hit a ton of home runs (only 29 over the two years), his offensive contribution was significant. Not only did he hit over .300, get on base roughly 35 percent of the time, and slug higher than .450 both years, but he did so in more than 500 at-bats each year. No other catcher, not even Hall of Famer Ernie Lombardi, slugged as high as .400 in as many as 400 at-bats each season. Danning's combination of durability and success made him the preeminent catcher in these two years.

Like many players, his career was cut short by serving in World War II, though arguably the amount of games caught had taken its toll by the time he enlisted after the 1942 season; both his '41 and '42 efforts were not nearly as good as '39–'40. Even so, Danning, from 1937 to 1942, made four All-Star teams, and his WAR of 14.6 ranks third among all catchers at that time. The only two ahead of him, Bill Dickey and Lombardi, are Hall of Famers. So are the two just behind him, Josh Gibson and Gabby Hartnett.

Following the war, Danning moved to the Valparaiso, Indiana, area with his wife, Diane. He worked in the insurance business—he'd played too early to qualify for an MLB pension—and did well enough at it that he could donate money to local baseball efforts. It was overdue. "I made $14,000 in my final year," Danning told baseball journalist Maury Allen in 1997. "I was as high as $18,000 after hitting .300 three years in a row."

Eventually, Valparaiso named a field after him, and a softball tournament was named in his honor as well. By the end of his life, Danning loved nothing more than to watch the game of baseball—he'd become a Chicago Cubs fan and would travel to a local restaurant to sign autographs and talk baseball with fans well into his 90s. When he died in 2004, his ashes were scattered at the field named for him. His daughter told *The Times of Northwest Indiana* she "could not have chosen a more extraordinary father."

Danning might have added to his career numbers had Adolf Hitler not intervened. He certainly would have done so had Mancuso not intervened. Despite both, he is our finest catcher, the man we as a people will rely on in the eventual cosmic baseball tournament between religions.

2. Mike Lieberthal

Bats Right, Throws Right
Philadelphia Phillies, 1994–2006
Los Angeles Dodgers, 2007

After spending a first-round draft pick on Mike Lieberthal, the Philadelphia Phillies had reason to believe they were watching the development of a star, when in his first full season, he hit 20 home runs at age 25. However, like many of his teammates on that 1997 Phillies team, along with the fortunes of the team itself, stardom and October success ultimately remained elusive.

Lieberthal followed with an injury-plagued 1998. In 1999 he had easily the greatest season of any Jewish catcher and one of the finest campaigns by any catcher, even goyim. He hit .300 with an on-base percentage of .363 and a slugging percentage of .551 on the strength of 31 home runs and 33 doubles. No Phillies catcher hit as many as 25 homers again until J.T. Realmuto in 2019. He also was awarded a Gold Glove for his defensive efforts, which included a 100-game errorless streak. At age 27, it seemed as if he was set to battle Mike Piazza for National League All-Star slots well into the 21st century.

Unfortunately, his body betrayed him. He appeared in 131 or fewer games in each season through 2006. He signed on with the Los Angeles Dodgers for 2007, but backing up the young, sturdy Russell Martin is no way to top that number, and Lieberthal finished his Dodgers career with just 77 at-bats and a lone RBI.

After calling it quits in June 2008, Lieberthal would seem to have a good case for GJB (Greatest Jewish Backstop): most home runs (150), RBIs (610), and a career slugging percentage of .446. Harry Danning's numbers are 57, 397, and .415.

Lieberthal also had about 1,000 more at-bats. However, it is hard to hold this against Danning. For one thing, any chance he had of playing after 1942 was eliminated by World War II. While in the service, he was told by an army doctor that his knee was "shot." And that was it. By means of comparison, Lieberthal was carried off the field May 12, 2001 with a torn anterior cruciate ligament. His ACL was replaced by a graft taken from a cadaver. A continuous passive motion machine hooked up to his bed, allowing him to rehabilitate as he slept. His daily isometrics and comprehensive physical therapy also helped him to return in time for the start of the 2002 season. "Cadavers, screws, an hour-and-a-half surgery," Lieberthal told *USA TODAY* in 2001. "Now it seems like players come back from anything."

Danning's injury was not so severe that he couldn't serve in the armed forces. His examination consisted of an army doctor using a slang term. Lieberthal, meanwhile, recovered in months from an injury he couldn't even stand on. So in evaluating the two of them, how do you penalize a guy for being too busy fighting World War II to play baseball and for being born too soon to enjoy modern medical miracles?

I asked Eve Rosenbaum to weigh in here, as she will periodically throughout the book. Eve is the director of player development for the Baltimore Orioles and a top prospect in the future Jewish general manager pipeline. She pointed out how much Danning probably had to go through, just in basic training, to prepare to serve in World War II. "The other thing I would bring up, just about the old-timey baseball catchers, is related to what you're saying in terms of the medical care," Rosenbaum said. "Catchers these days, we just know so much more about—not just big knee surgeries but just how to treat them on a day-to-day basis to keep their knees fresh...There is so much more we know about the work to do with them and the athletic training room and the gym to keep them more fresh that we didn't know in the '30s. I think in the '30s we're just going out there and [having them put] on the gear and squatting."

Though he acknowledged he is not an unbiased observer, Ruben Amaro Jr.—a former teammate of Lieberthal's—made the case for his player. "You're talking about a guy who was a 30-home run catcher," Amaro Jr. said in a May 2021 phone interview. "There's not that many. The guy that was an All-Star, and it's just difficult to find offensive catchers. The great ones, like Piazza, are in the Hall of Fame...And Liebe was certainly a great offensive catcher."

Purely as a statistical exercise, the two are basically dead even. Lieberthal accumulated 15.3 WAR in 1,212 games. Danning checks in at 14.6 WAR, but he did it in just 890 games, making him more valuable on a per-game basis. Add to that Danning's service in WWII (arguably, had Danning and the Allies not prevailed, Lieberthal never gets the chance to play), and Harry the Horse gets the edge.

3. Brad Ausmus

Bats Right, Throws Right
San Diego Padres, 1993–1996
Detroit Tigers, 1996, 1999–2000
Houston Astros, 1997–1998, 2001–2008
Los Angeles Dodgers, 2009–2010

Brad Ausmus, born and raised in Connecticut, came from an academic background—his father was a professor of European history—and so it came to pass that his parents would let him play baseball only if it didn't interfere with his ability to get an Ivy League education since he'd been accepted to Dartmouth. Ultimately, that's just what Ausmus did, earning a degree in government in 1991 while attending classes in the offseason.

His father is Protestant; his mother, Linda, is Jewish. And he got an education from her as well—she took Ausmus to a Ku Klux Klan rally as a child, so Ausmus could see that there is hatred in the world for people with his background.

Ausmus could have been the great Jewish frontline player New York has craved since John McGraw signed Moses Solomon to be the "Rabbi of Swat" in 1923. Instead, the 1987 draft pick of the New York Yankees, Ausmus was selected instead in the expansion draft to stock the Colorado Rockies for the 1993 season. Ausmus never played for the Rockies either, getting dealt to the

San Diego Padres in a five-player deal highlighted by Bruce Hurst. It was a feeling he would need to get used to—he was traded by the Padres and by the Houston Astros along with getting dealt twice by the Detroit Tigers (though unlike fellow catcher Harry Chiti, he was never exchanged for himself).

Even at that point, Ausmus' career path was clear: his career minor league slash line was .259/.331/.327, foreshadowing a major league career of .251/.325/.344. Even as a high school player, a future big leaguer, Ausmus would get bunts down to advance the runner. He was a high-IQ, smallball catcher from the earliest parts of his career.

Despite an undistinguished offensive career, Ausmus has made a living with his defense and durability. Ausmus caught 480 of 1,374 would-be base stealers, a success rate of over 35 percent, while playing in at least 117 games every year from 1996 to 2007, including 150 for the 2000 Tigers. His reputation for blocking balls as well as anyone is borne out by the numbers as well—1,938 games caught, just 61 passed balls. (For comparison, in 2,088 games through September 2021, future Hall of Famer Yadier Molina has allowed 93 passed balls.)

Ausmus won three Gold Gloves, but his only All-Star appearance in 1999 came in a different campaign. Fittingly, in that All-Star appearance, he threw out Brian Jordan attempting to steal second base.

Still, respect came slowly to Ausmus, who despite his excellent work behind the plate, did not win his first Gold Glove until age 32 with the Astros in 2001; he then quickly nabbed his second in 2002 and another in 2006. Like Steve Yeager, Ausmus saw significant action in October, playing the role of starting catcher for five postseason Astros teams and made his World Series debut in 2005, thanks in large part to his home run in Game 4 of the National League Division Series against the Atlanta Braves. Houston eventually won the classic in 18 innings. His career postseason line of .245/.304/.377 isn't far from his overall career numbers of .255/.328/.353.

Ausmus was understood to be a future manager well before his playing career ended and fulfilled that destiny first with Team Israel in the 2013 World

Baseball Classic, then as Tigers manager with middling results from 2014 to 2017.

In a different era, Ausmus might have been considered one of the greats. But with base stealing deemphasized and power considered the key, a catcher who prevents thefts and provides little pop is less valuable than ever. The trade by the Yankees robbed Ausmus of his chance to shine before millions of his own religion. And Lieberthal's gaudy offensive numbers overshadowed him even among his own faith and position. Perhaps in this day and age, good defensive catchers are meant to be seen and not heard.

Ausmus gets the nod over Yeager, though like the top two guys, Ausmus and Yeager are very close. There is even an argument for Ausmus at the top spot because his WAR of 16.5 tops both Danning and Lieberthal in career value. Ultimately, Ausmus and Yeager were very much the same player. Yeager's OPS+ of 83 edges Ausmus' 75, but Ausmus' durability far outpaces Yeager's (only two years with more than 117 games, and only five seasons topping 100). Ausmus also gets extra credit: his maternal grandfather was a rabbi.

4. Steve Yeager

Bats Right, Throws Right
Los Angeles Dodgers, 1972–1985
Seattle Mariners, 1986

Steve Yeager is a favorite of mine. He was one of the few Members of the Tribe to receive Hall of Fame votes (two in 1992), he was the cousin of an astronaut, an area which, like the National Pastime, Jews do not have the presence we have in, say, the legal profession. He was a terrific defender, catching 365 of 960 would-be base stealers (38 percent). His offensive totals are also undervalued by virtue of playing in a poor offensive era and one of the best pitchers' parks (Dodger Stadium) in baseball history.

Yeager was drafted by the Los Angeles Dodgers in the fourth round of the 1967 draft and debuted in 1972. After a strong 94-game stint in 1974 (.266 with 12 homers in 316 at-bats and plus defense), he took over full time from Joe Ferguson in 1975. He went on to hit double-figures in home runs six times in his career, though his batting average quickly became his offensive Achilles heel (he hit over .228 just once in his last nine seasons). That's a deceiving stat since he walked and hit enough home runs that his offense, especially at the position, was more than sufficient for an everyday starter on a perennial contender.

Yeager's offense was considered a bonus by managers Walter Alston and Tommy Lasorda, however, who were thrilled with his defensive prowess. It is hard to argue with the results: in his 15 seasons Yeager's teams captured six division championships, four pennants, and a World Series title in 1981. A closer look at the stats would indicate that Yeager was more than incidental to his teams' successes. His batting, on-base percentages, and slugging percentages were .228, .298, and .355 in the regular season; he raised those to .252, .317, and .449 in the postseason. (One obviously faces better pitching in the playoffs, making that jump even more impressive.) He became particularly prodigious on baseball's biggest stage: in 58 World Series at-bats, he hit .298 with a slugging percentage of .579. His 1981 October Classic performance earned him a share of the World Series Most Valuable Player award. Not bad for a defense-first catcher.

The argument for Yeager as GJB is closer than it would appear; basically, if one values catcher defense and World Series MVPs very, very highly, he is your man. He leads the pack in career WAR, too, at 17.9. Yeager continues to hold two records—most career home runs by a Jewish catcher who posed for *Playgirl* (102) and most consecutive *Major League* films acted in by a former World Series MVP (three).

Yeager was also an innovator in the area of safety, inventing the catcher's neck protector after shards from a broken bat by Bill Russell lodged in his throat. Fittingly, not only did Yeager come up with the solution, but he also was back in the lineup three weeks later despite suffering—and this is not an injury I have ever heard anyone experiencing other than Yeager—a punctured esophagus.

5. Jeff Newman

Bats Right, Throws Right
Oakland Athletics, 1976–1982
Boston Red Sox, 1983–1984

No one will ever confuse Jeff Newman with the predecessors on this list. The top two played at a star level; the next two were good enough to start for championship teams. But Newman's ability to handle pitchers, hit home runs, and throw out would-be base stealers led to a long career first playing the game, then teaching it.

For the purposes of this book, 1970 looms large in Newman's life—he was drafted in the 26th round by the Cleveland Indians and a year after marrying his high school sweetheart, Diane Rosen, he converted to Judaism. But Cleveland employed Dave Duncan, the future pitching coach, as its regular catcher by the time Newman reached the high minors. And just like Newman, Duncan was a low-average, power-hitting catcher who could throw out runners. So the Oakland Athletics were able to purchase Newman in time for the 1976 season, but he and Diane had decided if he didn't make it to the big leagues in 1976, he'd call it a career. They'd tired of the itinerant life, which included Diane working the midnight shift at a Reno casino as a blackjack dealer. But in July 1976, Newman got the call. In his first official plate appearance, he drove in two with a single against Mark Littell of the Kansas City Royals. By 1977 he was Oakland's regular catcher.

As in the minors, Newman's flashier skill was hitting home runs. Newman hit nine of them in 268 at-bats in 1978, then socked 22 in 1979, and followed that with another 15 in 1980. Unfortunately, he had no other corresponding offensive skill. His inability to take a walk (just 70 over those three years and 1,222 at-bats) combined most unfortunately with batting averages of .239, .231, and .233. By 1981 Oakland turned to Mike Heath in a timeshare at the position and then traded him to the Boston Red Sox in a deal that brought back Carney Lansford.

Newman did stick around for another few years, largely on the strength of his glove. Newman threw out 160 of 406 attempted base stealers, a career percentage of nearly 40 percent, and in his first two big league seasons, stealing on Newman was a worse-than-even proposition. And his ability to handle pitchers led to a long, distinguished coaching career, including a time in 1986 as interim manager in Oakland. "It's a matter of experience," Newman told the *Fort Worth Star-Telegram* in July of 1976, discussing how he calls a game. "I know hitters because I've been around a long time, but a lot of catchers are in the same position. The key to working well with pitchers is to know them well enough to be able to get in sync with them. You have to establish a rhythm with each pitch. You have to sense his rhythm on a given day and stay in sync with him, which will help his frame of mind."

Not only did his knowledge serve him well, but it also brought us the potential first ever Jewish father-son managerial combination. After playing three years in the Pittsburgh Pirates' minor league system, his son Ryan is the skipper for the Winston-Salem Dash, high A franchise for the Chicago White Sox.

6. Joe Ginsberg

Bats Left, Throws Right
Detroit Tigers, 1948–1953
Cleveland Indians, 1953–1954
Kansas City Athletics, 1956
Baltimore Orioles, 1956–1960
Chicago White Sox, 1960–1961
Boston Red Sox, 1961
New York Mets, 1962

Delightfully, this new edition of *The Baseball Talmud* allows me to take advantage of data that wasn't around for the first version. Joe Ginsberg hit .241/.332/.320 for his career. But we needed to take the word of his contemporaries to evaluate his defense, which was the obvious reason he stuck around for 14 years. That's no longer true.

So what do we know now? Well, we know he threw out 108 of 283 would-be base stealers, good for a mark of 38 percent, thanks to Baseball-Reference.com. We know he was signed by his hometown team, the Detroit Tigers, but missed two full seasons after getting drafted by the army at the tail end of World War II. Still, by 1951, after going through the Paul Richards Finishing School for Catchers, Ginsberg earned the starting job, posting a solid .260/.355/.385 line.

Ginsberg, unlike Brad Ausmus and Steve Yeager, also does not get extra credit for playing for championship teams. He played for losing teams throughout his career in eight of 13 seasons and, in three of the four years he didn't, he played a grand total of 49 games. He did have a reputation for clutch-hitting, though, and the numbers bear that out. His slash line—in 426 plate appearances defined as "late and close" by Baseball-Reference.com—jumped to .280/.366/.352.

It is fair to wonder if he hadn't complained about his playing time in 1954 with Cleveland Indians—earning him a trip to the minors—whether things could have shaken out differently for him. In a pair of eight-team leagues, starting gigs were at a premium.

Ginsberg was able to shine in the Pacific Coast League for the Seattle Rainiers in 1955, hitting .290 as their starting catcher and leading them to the PCL title. However, his success bred a return to major league also-random, when he was purchased by another kind of farm team, the Kansas City Athletics. His career continued in that vein, finishing with five at-bats for the 1962 New York Mets, the losingest team of them all. But his career minor league line of .285/.372/.401—mostly accumulated in the high minors—hints at what might have been.

7. Moe Berg

Bats Right, Throws Right
Brooklyn Dodgers, 1923
Chicago White Sox, 1926–1930
Cleveland Indians, 1931, 1934
Washington Senators, 1932–1934
Boston Red Sox, 1935–1939

It's hard to add anything to the legend of Moe Berg—backup catcher, spy, and linguist, though certainly not in that order. I suspect that no one would have been more excited to use the Internet than Berg—the man collected so many newspapers that wherever he was living would have piles of them stacked high on his floor. He was an information junkie before the information age.

As a player, Berg was said to have originated the term "good-field, no-hit," and justifiably so. His career line of .243/.278/.299 was amusingly enough accumulated during an extreme hitters' era. So his true offensive value was below that. Still, he was perceived as valuable enough to stick around for 16 seasons in professional baseball, though again much of that allure was due to the belief that he could—and did—teach much to his teammates. His career high in at-bats was 352, and he only topped 200 at-bats one other time in 16 years.

But Berg was more than simply smart for a baseball player. In a sport where merely getting caught reading a book, regardless of its author, gets a player tagged with a virtual monocle, Berg put off returning to the Brooklyn Dodgers for spring training 1924 in order to complete his studies at the Sorbonne. He was added to the first major league baseball touring team in 1934 because he could speak Japanese like a native. He served as a panelist on the radio quiz show *Information Please*, which served as a broadcast version of the Algonquin Round Table (with many crossover members) in the 1930s and '40s.

I think there's a case to be made that the things that kept him from a satisfying life probably held him back as a baseball player, too. He was easily bored with his coaching work after retiring, his spy work, and many of his other pursuits. (He got his law degree from Columbia University in 1925 but stopped practicing law after a single winter at it.)

Berg had excelled at Princeton University as a shortstop, and the Dodgers saw enough in him to give him regular time in 1923, when he was the youngest player in the majors, and asked him back in 1924. (Without Berg that team went on to win 92 games, so it's not as if they were bereft of talent.)

One suspects that had Berg devoted more of himself to a single pursuit, the last 15 years of his life, in which he suffered from depression and lived with friends and relatives, might have been happier. Had he focused on baseball, he also might have reflected on a far more successful baseball career. However, his failure to do so makes it hard to think of anyone, living or dead, who would be more interesting at a dinner party.

8. Norm Sherry

Bats Right, Throws Right
Los Angeles Dodgers, 1959–1962
New York Mets, 1963

Between his brother (Larry Sherry, the 1959 World Series MVP), his teammate protégé (Sandy Koufax, one of the great pitchers, Kosher or *treif*), and those he helped develop as a coach and manager (including Hall of Fame catcher Gary Carter), Norm Sherry had quite an impact on the world of baseball in general, and Jewish baseball in particular, during a short but sweet major league career. Sherry, nee Scharaga (with a family that fled Europe in the latter decades of the 19th century), presaged the journey of the team he signed with, the Dodgers, as his family moved from the east coast to Los Angeles, just blocks from Fairfax High School.

While the Dodgers signed him in 1950, he became a victim of a talented farm system organized by Branch Rickey and spent eight seasons in the minor leagues before getting to Los Angeles in 1959. Though he got into just two games, he was able to see his brother shut down the Chicago White Sox and help the Dodgers win their first post-betrayal title.

While Sherry served as backup to the capable John Roseboro from 1960 to 1962 for the Dodgers and managed a very impressive .283 average, .353 on base percentage, and .503 slugging in 138 at-bats in his first year (his subsequent production was not as prodigious), his largest contribution to the Dodgers, and indeed to baseball, was finally convincing a hard-throwing project named Koufax to take just a bit off of his fastball and throw more breaking pitches in exchange for control during spring training of 1961. "We had many talks," Sherry told the *El Paso Herald-Post* in 1972. "It's nice that he always gives me the credit for helping make him a pitching star."

Koufax, who had considered quitting baseball after a lackluster 1960 season, set the single-season National League strikeout record for lefthanders in 1961, a mark which stood until Koufax broke it again in 1963 and then a third time in 1965.

Sherry, meanwhile, did not find a similar path to stardom, hitting .256 and .182 behind the durable Roseboro before he was sold to the New York Mets following the 1962 season. Sherry played in a career-high 63 games for the 1963 Mets but batted just .136, thus ending his career. It also ended the automatic Jewish catcher's seat on the Mets bench he inherited from Joe Ginsberg when Sherry did not return in 1964 and Chris Cannizzaro failed to convert.

Sherry went on to manage for years in the Dodgers' and Angels' systems and briefly took the reins for the major league Halos in 1976–77. He found out he was succeeding Dick Williams when Red Patterson, the longtime public relations official for the Angels, handed Sherry a press release and asked him to read it out loud.

He went on to serve as pitching coach with the Montreal Expos, San Francisco Giants, and elsewhere with distinction. In Montreal his explicit role was to turn Carter, an offense-first catcher, into an asset behind the plate. It's hard to argue anyone other than Carlton Fisk can live up to Carter's two-way career contributions, and Sherry received a significant amount of the credit for that from the media covering the Expos at that time.

So what was responsible for Sherry's success as a baseball man? As Sherry explained it to Phil Pepe in 1976: "I'm not sure why backup catchers seem to wind up as managers. Maybe because as a catcher you get to work with the pitchers, and everything is in front of you. You're in the game more. Patience is an important part of managing, and when you struggle all your life, you learn to be patient. I can sympathize with the players who aren't starting. I know what it is not to play."

9. Jesse Levis

Bats Left, Throws Right
Cleveland Indians, 1992–1995, 1999
Milwaukee Brewers, 1996–1998, 2001

Scouting is an imperfect science.

Jesse Levis, a Philadelphia product, was drafted by his hometown Phillies out of high school after earning all-county honors as a catcher his senior year. A Major League Baseball scout told the *Philadelphia Daily News'* Ted Silary that Levis was "the best catcher in this area; that's talking high school and college." Levis' big rival in the area? Phoenixville High School was led by a young first baseman named...Mike Piazza.

Levis elected to attend the University of North Carolina rather than accept 36th-round money out of high school. The delay paid off, as he signed with Cleveland after the Indians made him a fourth-round pick three years later. (Piazza, meanwhile, played junior college ball and was a sixty-second 62nd-round pick by the Los Angeles Dodgers and only as a favor to his father Vince, a friend of Tommy Lasorda's. He turned out okay.)

Levis made his way up the organizational chain, posting relatively unremarkable stats along the way with the exception of his ability to make contact and reach base for free. Each season until he reached the majors, Levis walked at least as often as he struck out; his season high in punchouts reached a paltry 42. However, Cleveland's All-Star backstop, Sandy Alomar, Jr., kept Levis from getting the opportunity to wow Cleveland's sizable Jewish population.

Finally, after a Triple A season that could not be ignored (.311 batting average, 413 on-base, and .454 slugging), Levis was shipped to the Milwaukee Brewers to serve as their catcher of the future. At age 27, it appeared Levis had finally arrived.

His on-base skills translated nicely, but the rest of his game did not make the transition. His on-base percentages for the two seasons were a respectable .348 and .361, but his slugging (.283 and .335) was far below par, and he threw out just 26-of-97 attempted base stealers (just under 27 percent).

Thus began a merry-go-round for Levis as an emergency backup catcher for hire, the guy who gets mentioned by announcers in the rare instance that both major league starter and backup fall victim to the injury bug. Levis garnered just 96 at-bats in the big leagues over the final seven years of his career while playing for the Tampa Bay Devil Rays, Indians, Atlanta Braves, Milwaukee Brewers, Cincinnati Reds, Phillies, and New York Mets organizations. He continued to judiciously weigh each errant pitch, finishing with a .380 career on-base percentage. He even got signed by his hometown Phillies and got to play all spring with them in Clearwater, Florida, while being managed by his boyhood idol, Larry Bowa, though he ultimately rode out the season in Triple A Scranton/Wilkes-Barre while being blocked in part by Mike Lieberthal.

Unfortunately, a foot injury befell him in a 2004 season that began with promise (he was hitting .370 at the time of the injury). He began his second career coaching—only to be stopped in his tracks by charges that he'd been masturbating in public view in his hotel room during spring training with the 2008 Boston Red Sox. The only witness soon recanted, but it took two years for prosecutors to drop the charges at a judge's behest for lack of evidence. "Hopefully, my reputation will be rebuilt, and I'll be able to prove again that I can really help an organization," he told the *Philadelphia Daily News* in

2010. "That's the bottom line. I think I have a lot to offer an organization as far as my knowledge and experience. So, hopefully, somebody will give me a chance."

Soon after that, his hometown Phillies did, and he resumed working as a scout until he was part of the 2020 COVID layoffs. In 2018 he was inducted into the Philadelphia Jewish Sports Hall of Fame.

10. Ryan Lavarnway
Bats Right, Throws Right
Boston Red Sox, 2011–2014
Baltimore Orioles, 2015
Atlanta Braves, 2015
Oakland Athletics, 2017
Pittsburgh Pirates, 2018
Cincinnati Reds, 2019
Miami Marlins, 2020
Cleveland Indians, 2021

Buck Showalter is one of the keenest baseball minds I've ever had the chance to interview. So this comment he made about Ryan Lavarnway in 2015 on the occasion of the Baltimore Orioles sending him down to Triple A Norfolk for everyday at-bats is one that's stayed with me: "I just don't think Ryan's swing and the things that he's capable of doing are conducive to playing once a week."

If that isn't the story of Lavarnway's career, man, I don't know what is.

Born to a Catholic father and Jewish mother, Lavarnway grew up idolizing Jason Varitek as a Woodland Hills, California, youngster. He wasn't Bar Mitzvahed but became more connected to his Jewish faith in high school and—after marrying a Jewish woman—practices the Jewish faith to this day.

He played at Yale University as a philosophy major, and Varitek's team, the Boston Red Sox, selected him in the sixth round of the 2008 draft.

Varitek enjoyed his last All-Star season that year at 36, and it sure looked like Lavarnway would come up and be his hero's successor—especially when injuries to Varitek and backup Jarrod Saltalamacchia earned Lavarnway a start on the final Tuesday of the 2011 season and he hit two home runs to keep Boston's playoff hopes alive one more day.

Baseball America ranked him Boston's ninth-best prospect in 2012 and scouted him this way: "Lavarnway generates plus power with a combination of strength and discipline. He works counts, lets pitches travel deep, and pounds the ball to all fields. His swing is relatively compact considering his long arms. Lavarnway's defensive improvement is a tribute to his intelligence and work ethic. He lacks athleticism and agility, but he has transformed himself from a dreadful receiver to an adequate one."

The issue is this: Lavarnway is fine behind the plate—nothing special—thanks to that arm. His plus bat carries the profile. Well, Showalter explained the rest. So over a 10-year career so far, Lavarnway has collected a total of just 486 plate appearances at the big league level with a paltry .217/.272/.345 line to show for it. In the primarily high minors, though, he's at .274/.365/.456 with 134 home runs in 3,867 plate appearances through the 2021 season.

He's also hit well for Team Israel, starting at catcher in the 2021 Olympics in Tokyo and hitting .350 with a pair of home runs. "Last night I played ping pong in the Olympic village rec center with athletes from Argentina, South Africa, and France while my teammates were hanging out and watching other events with athletes from Hungary and Romania," Lavarnway tweeted in the summer of 2021. "I keep having to pinch myself to remind me this is real!"

He returned to the United States in August, hit five home runs in six games for the Triple A Columbus Clippers, got called up by the Cleveland Indians, played sparingly, and was sent back down to Triple A.

It's never been a more barren landscape for catchers with plus bats, so there's still time for Lavarnway. Someone, though, ought to sign him and let him play every day. Dan Szymborski's ZIPS projection on FanGraphs for

Lavarnway is .235/.309/.371, which is certainly better than some catchers are going to put up in 2022.

11. Skip Jutze

Bats Right, Throws Right
St. Louis Cardinals, 1972
Houston Astros, 1973–1976
Seattle Mariners, 1977

Some people are born Jewish; some people have Judaism thrust upon them. So it was for Skip Jutze, not born and raised a member of the tribe despite the Semitic syllable in his last name. But growing up in Queens, peer pressure to don a yarmulke and consume gefilte fish must have been overwhelming, and Jutze eventually bowed to the inevitable and converted.

A multi-sport star who drew notice for his work quarterbacking at Central Connecticut State (including a school-record 298 yards passing in a 1965 game against Trenton State, a mark that stood for 28 years), Jutze was drafted twice in high rounds before signing his third time around as a fourth-round pick of the St. Louis Cardinals. His .324 batting average and .455 slugging at Triple A Tulsa earned him a cup of coffee in St. Louis, in which he threw out 12 of 18 would-be base stealers. After the season he was shipped to the Houston Astros in a four-player deal and received the bulk of the playing time for the 1973 Astros. It did not go well. By August 4 he even had a theory for his struggles, which he shared with Tom Duffy of the *Tampa Bay Times*. "At the start of the season, I had a 'stashy and hair down to here," Jutze said. "But we went to New York, and my wife said, 'Cut it.' I haven't had a hit since then, hardly."

But a closer look at Jutze's 1973 season largely rebuts the Samson-like idea that his wife and lack of hair were to blame for his poor hitting. When Jutze and the Astros arrived in New York on July 9, he had a season slash line of .256/.316/.298. By the time of this interview, yes, his production had dropped to .155/.183/.155 during the intervening few weeks.

At the end of the interview, however, Jutze revealed that he was actively growing out his hair and moustache. Nevertheless, from August 4 on, his hitting failed to return to his pre-shearing days over the final two months of the season. By October rumors had the Astros actively shopping him in a potential deal for Jerry Reuss. He seemed destined for a forgotten career with the Astros, accumulating 198 at-bats over three seasons from 1974 to 1976, failing to hit very much, and allowing 48 of 65 baserunners an Enron-like environment for larceny. He had no home runs in his entire career through 1976.

Then the gods looked down upon Jutze and cried out: expansion! Jutze was traded to the newly-created Seattle Mariners, who went ahead and started him on April 12, 1977. Unlike in his previous 547 major league at-bats, Jutze finally got a pitch he could drive. Jutze rode his new power to the tune of three long balls in just 109 at-bats. Even so, once he failed to make the 1978 Mariners, he turned down a player/coach position with Seattle's Triple A team, the San Jose Missions, but as *The Tacoma News Tribune* reported at the time, he refused. "I'm going home," he said. "I'm not going around, begging other clubs for a job."

Inducted into CCSU's inaugural Hall of Fame in 1979, Jutze, like in Joe Ginsberg's magical 1955 before him, J proved that Seattle is a very hospitable place for Jewish catchers. One would hope that Mariners' management will pick up on this trend—it is no accident the franchise has never even been to a World Series, and current catcher Tom Murphy—not Jewish—has an average around the Mendoza Line.

12. Eric Helfand

Bats Left, Throws Right
Oakland Athletics, 1993–1995

Drafted by the Oakland Athletics in the second round of the 1990 draft, he was supposed to be the next Gene Tenace. He wasn't, though a large number of smart baseball folks sure thought he would be.

On the heels of a solid 1991 minor league campaign, Helfand built on it in 1992, hitting .270/.369/.430 between high A Modesto, earning Cal League All-Star honors (he was the All Star Game MVP, too), and Double A Huntsville.

That drew the attention of Florida Marlins general manager Dave Dombrowski, who selected him 18th overall in the Marlins' portion of the expansion draft just ahead of Joe Girardi, who went to the other new team in Colorado, and before the Marlins picked Bryan Harvey, their first great closer, or even Jeff Conine, better known as "Mr. Marlin." And no less an authority than A's GM Sandy Alderson responded by re-acquiring him for Oakland, giving up Walt Weiss, the team's starting shortstop during its Bash Brothers heyday, to keep him as part of the Athletics' future. "He's smart, he works hard, he's not excitable, and he listens," his Modesto manager, Ted Kubiak, told *The Modesto Bee* in November 1992. "It's difficult to find all of those things in one guy."

But his offense regressed in 1993, and his slash line dropped to .228/.333/.391, though he did earn his first call-up to Oakland. In 1994 he spent much of the year with Oakland, but he didn't play often behind Terry Steinbach and Scott Hemond. Tony La Russa wanted three catchers, however. "Definitely, this is not helping Helfand," La Russa said of the situation.

Not exactly ideal at a position that requires repetition to master it. After the 1995 season with Steinbach showing no signs of aging, Helfand was granted free agency and signed with the Cleveland Indians. But while playing for Buffalo, Cleveland's Triple A club, Helfand's bat disappeared, and he slashed .209/.350/.306 line in 1996. Though he improved to .315/.401/.487 with the San Diego Padres' Triple A team in 1997, his ability to throw out runners had betrayed him—just a 14 percent mark—and he never saw any big league action again. He finished with a career .171 batting average in the majors over 105 at-bats while hitting a respectable .248/.350/.381 in 1,954 minor league at-bats.

That 1990 draft was a rough one for the A's. Their first-round pick? Todd Van Poppel. In the supplemental round? Kirk Dressendorfer. Some rare misses for the team with a history of drafting more Reggie Jacksons than Steve Chilcotts.

13. Garrett Stubbs

Bats Left, Throws Right
Houston Astros, 2019–present

It's getting late early for Garrett Stubbs, one of my favorite Jewish prospects at the moment. This is how it works too often for catchers, especially college catchers. There's a learning curve to hitting professional pitching. Improving that craft as you rise in the minor leagues and doing it while taking on the responsibilities of calling a game is no easy task.

This is even true for a guy like Stubbs, a cerebral backstop who won the Johnny Bench Award as the top college catcher with USC in 2015. Back then, his college coach, Dan Hubbs, described him this way to *The Desert Sun*: "He has the ability to do a lot of different things on offense as well as defense. I haven't seen that combination with anybody else."

That earned Stubbs a call from the Houston Astros in the eighth round of the 2015 Major League Baseball Draft, and he's been an elite defensive catcher at every level, throwing out 42 percent of those who run on him. My favorite part of his game is what he does in return. Stubbs stole 20 bases his senior year at USC, and it wasn't a fluke. He's nabbed 51 steals in 56 attempts. Succeeding that consistently is the mark of a truly great baserunner.

But the Astros didn't seem to know what to do with him. One spring, they had him learning second base with Craig Biggio and they've had him in some corner outfield spots during spells with the big club. His bat hasn't really translated in his limited MLB appearances, though he posted a .265/.418/.363 line with Triple A Sugar Land in 2021.

And with regular catchers at the MLB level like Martin Maldonado and Jason Castro, Stubbs had a real opportunity to take this job and run with it in Houston after his cameo in the 2021 World Series. Add in the ability to play multiple positions, and his long-term prospectus gets even better. But he'll be plying his trade in Philadelphia, not Houston, thanks to an offseason trade to the Phillies. He'll get an opportunity to back up J.T. Realmuto, but his path to everyday play should be blocked for a while. Dan Szymborski's FanGraphs projection has him in ZIPS at .228/.290/.349, so he's going to have to best that to grab ahold of a job playing multiple positions and occasionally spelling Realmuto.

14. Bill Starr

Bats Right, Throws Right
Washington Senators, 1935–1936

Son of Russian immigrants Isaac and Esther, Bill Starr made his name not as a player but as a trailblazing executive. His playing career included 24 at-bats with the 1935 Washington Senators, but he had a more significant minor league career. He displayed an early interest in baseball—not so much in Hebrew School. "In later years as a catcher in professional baseball, I was convinced that my manual dexterity derived from the skill I developed in avoiding the rebbe's attempts to use my knuckles for his batting practice," he recalled in his memoir, *Clearing the Bases*.

He went on to play several more years in the Pacific Coast League, then both independent of Major League Baseball and considered the top minor league. In 1937, en route to hitting .219 for the then-minor league San Diego Padres, he pinch hit for teammate Ted Williams. (Astonishingly, his manager, Frank Shellenback, was nevertheless retained in 1938.) A broken leg ended Starr's playing career at 28.

In 1944 he was part of a group that purchased the Padres, and Starr took over day-to-day operations. He signed the league's first African American ballplayer, John Ritchey. And he didn't stop there, adding stars like Luke Easter and Minnie Minoso. By the end of the decade, Starr had a working agreement with the Cleveland Indians, whose general manager is also familiar to you: Hank Greenberg.

In the early 1950s, Starr made a push to turn the PCL into a third major league, which was a legitimate idea both in terms of league quality and geographical breakdown. (There were no baseball teams west of St. Louis.) However, the PCL effort failed, and Starr sold his share in the Padres at a large profit in 1955.

Starr went on to become a successful real estate developer, and while no Moe Berg, Starr published a 1989 book contrasting modern baseball with the baseball of his youth. It's an extremely readable book, making a strong case for the players of the 1920s and 1930s through reporting and interviews, challenging a lot of my long-held beliefs as a strong proponent of statistical analysis in baseball. I highly recommend it. He also became a founding member of the San Diego Jewish Community Center. So that Jewish education came in handy, too.

15. Ike Danning

Bats Right, Throws Right
St. Louis Browns, 1928

Ike Danning was the older brother of Harry the Horse, and his 3-for-6 career major league batting record gave him a batting average of .500, 133 points higher than the all-time career leader, Ty Cobb, though in 11,428 fewer at-bats. The Dannings were one of six sets of Jewish brothers to play in the major leagues. Ike was six years older and overshadowed by his younger brother. But Ike still had a long, successful minor league career even as the major leagues failed to fully appreciate the value of a catcher who gets hits half the time.

In 1925 the elder Danning earned front-page acclaim from the *Los Angeles Times*. Robert Ray described Danning and his teammate, Pat O'Shea, as "a couple of youngsters who [Vernon Tigers manager Rube] Ellis picked up from local semipro ranks." Danning homered and drove in four runs, earning himself a $10 bill from Vernon owner Ed Maier, who made a practice of slipping a ten-spot to one of his players any time he homered.

After Danning finished playing baseball, he went on to a long career working in the movies at 20th Century Fox. But his baseball background came in handy. Sidney Skolsky reported in his June 27, 1951 column, "Hollywood Is My Beat," for the *Los Angeles Evening Citizen News* that Dan Dailey is "practically in 'spring training' to get ready to play Dizzy Dean in *The Pride of St. Louis.*" His baseball coach? That's right: Ike Danning.

However you feel about the film as a whole, I've reviewed the movie and Dean's old windup, and Danning really got Dailey to pitch just like Dean.

16. Frank Charles

Bats Right, Throws Right
Houston Astros, 2000

Arguably the finest Jewish catcher in modern indy-league baseball, the career of Frank Charles promised so much more when he was drafted in the 17th round out of Cal State-Fullerton. Frank tore up the Northwest League, a low A level minor circuit, hitting .318/.374/.510 as a rookie. Though he was old for the league, it was an auspicious beginning. As sportswriter Jim Price saw it, Charles was the "nemesis of the Spokane Indians," with Price noting Charles had 17 hits in 41 at-bats playing for Everett and against Spokane.

The San Francisco Giants rushed him, giving him just five A ball at-bats, then sending him to high A, where he struggled in San Jose, hitting .290/.322/.353 in 1992. Oddly, the Giants then gave up on him, and he was signed by the St. Paul Saints, owned by Bill Veeck's son, Mike, in 1993. After a year in the Northern League, Charles was hitting .171 on July 11 when his then-girl-friend, Noelle Ponsetto, visited. Charles credited the visit with turning his season around, one in which he finished the year at .273, though his manager Tim Blackwell joked to the *Minneapolis Star Tribune*, "I'd like to think I had something to do with it."

The Texas Rangers saw enough to sign him for the 1994 season. He reached Double A, but Texas did not have a spot for him, considering they had an in-prime Ivan Rodriguez behind the plate. History might have been different if the replacement players brought in by Major League Baseball owners in the spring of 1995 during the labor battle with MLBPA had been allowed to play. Charles was a Texas replacement player that spring before returning to their minor league system when the strike was settled. Then the Giants gave him another try, but despite a strong .287/.323/.474 line in Double A Shreveport, he was on to the San Diego Padres system in 1999, then the Houston Astros in 2000.

But after signing with Houston and holding his own at Triple A New Orleans in 2000, he made his way to the big club as a September call-up. On seemingly the only Houston team not to play meaningful September games (the 2000 edition finished 72–90), Charles managed three hits in seven at-bats—good for an Ike Danning-esque .429 batting average. His lone start came on October 1, and he made good, hitting a two-run single and nursing Chris Holt through seven stellar innings in a 6–1 Astros win against the Milwaukee Brewers.

He played several more seasons, even putting up a .300/.339/.495 line for the Northeast League's North Shore club, but he never made it back to the show. With catchers slow to develop, the Giants quick to give up on him, and Pudge blocking the way in Texas, it is fair to wonder if Frank Charles might have had a better career in a different system.

17. Harry Chozen

Bats Right, Throws Right
Cincinnati Reds, 1937

Pasadena, California's own Harry Chozen played 17 years in the minor leagues and one solitary game in the big leagues on September 21, 1937 as one of the backup catchers to Ernie Lombardi, one of the few bright spots on an eighth-place team. Chozen earned his way into that moment, though. The Cincinnati Reds signed him in 1935 and assigned him to Class D Lake Charles, where he hit .321. Promoted to Class C El Dorado in 1936, he hit a respectable .261 with

13 home runs, then dominated in 1937 with a .339 batting average and 14 home runs—fantastic numbers for a catcher. He was the MVP of the league as voted by the sportswriters of the right-team circuit.

As the *Pasadena Post* reported on August 1, 1937, "the husky young catcher" led the Cotten States League in batting, while his brother, Mike (listed as Myer on Baseball-Reference.com), was hitting .292 for Jackson in the Southeastern League. (Mike or Myer went on to play in the league for years, along with logging some PCL time—clearly a good ballplayer in his own right.)

Chozen collected one hit in four at-bats, playing the second game of a doubleheader, a 10–1 loss to Dolph Camilli's Philadelphia Phillies. And according to *The Cincinnati Enquirer* the following day: "He produced a foghorn voice that is louder than anything heard at Crosley Field this year." To be fair, I think that's on the 1937 Reds, who finished 56–98.

Chozen's Major League Baseball career was over—he also had short stints as a boxer and a radio singer—but his minor league travels had just begun, even putting in time as player/manager with the Newport News Builders while hitting a stellar .312. Chozen was out of baseball in 1943 but by choice—he had been recruited by, among other teams, the Elmira (New York) Pioneers. But he was back—just a player again—for a franchise that began in Knoxville in 1944, then relocated midseason to Mobile, Alabama.

And in 1945 for the Mobile Bears, Chozen had his best season yet at age 29. Not only did he hit .353, but he also set the Southern Association hitting streak record with hits in 49 straight games. His reward? Two weeks later he got called up to the army, and his season with Mobile ended a few weeks early.

But less than a week after getting called up came V-J Day, and Chozen was back in 1946, continuing his minor league tour to Memphis, Greenville, Miami Beach, Pine Bluff, back to Lake Charles, and finishing in Greenville, Mississippi, with the Bucks in 1952. Even then at age 36, Chozen hit .271 while assuming managerial duties once more and general manager duties as well.

But by 1953 no baseball opportunities arose, and Chozen returned to his Lake Charles home, where he went into the insurance business and, according to the *Abbeville Meridonial*, "married a Lake Charles girl." Not that he could stay away from the game he loved: by 1954 he was the president of Lake Charles Little League.

18. Bob Berman

Bats Right, Throws Right
Washington Senators, 1918

Bob Berman played in just two games for the Washington Senators and never batted. A New Yorker raised on the Lower East Side at PS 42 and Evander Childs High School, he told *The New York Times'* Ira Berkow in 1988 that his father had supported his baseball playing, but his mother had preferred he become a Latin teacher.

Nevertheless, his career reached a crest at Sportsman's Park in St. Louis, when Berman got the call to enter the game in the ninth inning of the Washington Senators' 6–4 win against the St. Louis Browns. Clark Griffith summoned, of all people, Walter Johnson to close it out, one of just 34 saves Big Train earned in his illustrious career (alongside his 417 wins). "I was a young kid, and Walter Johnson was like a god to me," Berman recalled. "People used to say, 'Wherever Johnson goes, Berman was sure to follow.' And I did, but he never seemed to mind."

Johnson struck out two and preserved the win. Berman went on to serve in World War I, then fulfilled his mother's wishes and became a teacher—P.E. and ballroom dancing, along with baseball coaching duties at Franklin K. Laine High School, where he mentored future major leaguer Bob Grim.

An elderly Berman couldn't remember what happened in the game by 1988, a few months before he died. But the emotion? That stayed with him: "It was the happiest day of my life."

2

First Base

With Hank Greenberg as the starting first baseman, not many backups are needed. Greenberg, a cultural icon, put up numbers that are historically great for any religion. No. 2 on the list is Kevin Youkilis, an extremely valuable player at multiple positions whose legendary batting eye has made him a cultural touchstone for two communities: Semitic and Sabermetric.

1. Hank Greenberg

Bats Right, Throws Right
Detroit Tigers, 1930, 1933–1941, 1945–1946
Pittsburgh Pirates, 1947

I hope you're as familiar with Aviva Kempner's fantastic film about Hank Greenberg as you likely are with Hammerin' Hank himself. It's a well-known fact that the war cost Greenberg a large portion of his career. However, the wrist injury he suffered 12 games into the 1936 season, a recurrence of a malady from the 1935 World Series, cost him his age-25 season, right between hitting .328/.411/.628 at age 24 with 36 home runs and 168 RBIs and his age-26 campaign, when he hit .337/.436/.668 with 40 home runs and 184 RBIs.

This was a serious hitter. His career slugging percentage ranks seventh all time, while his on-base-plus-slugging, or OPS, is eighth all time. Consider that his career is missing five peak years but contains all of his decline, and his rate stats are even more impressive. That career line of .313/.412/.605 translates to an OPS+ of 159. Let's put that in a historical context: among hitters with at least 6,000 plate appearances in baseball history, that ranks Greenberg 12th all time. Those ahead of him: Babe Ruth, Ted Williams, Barry Bonds, Lou Gehrig, Rogers Horsby, Mickey Mantle, early star Dan Brouthers, Ty Cobb, Jimmie Foxx, Mark McGwire, and Stan Musial. That's it. That's the whole list. (Mike Trout, at 5,660 plate appearances through September 2021 and a 176 career OPS+, will likely join this list next season.) That means Greenberg's OPS+ is ahead of...well, everyone else in baseball history: Hank Aaron; Frank Thomas; Tris Speaker; Willies Mays/McCovey, and Stargell; Joe DiMaggio; David Ortiz. It's a remarkable level to reach as a player.

But measuring Greenberg has to move beyond simply baseball. For instance, it is to take nothing away from Jackie Robinson, but while the struggle to integrate baseball was unimaginably difficult, Brooklyn was the perfect place, politically and culturally, for such an endeavor to take place. Robinson faced unfathomable hatred in so many ways during his lonely journey. But at home, at least, a progressive community was there to embrace him.

By contrast, the world, and in particular the major league city that Greenberg called home when he got to the big leagues, was arguably the toughest time and place a Jew could have gone to establish himself in the public eye. Greenberg got to Detroit to stay in 1933—the year Adolf Hitler took over in Germany. Detroit's most famous citizen, in fact the city's raison d'etre, was Henry Ford. He published a newspaper, which unceasingly railed against Jews, and a collection of the newspaper's columns was published in book form as *The International Jew—the World's Foremost Problem*. Reportedly, Mr. Hitler was one of his readers and admirers. Ford went on to blame "International Jewish bankers" for World War II after receiving the highest award a foreigner could receive from Hitler's government. Ford was nice enough to suffer a stroke when shown films of the Nazi concentration camps, according to a collaborator of his. I suppose it was the least he could do.

Along with Ford's presence shadowing Greenberg's city was the leading voice of public Catholicism in the 1930s, Father Charles Coughlin, whose weekly radio sermons were estimated to reach more than 40 million people weekly at their peak. Coughlin pinned the Russian Revolution and the Great Depression on the Jewish people from his pulpit in Royal Oak, Michigan—just outside of Detroit.

Into this situation, and a city ravaged by that Depression and looking for scapegoats, stepped Greenberg. One can only imagine the degree of difficulty. And even when he made good, there were not scores of Jews ready to join him—Robinson had a Black teammate before the year was out, and African Americans in the major leagues were commonplace by the early 1950s. Greenberg, for his career, was the symbol of the Jewish people, and all that it entailed.

This is not to disparage what Robinson accomplished. Of course, Robinson had a barrier of nearly 50 years to break, while other Jews had played in the major leagues around the time Greenberg came up. (John McGraw was desperate for a Jewish star, but New York Giants scouts had apparently dismissed the local boy, Greenberg. Given their lack of success with the Jews they did sign, this is not surprising.) To attempt to quantify or compare what the two men did is impossible. To Greenberg's credit, he often told his son that, "He never knew what having it bad was until he saw how they treated Jackie Robinson," and Greenberg also was one of the first players to publicly offer encouragement to Robinson during the trailblazing star's rookie year. The point is not to play the two men off of each other. Rather, the Robinson tale that is being told again and again is an incomplete one without the story of his immediate predecessor, Hank Greenberg.

2. Kevin Youkilis

Bats Right, Throws Right
Boston Red Sox, 2004–2012
Chicago White Sox, 2012
New York Yankees, 2013

The man whose discerning ability to navigate balls and strikes once led me to drive five hours, back when I was in college, to stand next to statistician Konstantin Medvedovsky and shower Youkilis with an ovation after a base on balls—college was wild—had a baseball career more than worthy of the early hype among people like us, who'd stay up all night playing *Baseball Mogul*, a baseball franchise simulation game developed by Clay Dreslough, that is as great as ever to this day.

Kevin was born and raised in Cincinnati, Ohio, where his father Mike built him a wooden batting cage in the backyard but never forced him to use it. He didn't have to. Youkilis stayed home for college at the University of Cincinnati, Sandy Koufax's alma mater, where Youkilis set records for home runs, slugging percentage, as well as that which he's become best known for: walks and on-base percentage.

He was drafted in the eighth round of the 2001 draft by the Boston Red Sox and continued his walking ways. He tied a minor league record by reaching base safely in 71 straight games, and while Youkilis climbed the organizational ladder, Oakland Athletics general manager Billy Beane reportedly coveted him. A number of conversations from Michael Lewis' book, *Moneyball*, detail the extent of Beane's lust for a Youkilis trade. In the film of the same name, Jonah Hill's character studies video of Youkilis, longing for a way to acquire him.

However, the Red Sox held on to him and are glad they did. He was a bit player on the 2004 Red Sox that broke The Curse of the Bambino but a star soon after. Although he didn't hit for much power in the minor leagues, he added it to his game in 2007, separating himself from the Dave Magadan comparisons that followed him for much of his early career. Mags was a good major league hitter, but without any pop, he failed to stick at his two positions—first and third base—as a regular.

Youkilis' fielding—he won a Gold Glove in 2007—only added to his overall value, an excellence beyond simple versatility. And by 2008 and 2009, he'd become a legitimate star, hitting 29, then 27 home runs in a pair of All-Star campaigns. His five-year run from 2007 to 2011 is truly impressive: a .294/.395/.517 line with 108 home runs for an OPS+ of 136. Among 167 players with at least 2,000 plate appearances during that five-year span, Youkilis ranked 17th in OPS+ ahead of stars like Hanley Ramirez, David Wright, and Chase Utley. And he was even better in October—his career postseason slash line was .306/.376/.568 with six home runs in 125 plate appearances.

In many ways, Youkilis' career looks like Al Rosen's—he got a late start to his major league tenure, and back problems ended his career at 34 in 2014 after a short stint in Japan. He also provided a Jewish flavor to meetings at first base with Ian Kinsler when the fellow Semite reached base. Kinsler told the *Ottawa Citizen* in 2009: "He'll just say, 'Happy Passover' or something like that. He's pretty into it. It's cool."

By the end of the decade, Youkilis had turned to the beer business, where he owns Loma Brewing Company and has a Twitter handle @GreekGodofHops. He'd gone back to school, too, getting his degree in business from U of C, which has retired his jersey No. 36. Many of his IPA names pay tribute to his various interests, but my personal favorite—born of his heritage and martial arts hobby—Jew-Jitsu.

In his final plate appearance with the Red Sox at Fenway Park—amidst trade rumors swirling in July 2012—he legged out a triple, then received a long-standing ovation from the Fenway crowd, who knew all he'd done to make his Red Sox champions. He makes beer, but he'll never have to buy one in the city of Boston.

3. Mike Epstein

Bats Left, Throws Left

Baltimore Orioles, 1966–1967

Washington Senators, 1967–1971

Oakland Athletics, 1971–1972

Texas Rangers, 1973

California Angels, 1973–1974

Often, top prospects get overhyped. But in Mike Epstein's case, not only was his baseball prowess touted, his mental facility also was the subject of press clippings. Even his physical resemblance to Mickey Mantle got him media attention.

Epstein, like Hank Greenberg roughly 30 years before, was a Bronx product, though he played his high school ball across the country at Fairfax High School in Los Angeles, like the Sherry brothers. He was a multi-sport star, excelling in both baseball and football, though he gave up football to avoid injury. He became an All-American at Cal-Berkeley, won a gold medal with the U.S. Olympic team in 1964, and was signed with a $20,000 bonus that same year by the Baltimore Orioles.

Even before his professional debut, Epstein was the subject of multiple items in *The Sporting News*. First, a young fan mistook him for Mantle in an airport and asked "Mr. Mantle" for his autograph. "Obligingly, Epstein wrote, 'Mickey Mantle,'" *The Sporting News* reported in its March 20, 1965 issue. "'I didn't want to break the kid's heart,' he said."

Two weeks later *TSN* profiled "Egghead Epstein: The Slugging Scholar" as he prepared for his professional debut with Stockton of the California League. "Writers need more than a pencil and paper when interviewing Epstein," Doug Brown wrote in the April 3, 1965 *TSN*. "They need a reference library, as well, for they hear words like 'inculcate,' 'adversary,' 'self-image' and 'defeatist,' along with quotations from Emerson and Socrates." The story goes on to describe an Emerson quotation Epstein left for a friend who was considering giving up baseball.

Epstein quickly supplied professional results to go along with his intellectual and imitational skills. He hit 30 home runs to lead the California League in 1965, and his power led a rival manager to label him "Superjew," which for some reason has never been the name of a comic book.

His stock soared still higher after Epstein hit over .300 again in 1966—this time for Triple A Rochester—with another 29 home runs. "He reminds me of a giant bomb waiting to go off," Orioles farm director Harry Dalton said. "He's a kid who could hit 50 home runs."

But the Orioles soon sent that bomb up the Potomac, trading Epstein to the Washington Senators for pitcher Pete Reichert. Epstein now found himself in a cavernous ballpark in the heart of the biggest pitchers' era in baseball history. His power numbers continued to impress, though the batting average did not stay above .300. Epstein hit nine, 13, 30, and 20 home runs from 1967 to 1970, though his batting averages were a more pedestrian .229, .234, .278, and .256. But his secondary numbers were particularly impressive, as Epstein drew plenty of walks, leading to on-base percentages of .331, .338, .414, and .371.

Epstein's 1969 was particularly noteworthy—he finished 25th in the MVP voting for a team that finished in fourth place. He finished ninth in home runs, though in just 403 at-bats. He was fourth in the league in home runs per at bat, and his OPS+ of 176 ranked sixth in the major leagues, just behind Harmon Killebrew and just ahead of Roberto Clemente, Hall of Famers both.

At age 28 in 1971, Epstein seemed poised to become a star. But as the Senators often did, they found it expedient to deal Epstein (and reliever Darold Knowles) to the Oakland A's for Don Minchner, Paul Lindblad, Frank Fernandez, and Washington's favorite trading target—cash.

Epstein picked up right where he'd left off in Oakland, hitting for power and reaching base a ton, even though he'd been sent to an even bigger pitcher's park, the Oakland Coliseum. His .234/.368/.438 line with 18 home runs in 329 at-bats was still good enough for third on the team in long balls and fourth in slugging percentage. The A's were no slouch team, either, winning 101 games and the American League West. He followed that performance with an even stronger 1972, posting a .270/.376/.490 line with 26 home runs in a career-high 455 at bats for the 1972 World Series champions. He even hit .283 against left-handed pitching, a career-long bugaboo for Epstein, though his power (22 of 26 homers) came against right-handers.

But owner Charlie Finley of the A's was never one to stand pat and he acquired a new catcher, Ray Fosse, who had yet to be pronounced "finished" by his collision with Pete Rose in the 1971 All-Star Game. That left the young Gene Tenace without a position. And Tenace was a low-average, high-walk, high-power hitter ready to play first base for less money—leaving Epstein without a position. (It probably didn't help that he'd had a fistfight with Reggie Jackson, that team's star among stars.) He was dumped to the Texas Rangers, newly arrived from their former life as the Senators, for reliever Horacio Pina.

Because life is never fair, Epstein found himself in another pitchers' park, Arlington Stadium. He was given just 85 at-bats before being discarded again—this time to the California Angels. But his swing didn't return right away, and by May 4, 1974, he was released by the Angels. He retired to a ranch near Lake Tahoe by 1975 to grow almonds and did not have a phone there. He said it was partly due to emotional burnout. But ultimately, he re-emerged, making a killing in the commodities business, ultimately moving his family to California so he could coach AAU and helping players, including his son, Jake, reach the professional ranks. Jake hit .336/.401/.552 in his lone minor league season, suggesting he, too, could have been in this book in his own right had he kept playing. I asked him why his career was so brief, and he answered on Twitter, "Haha, you will have to ask the Angels!"

A rendering of Epstein's career suggests that he was never fully appreciated in his time. Given his secondary skills, like drawing walks, if an Epstein were to find his way to the major leagues today, sabermetric disciples all over the country would be clamoring for him. And in a hitters' era, Epstein likely would have posted numbers too strong to ignore—let alone ones that allowed him to go from starting first baseman on a world champion to out of baseball in just 18 months.

Epstein became a wandering coach, teaching hitting to minor leaguers in both the San Diego and Milwaukee systems, and currently runs a successful hitting school along with Jake. With a modern statistical lens, let us all look past his career batting average and see that the sum of his contributions as a hitter were quite good, if not Super. But as Emerson wrote, "To be great is to be misunderstood."

4. Ron Blomberg

Bats Left, Throws Right
New York Yankees, 1969, 1971–1976
Chicago White Sox, 1978

The ironic part of Ron Blomberg being primarily remembered for his role as baseball's first-ever designated hitter is that his athletic profile runs entirely counter to the general perception of the oafish, one-dimensional ballplayer we've come to associate with the position.

Blomberg was the son of Sol and Goldie Rae Blomberg, who operated a jewelry store in Atlanta. He was a multi-sport star at Druid Hills High School in Atlanta, earning *Parade* All-American honors in baseball, basketball, and football. He received 125 college basketball scholarship offers, even drawing a recruiting visit from UCLA's John Wooden. Football was no different—he got 100 gridiron scholarship offers as well. His first mention in *The Sporting News* was May 20, 1967—for his running: "Another highly regarded prospect is Ron Blomberg, a right-handed throwing and left-handed hitting first baseman... whom most of the ivory hunters say can 'do it all,' Blomberg has been clocked in 3.8 seconds going from home plate to first base."

He was the top overall pick in the 1967 draft, going ahead of future big league standouts Jon Matlack, John Mayberry, Ted Simmons, and Bobby

Grich. Just more than two years later, he made his way to New York for a brief callup. Just two years later, he was up to stay.

His minor league tenure was similar to his major league career—he hit very well when healthy, but injuries were a problem he never could conquer. His minor league slugging percentage was .461 with two seasons above .500—but his season high in home runs was just 19 because his season high in at-bats was a mere 384.

The 1971 New York Yankees were a team in transition. Blomberg easily supplanted Danny Cater at first base, while young stars like catcher Thurman Munson and center fielder Bobby Murcer (who hit .331 with 25 home runs, drawing comparisons to Mickey Mantle in the process) seemed to portend success just ahead. "When I'm finished playing, I'd like them to have a monument of mine out there," Blomberg told UPI's Milton Richman in 1971.

But after Blomberg's rookie season, a spectacular debut by any measure (.322 average, seven home runs in 199 at-bats—good for a .477 slugging percentage), the Yanks went out and got 37-year-old Felipe Alou to block the position of first base for the 1972 season. Nevertheless, Blomberg and Alou ended up each appearing in 95 games at the position in 1972, and the 23-year-old Blomberg easily outhit Alou. While his average dipped to .268, Blomberg hit 14 home runs in 299 at-bats, slugging .488 in the process. He also continued to show the ability to not strike out. After 14 walks and 23 strikeouts in his 1971 campaign, he walked 38 times and struck out just 26 times. He would go on to walk more than he struck out—the walks were infrequent, but the whiffs were remarkably rare for a power hitter. He struck out just 140 times in 1,333 at-bats. By contrast, contemporary slugger Dave Kingman struck out 122 times in 1973 alone—in just 305 at-bats.

The 1973 season saw Blomberg come closest to realizing his seemingly unlimited potential. After hitting just .188 through April 29, he managed a 4-for-4 day to break out of his slump against the Minnesota Twins. He would not falter again for some time, getting most of the starts at designated hitter. (Jim Ray Hart filled in for him some, due to nagging injuries.) Blomberg pushed his batting average above .400, earning the cover of *Sports Illustrated*, among others.

Blomberg topped .400 as late as June 28, but a summer-long slump eroded that mark to a still great .329 average with 12 home runs and just 25 strikeouts in 301 at-bats. With Graig Nettles now manning third, Doc Medich holding down a rotation spot, and Sparky Lyle closing, the Yankees and Blomberg looked ready for the big time. Though the Yankees got to the World Series by 1976 and won it in 1977, Blomberg was not a large part of the renaissance. His 1974 season was nearly as good as his 1973 campaign—.311 average, 10 home runs in 264 at-bats for a .481 slugging percentage, and just 33 strikeouts.

But he suffered knee and shoulder injuries that limited him to just 106 at-bats in 1975 and a mere two at-bats in 1976. Fully rehabilitated, Blomberg looked to resume his career in 1977, but a collision with an outfield wall—plus Chris Chambliss, Carlos May, and Lou Piniella blocking the way at first base and DH—rendered Blomberg's 1977 a moot point.

After the 1977 season, he signed as a free agent with the Chicago White Sox. But the injuries had collectively sapped much of Blomberg's talent from him, and he managed just a .231 average in 156 at-bats before calling it a career in the spring of 1979, when he failed to make the team out of spring training. "It was my knee," Blomberg told Dave Anderson of *The New York Times* in 1978. "I was the only one who knew how much it hurt. It just didn't come around after the operation."

It is an exercise in futility to speculate on how good Blomberg, if healthy, might have been. Even with all that he suffered through, he ended with career marks of .293 batting average, a .360 on-base percentage, and a .473 slugging percentage. His 52 home runs in 1,333 at bats translates to 20–25 per season had he ever been fully healthy. His stats are also undervalued by his era. His career OPS+ of 140 in 1,493 at-bats is the mark of a true star. Mike Epstein's sparring partner, Reggie Jackson, reached the Hall of Fame with an OPS+ for his career of 139.

Blomberg signed on in the spring of 2007 to manage the Bet Shemesh Blue Sox in the inaugural season of the Israeli Baseball League. He's published multiple books, highly entertaining ones, and works as a motivational speaker to this day. His legacy is secure. But it's hard not to look at his career and think that with good health, we might be talking about one of the best who ever lived.

5. Phil Weintraub

Bats Left, Throws Left
New York Giants, 1933–1935, 1937
Cincinnati Reds, 1937
Philadelphia Phillies, 1938
New York Giants, 1944–1945

It is nearly impossible to understand how Phil Weintraub did not become a star first baseman in the major leagues. His statistical profile is one of a fine hitter—both superficially in the tools used to evaluate at the time and in the modern era. His career batting average was .295, and by the more exact measures we have today, his OPS+, which measures how his on-base percentage-plus-slugging measures against the league he played in, was 132 (100 is average). For a modern comp: Rhys Hoskins' OPS+ is 129.

After playing at Loyola College of Chicago, Weintraub joined the New York Giants in 1933. He received just 15 at-bats for the world champions, as another left handed, line-drive hitter, player/manager Bill Terry, manned first base.

Imagine a young Weintraub—a potential star, a figure of glamour, who reportedly owned 100 different suits—establishing himself as a star in New York, home to an enormous Jewish population. His popularity would have been impossibly huge. But the Giants let Weintraub go to Nashville of the Southern Association for more seasoning in 1934, and like Terry in 1930, Weintraub hit .401, becoming the first man to ever top .400 in the league. He hit 16 home runs in just 372 at-bats. He drove in 87 runs. He walked 68 times and struck out on just 36 occasions. He hit three home runs in a game. He was called up late in the season and hit .351 for the Giants. *The Sporting News* said of Weintraub in December 13, 1934: "The Giants don't know what they're going to do with Phil."

The answer in 1935 was to bury him on the bench. Terry hit .341, while the offense provided by outfielders Mel Ott, Jo-Jo Moore, and Hank Lieber (all three 26 and younger) left few at-bats for Weintraub. But Terry was 36 in 1935. Surely, Weintraub had to be the heir apparent!

Instead, Terry shipped Weintraub, along with pitcher Roy Parmalee, to the St. Louis Cardinals for middle infielder Burgess Whitehead. Injuries limited Terry in 1936, but the middling Sam Leslie, not Weintraub, was there to step in. Meanwhile, in St. Louis a young man took over at first base named Johnny Mize. Cardinals general manager Branch Rickey soon saw that he had no need for Weintraub and parted with the thing he liked more than almost anything: a young player with unrealized potential in exchange for the thing he liked even more, money.

The Cincinnati Reds kept him in the minors for the rest of 1936, even though he was hitting .371 in the International League with 80 RBIs at the time of the deal. They made little use of him in 1937 as well. Les Scarsella and Buck Jordan were the obscure names that prevented Weintraub from a full trial. He came full circle, returning to the Giants in July but received just nine at-bats for New York. Johnny McCarthy was the choice this time, even though the rate stats for his career-best season (.279/.322/.410) pale in comparison to Weintraub's season line of .274/.348/.430 in 179 at-bats.

Weintraub was promptly dumped by the Giants again to the unaffiliated minor league club in Baltimore. He was then purchased in June 1938 by the Philadelphia Phillies, who offered him a chance to play regularly for the first time in the major leagues. Weintraub did not disappoint, hitting .311 with a .422 on-base percentage in 351 at-bats and even collected the final hit in the Phils' old park, the Baker Bowl. The Phillies promptly sold him to the Boston Red Sox at season's end.

While his rights were controlled by the Red Sox, Weintraub's chances of helping the major league club were remote at best. The incumbent, Jimmie Foxx, went out in 1939 and hit .360 with 35 home runs. Weintraub echoed Foxx's production with Minneapolis of the American Association, hitting .331 with 33 home runs in 1939. The next year, 1940, was the same story: Foxx hit .297 with 36 home runs for the Sox, and Weintraub hit .347 with 27 home runs for the minor league Millers.

Then came the war. Foxx slowed down, but Weintraub continued slugging in the minors. He was well past 30, and the draft board had declared him unfit for service. Foxx was replaced at first by Tony Lupien, who proved to be, well, no Jimmie Foxx.

Weintraub's rights were shipped to the St. Louis Browns, then reacquired by the Giants for a third time. The 36-year-old Weintraub showed he still had pop left in his bat. For the '44 Giants, he hit .316/.412/.524 in 361 at-bats with 13 home runs. That included a memorable day on April 30, 1944, against the Brooklyn Dodgers at the Polo Grounds, when he drove in 11 runs in a 26–8 win. The 11 RBIs are one short of the all-time mark for a single game held by Jim Bottomley and Mark Whiten.

Weintraub followed that in 1945 with a .272/.389/.417 line and another 10 home runs at age 37. Two of these came on the occasion of New York's home opener in support of winning pitcher and fellow Jew Harry Feldman. The 1946 Giants had five Jews. Weintraub was not one of them. The Giants had traded for Mize, and Weintraub's major league career was over. He was released in July 1946.

How good was Weintraub? Terry, his manager, predecessor, and bete noir, finished with an OPS+ of 136 en route to the Hall of Fame. Weintraub, who couldn't get a real shot at regular playing time, finished just behind Terry at 132. Even Weintraub didn't understand why he never got his opportunity. "I frankly don't know why I was a minor for so long, but I suppose the final explanation is that is just baseball," he said, according to SABR. "It certainly is a strange game."

It isn't hard to imagine a different career path for Weintraub that would have included enshrinement as well.

6. Ike Davis

Bats Left, Throws Left
New York Mets, 2010–2014
Pittsburgh Pirates, 2014
Oakland Athletics, 2015
New York Yankees, 2016

I will believe, to my dying day, that Ike Davis' could have had Freddie Freeman's career—if not for an obscure disease that's utterly destroyed many other players as well throughout professional sports.

Let's review their paths and when they diverged. Ike Davis was a schoolboy star growing up in Scottsdale, Arizona. His father, Ron Davis, had a long career, but he's Baptist. It is Ike's mother, Millie, who places him in this book. Ike is self-described as "culturally Jewish" with a clear understanding of his heritage and an appreciation for the history of his own family—his great-aunt is a Holocaust survivor, and he met with descendants of Holocaust victims during his time with the New York Mets.

Davis went onto Arizona State, and in 2008 the Mets selected him in the first round of the Major League Baseball Draft. Freeman, meanwhile, was tabbed in the second round of the 2007 draft by the Atlanta Braves. The two posted similar minor league numbers—an OPS of .839 for Freeman in the minors, .819 for Davis, including a slow start in Brooklyn—and they both broke into the big leagues in 2010. By March of 2011, this is how *The Bergen Record*'s Bob Klapisch described the two: "The Braves think Freeman, a left-handed hitting first baseman, will be a notch better than Ike Davis, which is no small endorsement."

This was the general view around baseball, but others had Davis ahead. The 2010 *Baseball America* top 100 prospect rankings put Freeman at 32 and Davis at 62, which is less a measure of the distance between them, and more points to the industry as a whole seeing them both as potential longtime regulars.

Freeman had played sparingly in 2010 but held his own in 2011 with a .282/.346/.448 line and 21 home runs. It was good enough for an OPS+ of 116, right in line with Davis' 115 in 2010. But in his second year, Davis was off to a huge start, going .302/.383/.543 with an OPS+ of 156, when he collided with teammate David Wright on a routine pop-up. The Mets misdiagnosed the injury several times, and ultimately, it cost him the rest of his 2011 season.

Still, by the time they got it right, an offseason of rest promised a 2012 with Davis good as new. At this point here's how the MLB comparisons looked between the two:

Davis: 183 games, .271/.357/.460, OPS+ 123

Freeman: 177 games, .277/.340/.444, OPS+ 113

Freeman was two years younger, but Davis had the clear advantage in performance to date. It's hard to make the argument for one over the other.

Well, in March 2012, Davis was diagnosed with Valley Fever, a malady that is incurable and is exacerbated by intense exercise. In true Mets fashion, they simultaneously attacked his work ethic for the next several years in leaks to the media while continuing to play him, ultimately flipping him at the trade deadline in 2014.

Freeman, meanwhile, continued along his path to stardom, won a National League MVP in 2020, and absolutely has a Hall of Fame case in the making.

Here's the two since Davis' Valley Fever diagnosis in March 2012:

Davis: 482 games, .224/.320/.393, OPS+ 99

Freeman: 1,368 games, .297/.388/.517, OPS+ 141

This is not an uncommon outcome for athletes with Valley Fever. Conor Jackson, a promising outfielder with the Arizona Diamondbacks, was diagnosed in the spring of 2009. His OPS+ was 104 before, 73 after. Johnny Moore, a point guard with the San Antonio Spurs, had racked up 26.6 win shares by his age-26 season in 1985 when he contracted Valley Fever. From age 27 on, his total win shares were 3.6.

Davis soldiered on, even attempting to reinvent himself as a pitcher late in 2017. In theory, less wear and tear from everyday play might have been a more fruitful path once he got Valley Fever, but without other suitors to help him keep trying, he retired after the 2018 season.

With many players here, we can only speculate, but I saw Davis play. Freeman is, too, a stellar first baseman who deserves every bit of the career he's had. It just should have been both of them.

7. Rowdy Tellez

Bats Left, Throws Left
Toronto Blue Jays, 2018–2021
Milwaukee Brewers, 2021–present

Rowdy Tellez has revitalized his career after a classic change-of-scenery trade in 2021. A beefy 6'4", 255 pounds, Tellez was a two-time *The Sacramento Bee* Player of the Year in 2012 and 2013 for Elk Grove High School but had a scholarship offer at USC and planned to go. The Toronto Blue Jays took him in the 30th round of the 2013 draft anyway and enticed him to give up an education for $850,000. He got to celebrate with his 93-year-old grandmother, then hopped on a place to Dunedin, Florida, where the Blue Jays assigned him.

The power was slow to show up in games, but he finally broke out with Double A New Hampshire in 2016, hitting .297/.387/.530 with 23 home runs. He never showed up on any top 100 prospect lists—playing first base at best, at worst designated hitter in his future—but he shot up Toronto's team-level prospect lists. And by 2018 he burst onto the scene with Toronto, hitting doubles in each of his first three plate appearances, all as he was grieving his mother, who'd died of brain cancer a short time earlier.

Tellez finished 2018 at .314/.329/.614, regressed some in 2019, before rebounding to .283/.346/.540 in 2020. (Clearly, the man knows how to weather adversity.) But a slow start in 2021 led to Toronto dealing him to the Milwaukee Brewers. Not only did he produce for the Brewers—a .272/.333/.481 line after the deal—he hit his first two postseason home runs in October. Add in the likely return of the designated hitter to the National League in 2022, and Tellez's future ceiling could land him ahead of Ike Davis and Phil Weintraub on this list. Dan Szymborski's ZIPS for FanGraphs is pretty high on him for 2022: .251/.316/.481.

8. Lou Limmer

Bats Left, Throws Left
Philadelphia Athletics, 1951, 1954

According to an April 5, 2007, obituary in the Jewish Telegraph Agency, long-time minor league slugger Lou Limmer became the first Jewish baseball player to ever hold the office of president in his synagogue. (In Limmer's case it was at Castle Hill Community Jewish Center in The Bronx). This seems like it would be a natural career move, something akin to how caterpillars become butterflies. First basemen are, by nature, talkers. Detroit Tigers first sacker Sean Casey was known as "the Mayor" for his gregariousness. The aforementioned Freddie Freeman doesn't have an enemy in the game, having forged relationships 90 feet from home. There is a combination of political conversing and a search for information that takes place all at once between the person manning the position and the baserunner.

Of the other Jewish first basemen, Hank Greenberg was certainly beloved enough to have become president of any congregation he desired (many thought Greenberg would be the president of the United States). Greg Goossen has shown his abilities as an actor—surely congregation political leader wouldn't be beyond him. And Ron Blomberg's talents at public speaking would surely lend themselves to the job.

That leaves aside the more obvious tactic, which would call for small-market teams, who cry poverty at a decibel level equal to synagogues on the High Holidays, to employ congregation presidents as first basemen. With most of them out of contention early in the season, what would they have to lose by sticking a lesser ballplayer into the bottom of the order, so that he may be able to kindly ask the passing baserunners for financial relief? Who better to target than baseball players? By their very inclusion in the major leagues, they are guaranteed to be making well over $500,000 annually. Only the presence of uniforms, which include identifying numbers and often names, would prevent the most valued Jewish charity of all, the anonymous kind. Still, it is an idea whose time has come.

The Philadelphia A's, no stranger to financial woes, were 50-plus years ahead of their time by employing Limmer, though they were likely persuaded more by his home run totals in the minor leagues (he hit 110 in his four seasons prior to his initial call-up in 1951 and a total of 244 in the minors, according to the Philadelphia A's Historical Society).

Mired in decades of penny-pinching by owner/manager Connie Mack, the Athletics had little talent on the field in 1951. And the hype around Limmer was considerable. Walter Johns wrote in March of 1951 for *The Danville Morning News* that "the A's consider him their number 1 player in the whole minor league system and believe he's ready for the majors."

Unfortunately for Limmer, Ferris Fain existed, a sweet-fielding on-base machine of a first baseman. While Limmer struggled to get at-bats, Fain won batting titles in both 1951 and 1952, long after Limmer had been returned to the minor leagues. Limmer hit .159 with five home runs in 214 at-bats, which isn't going to strike fear of job insecurity into the heart of any batting champion.

He did participate in a bit of Jewish baseball history, however, hitting a home run off of the Tigers' Saul Rogovin, as Joe Ginsberg caught him on May 2, 1951. It was the first, and thus far only, Jewish battery and hitter in major league history.

Fain was eventually shipped out as the A's attempted to retool, and Limmer got his second and final shot in 1954. This time around, he hit .231, slugged 14 home runs (second on the team), and even managed the last home run in Philadelphia A's history. His long home runs during the pregame festivities even earned him the double-edged nickname "Babe Ruth of Batting Practice."

But attendance had fallen to just 304,666 for the season. From that perspective even Kansas City can seem like greener grass, so the A's took off, leaving Limmer behind in the minor leagues—this time for good.

But in case you wondered whether Philadelphia left its mark on Limmer, where he'd been a hero to many in the Jewish neighborhood of West Philly, wonder no more.

Max Silberman, vice president of the Philadelphia A's Historical Society in 2002, told *The Philadelphia Inquirer* that in 1998 he'd suffered a stroke and spent some time in the hospital. At 1:00 PM each Saturday he was there, the phone rang. It was Limmer, who'd gotten to know Silberman through his efforts to keep the A's memory alive. "He called me every Saturday at 1 in the afternoon to say he prayed for me at synagogue," Silberman said. "I cried for days because I meant something to him after he meant so much to me."

It is hard to imagine a slugger the quality of Limmer languishing in the minors for his entire career in the era of the six-year minor league free agents and 30 teams. He won two minor league batting titles and finished in the top five of his league on seven different occasions. Had the Athletics utilized him as Castle Hill Community Jewish Center did, perhaps Philadelphia would have two teams still.

9. Greg Goossen

Bats Right, Throws Right
New York Mets, 1965–1968
Seattle Pilots, 1969
Milwaukee Brewers, 1970
Washington Senators, 1970

I've included all those who can be considered Jewish by the definitions of any Jewish sect or those who self-identify as Jewish. It seems Goossen was "perplexed" why he was included here, something he expressed in the interview that formed the basis of his 2011 obituary in *The New York Times*. I don't wish to argue with the dead, but his father was Jewish, though Goossen was a practicing Roman Catholic. Moreover, the fact that he was simply confused, but not outraged, means we'll leave him here for the second edition as well.

Goossen was, like Ed Kranepool, a young player who lost his prime development years playing for the early New York Mets. Those Mets were desperate for talent, so Goossen, Ron Swoboda, and many others, who could have benefited from minor league time, instead provided a sense of hope to fans as the Mets found 10th place each year.

When he did play in the minors, he excelled, even though he was young for the league. As a 19 year old with Single A Auburn, his slash line was .305/.395/.573. A year later at age 20 with Triple A Jacksonville, he was still productive, hitting .243/.346/.475 with 25 home runs while playing behind a young hurler named Tom Seaver.

Plucked away by the expansion Seattle Pilots in 1969, Goossen experienced a magical season, hitting .309 with 10 home runs in just 139 at-bats with a .597 slugging percentage. But his magic did not travel with the franchise to Milwaukee, and after slumping to .255, then .222 after being purchased midseason by the Senators, he never returned to the major leagues. He is memorialized in many stories you can find in Jim Bouton's *Ball Four*, however, and one of the few players Bouton spoke of with respect.

He was quick-witted, pointing out that the Mets let him go in 1968, only to win it all in 1969. "You don't think they tried to tell me something, do you?" he mused in 1971.

Between major league, minor league, and international teams, Goosen played for 38 clubs, he told the *Los Angeles Times* in 1991. "Either everybody wanted me, or everybody wanted to get rid of me," Goossen said. "I could never figure out which one it was."

After bouncing from job to job, Goossen did find a post-baseball home acting in films, primarily with Gene Hackman, who also insisted Goossen be his stand-in. Although it is hard to fashion an argument that Goossen made a huge difference for his oft-losing major league teams, is it possible that his presence was the difference in Hackman's finest films.

Five Best Gene Hackman Movies with Greg Goossen

1. *The Royal Tenenbaums*
2. *Unforgiven*
3. *The Birdcage*
4. *Get Shorty*
5. *The Firm*

Five Best Gene Hackman Movies without Greg Goossen

1. *The French Connection*
2. *Reds*
3. *Hoosiers*
4. *Superman*
5. *Crimson Tide*

10. Nate Freiman

Bats Right, Throws Right
Oakland Athletics, 2013–2014

The tallest Jewish player in Major League Baseball history, big Nate Freiman should have gotten more of a chance to prove himself. But the very reasons he didn't—already in place by the time he climbed the minor league ladder—were understood not only by Freiman, but also by those closest to him.

So it was conveyed to me, when I had the chance to chat with Marjorie Freiman, Nate's mother (though she referred to him as Nathan throughout that and our subsequent conversation). She had an appreciation for what he'd done, not what circumstances might have prevented him from doing.

The Freimans are a family of educated people. Both Marjorie and her husband have law degrees. Marjorie herself is an educator. So the fact that

Nate stayed in school, earning his degree at Duke before embarking on his professional career, meant a later start. (It also meant he's the all-time leader at Duke in home runs, incidentally.) "We're treating every day he has with this team as a gift," Marjorie told me at Yankee Stadium in 2013, as we stood watching Nate take batting practice. "We didn't know how long it was going to last. And as a parent, we want to mostly convey to him: he's made it. Whatever happens from here, he's made it to this level."

The San Diego Padres selected Freiman in the eighth round of the 2009 draft and they were conservative with him—one level a year—despite evident success in each new city with an OPS north of .800 each year, batting averages in the .280s and .290s, and power production to spare. But time was running short, and he'd started late. "The only thing we've ever wanted is for him to have a chance," Marjorie said as she stood in the first row of seats behind home plate. "And being from the northeast and a kid who wanted to go to college and finish college, he knew he was going to have to work two times or three times as hard. And that wasn't daunting to him. We just always hoped he'd get the chance."

The Houston Astros, wisely, took him in the 2012 Rule 5 Draft. Very few people take the time to consider what a Rule 5 draft does to Jewish education in this country. "I was at the temple. I was in a Torah class, and my husband texted me and said, 'Nathan just got picked up', and it's very obviously jarring for him from one minute to the next. You have to be in this business with a certain zen outlook," Marjorie said, chuckling, "because you know it's a fickle business, and in one day, everything can change."

But the Astros then unwisely allowed him to be exposed on waivers in the spring of 2013, when he was snapped up by the Oakland A's. So there stood Freiman, in early May of 2013, about to take on CC Sabathia and the New York Yankees. He had something to prove to three different organizations—his current one and the two others that hadn't believed in him.

You can imagine the thrill for Freiman and his entire family when he went 3-for-3 that night, including three hits against Sabathia. The Wellesley,

Massachusetts, family—Boston Red Sox country—took particular pleasure in seeing it happen against the Yankees.

It was part of a magical May for Freiman, who finished the month at .351/.415/.514 and earned American League Rookie of the Month honors. For the season he checked in at .274/.327/.389, right at league average, and most of his damage occurred against lefties. (He easily outpaced every first baseman and designate hitter on the Astros, the team that let him go, by the way.)

Freiman provided more of the same in 2014, but instead of platooning him with Brandon Moss, the A's used him in just 36 games, cycling in others like a late-career Adam Dunn and Daric Barton, again limiting his ability to grow as a player. By 2016 he was a Long Island Duck, an indy league team, trying to get back into affiliated baseball during the season, and crushing baseballs in the Mexican League as well, all to no avail.

Do I think there should have been a place for a certified lefty-masher (he'd even by his 2016 season in Double A Portland elevated his ability to hit right-handers as well) who handled first base well in the big leagues? I do. Does the fact that I met his mom make me even more sympathetic to this idea? Well, sure. But the data is there.

Did I mention he absolutely crushed the ball when he played for Team Israel? Well, he did—four home runs and a .417 average as Brad Ausmus' first baseman and No. 3 hitter in 2013 and a .273/.429/.636 line in the 2017 World Baseball Classic. "For some of our guys, playing in the tournament was not only a chance to represent an ancient religious conviction, but also a way to inspire a new generation of baseball players in Israel," Freiman wrote in The Players' Tribune in 2017. "For others, it was an adventure, an opportunity to compete on a world stage. And for many of us, it was a chance to show that we still have what it takes to play pro ball."

And thanks to Freiman's hitting, Team Israel reached the Olympics for baseball for the first time in 2021.

By then, Freiman had retired from the game—an MBA from Duke beckoned when he retired in 2018, then a job in the Cleveland organization as assistant director of player development, which is where you'll find him as this book goes to the printer. There's no tragedy here, just a group of extremely capable people who have come together—Freiman and his wife, the former LPGA golfer Amanda Blumenhurst, have an adorable family. I highly recommend following her on Twitter for video updates.

That night in New York was a triumph. It was understood by everyone then to enjoy the moment. Wisdom then, wisdom we can all heed now. "What a thrill it was," Marjorie told me by email a few days after it happened. "To see Nathan in the box facing CC Sabathia was surreal in and of itself. To see him get 3 hits in Yankee Stadium [even though it's the new one], against a team he has grown up watching and which is the most storied franchise in the league—and which Boston faces so often every season—was the experience of a lifetime. Our cousins took the entire family [more than 20 of us] to Peter Luger for dinner after Saturday's game and we had a wonderful time. The boys all sat with Nathan and Amanda and asked them dozens of questions; he signed baseballs for each of them, and we celebrated my nephew's 19th birthday together. An unforgettable weekend."

11. Jake Goodman

Bats Unknown, Throws Unknown
Milwaukee Grays, 1878
Pittsburgh Alleghenys, 1882

How can I fail to honor the memory of Jake Goodman, a Jewish first baseman who finished fifth in the National League in home runs in 1878? Well, the total that catapulted him to fifth was one home run. (When they call it the Dead Ball Era, they aren't kidding.) He finished seventh in the league in strikeouts and 10th in total outs made.

The Grays weren't much better as a team, finishing at 15–45, though based on their runs scored and runs allowed, they should have been closer to 19–41.

Like a guest too polite to make a host uncomfortable any longer, the Grays politely bowed and ceased to exist.

Goodman resurfaced with the 1882 Pittsburgh Alleghenys of the American Association, the forerunner to today's Pirates. (Pittsburgh merged into the National League in 1887.) There, Chappy Lane proved to be no contest for Goodman in the first-base battle. Lane hit just .175 while Goodman batted a robust .317, though his home run total dropped slightly, to zero. Nevertheless, Pittsburgh went with the younger Ed Smallwood in 1883, releasing Goodman and ending his major league career. His playing career continued in the minors in places like Trenton, New Jersey, and Lancaster, Pennsylvania, before returning to his hometown of Reading, Pennsylvania, post-playing career to work in an iron mill until passing away at an early age in 1890. "Jake was a fine first baseman and a good hitter," reported *The Chicago Inter Ocean* in 1890. "Jake stood over six feet in his stockings, and could coach in a high key."

12. Josh Satin
Bats Right, Throws Right
New York Mets, 2011–2014

Josh Satin reached Cooperstown early. His Valley Vipers played in the Field of Dreams Tournament in 1997, and 12-year-old Josh led off and scored three times in a 13–1 win against the Florida Gators. This would be the high point for most players but not Satin, who went on to star at Harvard-Westlake High School, then make the all-American team playing at Cal-Berkeley, following a Bar Mitzvah attended by future fellow Team Israel player Blake Gailen.

It was enough to earn him a sixth-round selection by the New York Mets in the 2008 draft—the same year the Mets picked Ike Davis in the first round, a bumper crop of Jewish Mets—and the two found themselves teammates in Brooklyn. Satin quickly displayed both a positional versatility that was promising—he could easily appear anywhere on the infield if his career had unfolded differently—and an on-base skill. By 2010 he'd mastered Double

A, hitting a combined .311/.399/.467 at high A St. Lucie and then Double A Binghamton, while producing plays in the field like a double play described by the *Binghamton Press & Sun-Bulletin* as "an over-the-shoulder catch in shallow right field and completed the play with a toss to second."

By 2011 he'd earned Mets organizational Player of the Year honors and debuted, playing some first, some third for the big club. As Steve Popper put it in *The Bergen Record* that September, "even with a September call-up, the team admitted that for him to make it in the majors he will likely have to be a utility player." Satin's career defensive metrics suggest he was an elite defensive first baseman and solid at both second and third, something I can confirm with the eye test.

Clearly, that was how the Mets saw him even after a 2013 in which he posted a .279/.376/.405 line and supplanted Ike Davis as regular first baseman for a time. That production was good enough for a 123 OPS+—for reference, Ben Zobrist that season in a similar super-utility role for the Tampa Bay Rays put up a 112 OPS+ and made an All-Star team. But the Mets of that time were not run as well as the Rays, and after New York gave precious little time to Satin on the 2014 team, he was off to the Cincinnati Reds as a free agent.

By then he was 30, and getting opportunities, especially in organizations that didn't draft and develop you, are hard at that advanced age. So it was in both Cincinnati and San Diego, Satin just provided organizational depth in both seasons. Satin did start at third base for Team Israel in both the 2013 and 2017 World Baseball Classic qualifiers but was already transitioning into his current career as a real estate investor.

13. Mike Schemer

Bats Left, Throws Left
New York Giants, 1945–1946

Mike Schemer, pride of Miami High in Florida, joined Jersey City, a farm club of the New York Giants, in 1940. He drew notice immediately: "He's a left-hander all-around, is a big boy, with lots of power," Smith Barrier wrote in in April 1940. Optioned to Class D Salisbury of the North Carolina State League, Schemer got off to a roaring start, hitting .400 into June, and finished as the starting first baseman on the all-league team.

Promoted to Class-C Fort Smith (Arkansas) Giants of the Western Association in 1941, Schemer kept on slugging with a .457 average through the end of May. "I kind of miss the sunshine," he confided to *Miami Herald* sports columnist Everett Clay. "It is only 110 in the shade up here, so you know how I miss it."

Clay pointed out a few weeks later that Giants manager Bill Terry was sending specific orders to Schemer to hit the ball the other way more, preparing him to be the heir apparent at first base. By July, Clay said four major league scouts had been to see Schemer in Fort Smith, and his average was still at an elite .371. Accordingly, that September, the *Springfield Leader and Press* reported that Schemer would be among the players who "will get their chance with the boys who make their home at the Polo Grounds" in the spring of 1942.

Elevated to the Class-B Jacksonville Tars, he tore up the South Atlantic League, too. By July 1942, with Schemer hitting .339, Terry was singing Schemer's praises to Schemer's hometown *Herald*. "I saw Schemer in two games at Jacksonville, and he looks great," Terry said, expressing the belief that he'd soon be in the major leagues. "The way he is hitting to right field, the picture has changed completely." He pronounced Schemer's fielding major league ready.

After working at a New Orleans shipyard during the offseason, Schemer was still touted by the press as the likely answer at first base for New York. The Army had other plans, and he reported instead to Camp Blanding on April 28. Discharged late in 1943, he returned from World War II in time to play 1944 with the Jersey City farm club. First base, however, was occupied by Phil Weintraub. And Schemer, incredibly, was ruled a free agent when the Giants failed to tender him a contract, a rare freedom for a player at that time. By 1945

Schemer was up with the big club as major league teams searched everywhere for able-bodied players.

Schemer acquitted himself nicely among the leftovers, hitting .333 in a part-time role (108 at-bats). He served as primarily backup, incidentally, for Weintraub. By 1946 he was only able to get a single at-bat, as newly-acquired Johnny Mize ate up the appearances at first base.

But he'd had a clear shot at the first base job in New York before world events intervened.

Schemer bounced around for a while after that, playing and managing with West Palm Beach in the Florida International League and pinch hitting for Sacramento of the Pacific Coast League. By the 1950s he was back in Miami, married, and playing in local softball leagues, bowling tournaments, and the occasional appearance at Old Timers' Days for the minor league Miami Marlins. He was active into the 1960s with the Miami Old Timers Professional Baseball Association, a kind of proto-SABR chapter.

An odd note, but one that seems too coincidental to be unrelated: a racing dog in the late-1970s tore through the Miami and area races for several years. That dog's name? Mike Schemer. Headlines like "Mike Schemer Romps In Stakes," "Mike Schemer Shortens Route," and "Hollywood dog breaks 37-second barrier" referred to Mike Schemer's racing time. I turned to the longtime sports journalist Howard Kleinberg for answers. In an email from his son, Eliot, Howard replied, "I didn't know there was a dog named after Schemer. But I seem to recall, from a hazy past, that Mike worked at a dog track."

As this book went to press, I had been unable to ascertain whether A) Mike Schemer the Person had any relationship with or connection to Mike Schemer the Dog and B) whether Mike Schemer the Dog was also Jewish.

14. Cody Decker

Bats Right, Throws Right
San Diego Padres, 2015

It would be a mistake to cast aside Cody Decker as simply a brief major leaguer, though his time in the show began and ended with 11 hitless at-bats for the San Diego Padres in 2015.

The man could play. He grew up in Santa Monica, hit .490 as a senior for Santa Monica High School, then was two-time All-Pac 10 playing for UCLA. He was selected by the Padres in the 22nd round of the 2009 draft and went on to crush 204 minor league home runs over 11 minor league seasons with a career slash line in the minors of .260/.341/.517.

But the biggest contribution Decker made to baseball came when he purchased the unofficial mascot of the 2017 Israeli World Baseball Classic team: Mensch on a Bench. Mensch first made an appearance on the team bench during WBC qualifying games in Brooklyn. Once Israel advanced, Decker attempted to get him a first-class ticket to the WBC in Seoul, settling for a duffel bag when that failed. "Every team needs their Jobu," Decker said. "He was ours. He had his own locker, and we even gave him offerings: Manischewitz, gelt, and gefilte fish."

Did that trick work like it did in the film *Major League*? Well, did Team Israel qualify for the 2020 Olympics?

15. Josh Whitesell

Bats Left, Throws Left
Arizona Diamondbacks, 2008–2009

After a stellar career at Loyola Marymount, the Montreal Expos picked Josh Whitesell in the sixth round of the 2003 draft, but no matter how much he hit, Whitesell couldn't get promoted. Despite 40 home runs over two seasons with Double A Harrisburg in 2006 and 2007, the now-Washington Nationals wouldn't so much as promote him to Triple A and even tried to sneak him through waivers during the spring of 2008. That's when the Arizona Diamondbacks picked him up, and a rebuilding Diamondbacks team seemed like a great fit for him to come up and hit.

The Triple A season in Tucson, Arizona, was a glorious one—.328/.425/.568, 26 home runs, 110 RBIs, Pacific Coast League Rookie of the Year—but all it earned Whitesell was the briefest of callups in September and a trip back to Triple A in 2009. Arizona elected to go with the final drops of Tony Clark's career and Chad Tracy in a platoon instead. That this failed was not just clear in retrospect but foreseeable. As Marc Hulet wrote in Fangraphs in January 2009:

"He's definitely earned a shot at a regular roster spot. Whitesell is cheaper than Clark, has more upside, and creamed right-handed pitchers in 2008 at Triple A to the tune of .342/.442/.602 in 342 at-bats. Admittedly, it is hard to know how a young player will adjust to a part-time role—and a high-pressured one at that. Whitesell, though, did well in 2008 with runners in scoring position by hitting .331/.438/.586. Truth be told, there are not many—if any— unimpressive numbers in Whitesell's statistics from 2008. He deserves a shot, and Arizona could certainly benefit from replacing Clark with the youngster and allowing Whitesell to get his feet wet as a pinch hitter while also playing regularly at first base against right-handed pitching."

To be fair to Arizona, Whitesell didn't hit much when he finally got the call in May 2009, but giving the young slugger the everyday job wouldn't have been a bad bet, especially given where Arizona was in the success cycle. Nearing 30, Whitesell elected to go to Japan, then the Mexican League in search of at-bats. It went well—his career overseas line was a fine .280/.373/.468. He'd probably have done similarly well with regular big league work.

16. Samuel Fishburn

Bats Right, Throws Right
St. Louis Cardinals, 1919

It is hard to imagine why Samuel Fishburn never got a chance to play—the St. Louis Cardinals gave him just six at-bats. He played one game at first, one at second for the Cardinals. But he was a shortstop by trade, having played 35 games for Reading of the International League before coming to the Cardinals. The Cardinals had a light-hitting shortstop named Doc Lavan, while their first baseman, Dots Miller, hit even worse. But Fishburn couldn't get into the lineup. In his one game at first, he made eight putouts without an error. At second base he had three perfect chances. He had a single and a double in six times at the plate. It was a small sample. But it certainly appears what Fishburn did was worthy of a second look.

He spent many years trying to get that second look before his retirement made headlines in his local paper, *The Morning Call*, in April 1925. "The lad who for four years was a star at Lehigh; who then went to the St. Louis Nationals; to several minor league clubs; thence to Northampton and later to Bangor, has announced he is through with baseball."

Fishburn himself said, "I'm a realtor now in the city of Bethlehem, and business will not permit me jumping around every evening and weekends playing baseball."

The writer of the unsigned article goes on to call Fishburn "a player of ability... the game suffers by his retirement."

And for the next 40 years until his death in 1965, that's what he did—becoming active in Democratic Party politics, joining the Old Timers' Baseball Association of the Lehigh Valley, and living right where he planned to: in Bethlehem.

His son Jay, according to lifelong friend Maury Pascover, became a passionate Philadelphia Phillies fan. Jay wrote to then-Phillies owner Ruly Carpenter in 1964, asking if he could be the first to order World Series tickets. Instead, Carpenter sent him two tickets to sit in the owner's box for Game One. Those of you who know what happened to the 1964 Phillies, however, know this story does not have a happy ending.

3

Second Base

In a 1976 *Esquire* Magazine article naming an all-Jewish team, the No. 1 Jewish second baseman was Hall of Famer Rod Carew. Indeed, the base hit machine finished with more than 3,000 hits, hit as high as .388 in a season, and earned a place in Adam Sandler's "Hanukkah Song."

Unfortunately, Carew isn't Jewish. He married a Jewish woman, but he did not convert. So much as we would like to claim him, he doesn't qualify any more than my childhood friend David Lopez qualified for complaining to his mother about being served "*goyische* corned beef" in eighth grade. He (Carew, not Lopez) also by career's end played more at first base than second base, meaning that had he converted, he'd merely be a backup to Mr. Greenberg in this book.

An excellent hitter and a much better fielder than Carew led my All-Jewish team at second base in the first edition of this book: Charles Solomon "Buddy" Myer. Though he finished with a .303 career batting average (Carew comes in at .328), their on-base percentages are nearly identical (.389 for Myer, .393 for Carew). The gap is wider than it would appear based on raw stats because Myer played in the hit-happy 1930s; Carew began his career in the 40-years-in-the-desert-offensive-era of the 1960s. Still, Myer is a fine choice for tops at second base.

The problem is: Myer's not Jewish either. I was fooled by his inclusion in, for instance, the International Jewish Sports Hall of Fame, an honor typically reserved for Jews. And to be fair, there were numerous press accounts referring to him as Jewish during his playing career. But Myer, a Baptist, didn't want to correct the record, worried it "would be taken the wrong way," according to his son.

This reminds me of a similar conundrum New York Mets catcher Mike Piazza faced in the early 2000s, when rumors swirled about his sexuality. Piazza faced an unenviable choice: if he wished to clear up the rumors that he was gay, he wanted to do so without making it seem as if being gay was anything to be ashamed of. Ultimately, he held a press conference to announce his heterosexuality, which was strange at the time and even stranger in retrospect but went to great lengths to reiterate that he'd welcome a gay player in Major League Baseball. In his autobiography a decade later, he added: "If I was gay, I'd be gay all the way."

I especially love that the International Jewish Sports Hall of Fame hasn't, well, kicked Myer out. They shouldn't! Someone who wished to be an ally to the Jews, even if wrongly inducted, deserves our respect. But he's not going to be in this edition of the book.

That said: second base is ably occupied by Ian Kinsler, whose career numbers are virtually identical to Myer's and whose Jewish background isn't in doubt. I should know: I met his Jewish father, a Bronx boy named Howard, who was excited to watch his son play at old Yankee Stadium. Kinsler went on to play for Team Israel in the 2021 Olympics. So we don't have to worry he'll turn out to be secretly Baptist. (Not that there's anything wrong with that.)

Others, like Andy Cohen and Jimmie Reese, are more famous for having played for John McGraw or roomed with Babe Ruth, respectively. Ultimately, the lack of depth at the position suggests that much as baseball is losing some of its finest athletes to basketball and football today, many of the would-be Jewish double-play combos may have found themselves in the medical or legal professions instead.

1. Ian Kinsler

Bats Right, Throws Right
Texas Rangers, 2006–2013
Detroit Tigers, 2014–2017
Los Angeles Angels, 2018
Boston Red Sox, 2018
San Diego Padres, 2019

Ian Kinsler, a multi-sport star out of Canyon del Oro High School in Arizona—a baseball hotbed, which produced guys like Chris and Shelly Duncan, Scott Hairston, and many more—was not highly regarded by Major League Baseball scouts. A 29th-round pick after completing his senior year, he chose not to sign with the Arizona Diamondbacks, though his father told *The Arizona Republic* that day that "it's every boy's dream." Nor were the scouts much higher on him following a college career that saw him play at Central Arizona, Arizona State, and University of Missouri. The Texas Rangers drafted him in the 17th round.

But his first full professional season in 2004 put him on the prospect map. He hit .402 with a .692 slugging percentage in A ball, followed that with a .300/.400/.480 line in his first exposure to Double A, and by 2005 was named the eighth-best prospect in all of baseball by *Baseball America*. The Rangers then converted him from shortstop to second base—not because of his own defensive shortcomings but due to the impending free agency of Alfonso Soriano. He hit .274 with 23 home runs at Triple A, and the Rangers dealt Soriano so Kinsler could have the second base job.

Back in 2007, I wrote this: "Defensively, Kinsler shows both his background as a shortstop and the recent conversion to second base within his performance. His range is unquestioned—he consistently gets to far more balls than Derek Jeter and led the major league in range factor in 2007. However, the by-product of his range has been to lead the major leagues in errors by a second baseman in both 2006 and 2007. Of course, errors are a lousy way to evaluate defense—Kinsler's 35 errors in his first two full seasons are similar to the total over that same span by Bill Mazeroski, widely considered the finest defender ever at the keystone position. Ultimately, I'd sooner take the chance that a wide-ranging defensive player will make more plays as he matures than that a player will start getting to more balls. And from seeing Kinsler play, there's little doubt in my mind that he will convert more of those plays in the coming years. Add plus defense to his offensive totals, and he needn't improve to make a claim as greatest Jewish second baseman—he merely needs longevity."

And Kinsler himself, when I spoke to him in the locker room of Yankee Stadium in 2007, put that goal on his radar: "That's something to shoot for," he said.

He got there. Kinsler's .319/.375/.517 line in 2008 put him into the first of four All-Star Games he'd play in, and if not for a thumb injury that cost him the last six weeks of the season, it might have been an MVP campaign for him. Kinsler's 257 home runs (with five 20-plus homer seasons and two 30-plus seasons), 243 stolen bases, two 30/30 seasons, and a career OPS+ of 107 while playing a vital position in the field is a strong legacy for all Jewish second basemen who come after him.

Defensively, Kinsler became a stellar performer at the position, winning a pair of Gold Gloves and racking up 15.1 of his career WAR in the field. His overall WAR is 54.1, by the way, which absolutely puts him in the running for Greatest Jewish Baseball Player if we're measuring by WAR alone (we're not, by the way); Koufax is at 53.1, and Greenberg is at 55.5.

A more interesting argument comes when measuring him against Mazeroski. Kinsler easily outpaces Maz in career WAR, and the modern defensive metrics all rank Kinsler among the best defenders at the position right through his final season in the major leagues. If Mazeroski is the Hall of Fame line at second base, Kinsler ought to be in Cooperstown. Even second basemen like Joe Gordon and Bobby Doerr have similar resumes, and both of them have plaques. This is no knock on them—Kinsler was that good.

And like so many of the other elite Jewish players, despite a lack of Jewish religious upbringing, the mere fact of playing baseball while Jewish seems to have tied Kinsler to his heritage. He became an Israeli citizen in 2020 and starred on the 2021 Israeli team that played at the Olympics in Tokyo in 2021. "At the time I agreed to do this, it just meant the opportunity to play more baseball," Kinsler said in July 2021. "But I needed to get my citizenship, and that meant diving into my family tree and going to Israel. Going through the whole process, going to Tel Aviv and Jerusalem, really understanding my heritage, it's made it such a really cool journey. It's something I'm a lot prouder to represent than when I first committed. Tapping into my history has really been special."

As his father, Howard, put it: "When he played and kids came up to him and said they loved him because he was Jewish, he told me he'd never had a grasp of that, of why...He understands the brotherhood of the people now. It's more real to him. And now it's more than just baseball. It's my happiness that he's getting interested in it."

Now Ian and his wife, Tess, are committed to growing the game in Israel. In a just world, players like Greenberg and Koufax would have represented Israel in the Olympics as well. But one of the true Jewish greats in Kinsler actually did.

2. David Newhan

Bats Left, Throws Right
San Diego Padres, 1999–2000
Philadelphia Phillies, 2000–2001
Baltimore Orioles, 2004–2006
New York Mets, 2007
Houston Astros, 2008

While David Newhan is not headed to the Hall of Fame, it is unlikely that any Jewish player has had a better month than Newhan's first after signing with the Baltimore Orioles in June of 2004. And to be sure, such a performance was unexpected. Newhan has Hall of Fame bloodlines, but they stem from the J.G. Taylor Spink wing of the Hall—where baseball's writers are honored.

Newhan was born and raised in California, getting the chance to experience the major leagues as he grew up. His father, Ross Newhan, was the esteemed baseball writer for the *Los Angeles Times* from 1967 to 2004. So Newhan received batting tips from Rod Carew while finding time to get Bar Mitzvahed at his conservative synagogue.

Recruited out of Cypress College to play at Georgia Tech for a season, Newhan became a sought-after player. He manned first base for a Yellow Jackets team that included shortstop Nomar Garciaparra, catcher Jason Varitek, and probably the best of the bunch, center fielder Jay Payton. But Tech coach Jim Morris had promised Newhan the second base job, so he transferred to Pepperdine University after one season. But there he played left field, winning All-Conference honors, and preparing for a life as a major league utility player, though he didn't know it yet.

The Oakland Athletics drafted Newhan in the 17th round, just like Ian Kinsler, but unlike Kinsler, a breakout offensive performance did not translate to organizational respect. Newhan converted to second base at the request of his Single A manager, then proceeded to outhit his double-play partner, future star Miguel Tejada. He hit .301 with a .538 slugging percentage—Oakland yawned, and Newhan repeated Single A. After three years with the A's, Newhan was dealt to the San Diego Padres, where he was finally able to advance, making his major league debut in 1999.

But Newhan's ability to hit in the minor leagues didn't translate to the big league level. He hit .140 in 1999 and, despite a strong spring landing him San Diego's second-base job in 2000, he was demoted after 37 at-bats with a .162 average. He was dealt to the Philadelphia Phillies, and his slump continued. His path then further diverged from success when he injured his arm slamming into an outfield wall—Newhan missed the 2002 season, and any major league success became extremely unlikely. Newhan was 29 entering the 2003 season, long past the sell-by date for prospects.

And despite Newhan's strong 2003 performance, hitting .348 for Triple A Colorado Springs, and a .328/.387/.557 line for Triple A Oklahoma in 2004, he did not get a call up by either the Colorado Rockies or Texans Rangers. On June 18, 2004, he asked for his release and signed with the Orioles, who had a roster need. What followed was extraordinary.

As a pinch-hitter Newhan got his first major league at-bat in three years that night. He crushed a 435-foot home run. Over his next 33 games, Newhan hit .403 with a .447 on-base percentage. He had three four-hit games. And he managed his hitting groove while constantly shifting positions—for the season he played 32 games at DH, 24 in right field, 19 in left field, 17 at third base, and two at first base. Notably, he didn't play any games at second base, his most comfortable position.

He finished 2004 with a .311/.361/.453 line, along with 11 stolen bases. The Orioles thought they had a building block for their future. "We value him," Orioles vice president Mike Flanagan told *The Baltimore Sun* in November 2004. "Everybody loves him."

But Newhan came crashing back to Earth in 2005, hitting .202/.279/.312. He split time between the Orioles and Triple A in 2006, the New York Mets, and Triple A in 2007. He struggled in the majors (.252 and .203 batting average) both seasons while excelling in the minors—putting up a .347/.413/.572 line with New Orleans in a pitchers' home park in 2007.

He signed with the Houston Astros for 2008, finishing his major league work with a respectable .260/.297/.404 slash line before a final season in the Philly minor league system in 2009. His .253/.312/.380 final numbers and an OPS+ of 82 represent a solid major league career, especially given his ability to play all three outfield positions, along with first, second, and third base.

And Newhan's baseball knowledge has been rewarded with an extensive post-playing career as a coach and manager. He skippered the Mobile BayBears in their final season in 2019 and spent 2021 coaching Pittsburgh's Double A Altoona Curve, where future stars like Oneil Cruz and Cal Mitchell showed significant growth under his tutelage.

3. Andy Cohen

Bats Right, Throws Right
New York Giants, 1926, 1928–1929

Before Hank Greenberg became the definitive Jewish American baseball icon, Andrew Howard Cohen was widely expected to be that man. And Cohen, geographically, made more sense. While Greenberg played in Detroit, a hotbed of anti-Semitism, Cohen played in New York, the Jewish capital of the United States.

Amazingly, there has never been a huge Jewish star in New York despite a large number of Jewish players. One can only imagine the media and popular swarm such a star would receive. Indeed, the reception for Cohen upon arrival in New York provides a glimpse into it. Cohen was not, however, a New Yorker by birth—he and his younger brother Syd, who went on to pitch in the big leagues as well, grew up in El Paso, Texas, and both attended the University of Alabama. The elder Cohen was a multi-sport star at Alabama, helping the Crimson Tide on the baseball diamond, the basketball court, and (of course) the football field.

Again worth noting—although many Jews point to Greenberg's success as a key in combating the stereotype that Jews aren't athletic, Greenberg was far from an athlete in the well-rounded sense—his lumbering gait made him arguably the slowest runner in the league for most of his career. Cohen's all-around abilities might have helped defeat this idea in a more comprehensive sense.

When Cohen finished in Alabama, he quickly signed with Waco of the Texas League, and it wasn't long before he drew the attention of major league scouts, hitting .319 as a 20 year old. New York Giants manager John McGraw purchased Cohen, intending to bring him to New York in time for the 1927 season—but was so impressed that he convinced Waco to let Cohen play some for New York in 1926 in exchange for the sum of $25,000. "The young Hebrew, Andy Cohen, was allowed to play second base—his first appearance in a National League game—and he surely looked and acted like the real article," *The Sporting News* wrote in its June 10, 1926 edition.

How big was Cohen's debut? A week later, *The Sporting News* made Cohen its featured ballplayer on page one. "Oi gevald!" screamed the *TSN* lead on June 17, 1926. "John McGraw has that Jewish baseball player he's been looking for these many years. At least, he thinks he has. The leader of the Giants, at this time, is not so sure what he's going to do with him, but the fact remains that the Jewish boy is in captivity, and that's something when it is considered Israel's children are the real dodos of the baseball woods." Thanks, *TSN*! Most of us were a generation removed from European pogroms... but thanks!

It gets better. "He is five feet eight, weighs 155 pounds, and has all the natural characteristics (physically) of his race—thick, dark hair, dark skin and keen mentality."

The 21-year-old Cohen hit .257 in 35 at-bats while failing to unseat the incumbent Frankie Frisch, the Fordham Flash. The Giants then traded one Hall of Fame second baseman for another, dealing Frisch for Rogers Hornsby, and Cohen was farmed out to Buffalo for more seasoning.

By the middle of June 1927, it was clear that Cohen had nothing left to prove at the minor league level. "Infielder Andy Cohen is showing high class ability in all departments of his game, his fielding being of sensational order, and his hitting of high proportions," *TSN* wrote on June 2, 1927. "His swatting mark recently stood at .431, which placed him at the top of the league in stickwork." He finished the season at .355.

How highly regarded was Cohen at this point? The Giants dealt away Hornsby—after he hit .361/.448/.586 with 26 home runs and 125 RBIs—to give Cohen a clean shot at the second base job. McGraw may have wanted Cohen for box office appeal, but no one wanted to win more than John McGraw. Clearly, he believed Cohen was the real deal.

And so did *TSN*, which had the April 19, 1928 headline: "Gotham's Gone Wild Over Andrew Cohen." The subheads are even better: "Work in First Week Establishes Youngster as a Star," and "New York Club Provides a Suite in Hotel for him That He May Meet Mobs of Worshippers."

Detailing the largest ovation in Giants history, when Cohen was literally carried off the field after notching three hits on Opening Day, *TSN* goes on to note, "Stories of the kid's life were hurried into the metropolitan newspapers, and his picture was flashed before enthusiastic crowds in the movie theaters."

Yes, even then, New York prospects were overhyped. Cohen did not live up to the clippings or adoration of that first week. By August, McGraw had moved Cohen down to No. 7 in the batting order, and Cohen lost some playing time to Randy Reese down the stretch. The Giants fell two games short of the pennant. Overall, Cohen had a decent first full season—he hit .274/.318/.403 with nine home runs at age 23. But in a time of offensive explosion, such numbers were not particularly distinguished, and his offensive contributions ranked eighth in his own lineup with an OPS+ of just 87.

As for attendance? Considering that in both the 1927 and 1928 seasons, the Giants finished with nearly identical records, both times finished two games out of first place, and that the only difference in the lineup was the presence of Hornsby in '27 and Cohen in '28, it would be fair to compare the two. In 1927 attendance was 858,190. In 1928 it was 916,191—a nearly seven percent increase.

Despite Cohen's middling 1928, *The New Yorker* took notice of the young second baseman with a Talk of the Town profile. Not only did Cohen receive "more presents this season than any other player," but Cohen "likes to make talks before boys' clubs. He reads both Will Durant and Edgar Guest and goes to most of the musical comedies." And the magazine also noted proudly, "His secret ambition is to go back and get his degree."

But 1929 held not only the stock market crash, but also the collapse of the Andy Cohen worshipping market. Cohen got the majority of the playing time at second base, but Reese got plenty as well—Cohen's at-bats dropped from 504 to 347. His overall numbers were a pedestrian .294/.319/.383, and he failed to provide much speed on the basepaths, swiping just three bases.

Cohen's major league time was over. As my great-grandfather did, Cohen made his way to Newark, playing second base for the Bears alongside fellow New York castoff Wally Pipp. But while Great-Grandpa stayed and built a world-class bakery, Cohen headed to Minneapolis, where he played world-class second base for the Millers of the American Association.

Thanks to Stew Thornley, who wrote the definitive Minneapolis Millers book, we know that Cohen played for a number of championship teams in Minneapolis, posting high batting averages and decent power numbers each year. Considering the high level of the Double A and that Cohen's career in the majors was snuffed out before he reached his prime, it is fair to posit that Cohen might have carved out a solid career in the bigs with just one more chance. His 1937 campaign—.320, 11 homers, 82 RBIs at second base—was not the mark of a man who couldn't hit big league pitching. For comparison, Phil Weintraub in 1939 hit .331 for Minneapolis. And a pretty fair hitter Ted Williams hit .366 for the 1938 Millers.

Cohen played through the 1942 season, finishing up in Elmira. For his minor league career, Cohen hit .288, a notable feat. Then he became a wandering minor league manager and sometime major league coach. He won league titles with both the Eau Claire Bears of the Northern League and the Denver

Bears of the Western League, showing himself to be both an effective manager and, it seems, an arctophile.

Cohen's moment of managerial glory came early in the 1960 season. Eddie Sawyer, who managed the Philadelphia Phillies through consecutive last-place seasons in 1958 and 1959, abruptly quit after Opening Day of the 1960 season. Cohen, who'd been on his staff, took over for Sawyer on April 14, 1960, and saw his starter, Curt Simmons, get knocked out in the second inning. But after reliever Ruben Gomez held down the Milwaukee Braves for three innings, Don Cardwell earned a six-inning victory in relief, even homering in his own cause. The Phils won the home opener 5–4 in 10 innings and quickly replaced Cohen with Gene Mauch. Did replacing an undefeated manager lead directly to the Phils' 1964 collapse just four years later, when the team blew a 6.5 game lead with 12 games left? It sure didn't help!

Cohen returned to his native El Paso and built from scratch the University of Texas El Paso baseball program with some help from his brother, Syd. He served as UTEP's first baseball coach from 1960 to 1976, so Philly's loss was El Paso's gain. The UTEP field has the unlikely name of Cohen Stadium in honor of the two men, and Andy Cohen is in the El Paso Baseball Hall of Fame. The headline in the *El Paso Times* when he died in 1988 called him "El Paso's 'Mr. Baseball.'"

And while his accomplishments fell short of Hammerin' Hank, Cohen was as well-known as any Jewish player of his time, except for Greenberg. Like Hank, he even inspired poetry:

Well nothing like that happened, but what do you suppose?
Why little Andy Cohen socked the ball upon the nose.
Then from the stands and bleachers the fans in triumph roared,
And Andy raced to second and the other runner scored.
Soon they took him home in triumph amidst the blare of auto honks,
There may be no joy in Mudville, but there's plenty on The Bronx.

—From "Cohen at the Bat," Author Unknown,
reprinted in *The American Hebrew*, April, 23, 1948

4. Sammy Bohne

Bats Right, Throws Right
St. Louis Cardinals, 1916
Cincinnati Reds, 1921–1926
Brooklyn Dodgers, 1926

The 1920s' Jewish version of Brent Gates, Sammy Bohne was certainly a fighter. His performance on the San Francisco sandlots earned him a shot with the St. Louis Cardinals at the age of 19—making him the youngest player in the league in 1916, though his 43 plate appearances preserved his rookie status. His work that season landed him on a tour of Hawaii with, among others, Shoeless Joe Jackson.

From there it was on to a super-utility role in the American Association, then the Pacific Coast League, only the interregnum of fighting World War I pausing his progress, before he resurfaced five years later with the Cincinnati Reds and laid claim on the second base job in 1921. He put together a fine rookie year, hitting .285/.347/.398 for an OPS+ of 101 and a plus glove to go with it. "He accepted ten chances without a wobble and was quite nifty in his performance in every respect," Jack Ryder of *The Cincinnati Enquirer* enthused in June 1921. "His Exhibition alone was worth the price of admission."

He was in the National League's top 10 in walks, runs, triples, and stolen bases—though the steals were negated some by his league lead in caught stealing.

But Bohne never lived up to his 1921 again; it would prove to be his highwater mark in virtually every category. He slipped to .274/.344/.360 in 1922 and in 1923 fell to .252/.316/.340. By 1924, he'd lost the starting keystone spot to Hughie Kritz, a fine player in his own right.

Bohne did score an important victory during that time. According to baseball historian Norman L. Macht, a journalist accused Bohne and a teammate of throwing games. Not only did Bohne deny the claim, but he also sued for libel and won—an awfully high legal threshold to cross. Such accusations were common following the Black Sox scandal of 1919—such victories by players accused were far rarer.

Macht also points out that Bohne broke up a no-hit bid by Dazzy Vance with two outs in the ninth on June 17, 1923. Clearly, the man had plenty of fight in him. Bohne went on to play with Vance late in the 1926 season after Brooklyn purchased him on June 15. But he hit just .201 in 1926 and headed to Minneapolis, where, like Andy Cohen a few years later, he played second base for the Millers. He hit .279 with 11 homers in 1927, .294 with a pair of longballs in 1928. By 1929 Bohne was a .241 hitter and a player/coach before getting into real estate and becoming a significant member of the San Francisco community for decades. He was even a pallbearer for Lefty O'Doul, when the baseball great died in 1969. Bohne died in 1977 in Menlo Park, California, not far from his San Francisco birthplace.

But back in 1929, he got perhaps his biggest hit. During a July 4 brawl between the Millers and the neighboring St. Paul Saints, Bohne's role in the fight earned him *The Minneapolis Journal* headline, "Sammy Bohne Doesn't Play, but Gets More Hits Than Those That Do."

5. Jimmie Reese

Bats Left, Throws Right
New York Yankees, 1930–1931
St. Louis Cardinals, 1932

Jimmie Reese was a baseball lifer. He was a bat boy for Lefty O'Doul and hit fungoes for Garret Anderson. He roomed with Babe Ruth and was honorary captain of an American League All-Star team that faced Barry Bonds. He was a batboy for the Los Angeles Angels when he was 11, signed his first professional baseball contract when Joe DiMaggio was 12, and was still coaching after Nolan Ryan retired. "It's all I ever wanted to do," Reese told the *Los Angeles Times* in 1988. "I don't know why."

He was still hitting fungoes with deadly accuracy into his 90s, something my early-40s back is amazed to know.

Reese grew up Hymie Solomon and changed his name, as many Jews did, to avoid anti-Semitism. The decision worked out well—in a charity game, catcher Ike Danning and pitcher Harry Ruby, the brilliant songwriter who penned "Hooray for Captain Spaulding" for Groucho Marx, decided to forgo signs and communicate in Yiddish. Reese, the covert Jew, went 4-for-4.

Reese had a long minor league career sandwiched around parts of three major league seasons. At age 28 he hit .346 for the New York Yankees—his roommate, Ruth, hit .359. While 1930 was one of the best offensive years in baseball history (the American League hit .288, and the National League hit .303), .346 is still .346.

But Reese's hitting tailed off in 1931 with a .241 average, and he followed with a .265 average with the St. Louis Cardinals in 1932. It seems as if there were only two eras Reese's glove wouldn't have kept him in the major leagues at second base—the late 1920s/early 1930s and the late 1990s into today.

But his work in the Pacific Coast League, a top-flight minor league, cannot be questioned. He earned raves for his glovework. Dennis Snelling called Reese "arguably the greatest fielding second baseman in Coast League history" in his definitive statistical history of the league. Reese hit plenty, too—notching a .337 batting average in 1929 for the Oakland Oaks and hitting .331 and .311 in his first two years back from the majors in 1933–34 for the Los Angeles Angels. He finished with 1,809 hits in the PCL, a legacy unto itself.

But Reese was just getting started, becoming a coach in Seattle, San Diego, even Hawaii. From 1972 until his death in 1994, he was the conditioning coach for the Angels. Nolan Ryan even named a son after him. So did catcher, coach, and manager Jerry Narron. His No. 50 was retired by the team. There were two Jimmie Reese Days held by baseball teams, and they happened 61 years apart. In 1927 with the Oakland Oaks of the PCL, he got $1,000 and a suitcase full of clothes. One of his teammates was Harry Krause, who was born in 1888.

The second came on August 28, 1988, by the Angels. Among those present was young center fielder Devon White, who played until 2001. "He was in his 90s, and his best friends were in their 20s," Bobby Knoop, who both played for and coached with Reese, told *The Orange County Register* in 1994. "Age was never a factor. And everybody he met in baseball was his friend."

White went on to win seven Gold Gloves, including one in 1994, the year Reese died. Reese coached Jim Edmonds, who won eight Gold Gloves and played until 2010. And Mark Langston, the left-handed pitcher, won seven as well, including one in 1994.

"I want to dedicate this to the memory of Jimmie Reese because he had a great deal to do with my fielding success, as well as the defensive skills of my teammates," Langston said upon receiving his award.

Now that is a baseball legacy.

6. Ty Kelly

Bats Both, Throws Right
New York Mets, 2016–2017, 2018
Philadelphia Phillies, 2017

Ty Kelly's an interesting guy. As you'd guess from his name, he's Jewish on his mother's side. He also was a communications major at UC-Davis, where he quickly drew the notice of pro teams, earning a spot in the Cape Cod summer league before getting selected in the 13th round of the 2009 draft by the Baltimore Orioles.

He showed defensive versatility and a plus-batting eye in his first three years in the Baltimore system, but even playing first, second, third, and the outfield while hitting .274/.369/.328 only got him a promotion to high A ball by 2012. He was running short on time before a power surge that season in Frederick helped catapult him through the Orioles' system. But before he could reach the big leagues, his transactional merry-go-round began—to the Seattle Mariners for Eric Thames, then to the St. Louis Cardinals for Sam Gaviglio, selected off waivers by the Toronto Blue Jays, signed as a minor league free agent by the New York Mets.

Finally, he forced his way to the bigs by hitting .391 for Triple A Las Vegas—a hitter's park but still. "I was told probably five years ago by Bobby Dickerson with the Orioles that the only way you get moved up is if you beat the league," Kelly told Tyler Kepner of *The New York Times* in 2015. "So I never really wondered why I wasn't getting moved up. I played well; it's great to play well and put up decent numbers. But for someone that's not a big-time prospect to get moved up, you've got to beat everybody. You've got to be the best in the league."

Kelly's played six positions in his big league time with the Mets and Philadelphia Phillies, but the hitting did not translate—just .203/.288/.323 in 158 big league plate appearances. However, he has proven useful as the successor to Josh Satin at third base for Team Israel and he's certainly not stopped hitting in the minors, where he posted a .418 OBP for the Long Island Ducks in 2021. Should Kelly get a Major League Baseball opportunity in 2022, Dan Szymborski's ZIPS for FanGraphs projects him to hit .202/.268/.283.

Kelly writes for one of my favorite newsletters, Mets Fix, putting that communications background into good use. And playing in the Olympics in 2021 made his Jewish grandmother, Gail, in Boca Raton, Florida, very happy. "I mean, she loves being Jewish," Kelly said. "She talks about her Jewish upbringing all the time, so this is really exciting for her."

7. Jake Pitler

Bats Right, Throws Right
Pittsburgh Pirates, 1917–1918

World War I stands unequivocally as a regrettable human tragedy. But for Jake Pitler, the resulting man shortage within Major League Baseball provided an opportunity. The 5'8" second baseman got his chance at the big leagues, when the Pittsburgh Pirates tabbed the 23 year old to man second base.

This was a hometown opportunity for the Beaver Falls, Pennsylvania, product and son of Frederick and Yetta, who'd emigrated from Russia. Once he got to the show, Pitler could have been forgiven for thinking he was still in the bushes. The 1917 Pirates were a terrible, terrible team. The Pirates hit .238 as a team. The team on-base percentage was .298. I mean, it was the Dead Ball Era, but still—these marks were terrible. Last or next to last in the league in nearly every vital offensive category, they scored 464 runs or almost three runs per game.

So just 192,807 fans turned out to see Pitler's one season in the spotlight, and all but one of his major league at-bats came during the 1917 season. And essentially, Pitler in 1917 *was* the Pirates. The team's line was .238/.293/.298, and Pitler's was .233/.297/.280. And it is safe to assume that Pitler had responsibility for a lot of ground balls on the right side of the infield—the regular first baseman was Honus Wagner, who was, after all, 43 years old. Hard to imagine the Dutchman calling off 23-year-old Pitler very often. "He was a smart player who knew his way around the infield, but he was strictly a glove man," sports editor of the *Pittsburgh Post-Gazette* Havey J. Boyle wrote in 1946. "That curve proved too much for him when he was up at the plate."

This scouting report dovetails with what followed. When the war ended, he played in the minor leagues for another 15 years, and much of that time came in the New York-Penn League. He even played semi-pro basketball in the offseasons. His playing career made him a natural candidate to manage in the circuit, and he piloted teams in Elmira, Scranton, and even Wilkes-Barre. Between his playing and coaching in Elmira, he came to consider that town his "second home away from home," and the town responded in kind by inducting him into its Baseball Hall of Fame.

Pitler went on to a long career with the Brooklyn Dodgers, managing their Pony League teams to back-to-back titles in 1939 to 1940 and coaching at the big league level from 1947 to 1957. He was important enough to the Dodgers that on September 18, 1956, the team held "Jake Pitler Night" and provided the coach with, among other things, a brand-new, two-tone Cadillac.

Rather than follow the team to Los Angeles, he stayed in the northeast as a scout. His reputation was built on observations such as recognizing that Gil Hodges, a walk-on at an open tryout, was a star-in-the-making.

Ultimately, evaluating a player like Pitler is extremely difficult because he spent so much of his prime playing in semi-organized circuits. But his value was clear that night in 1956 at Ebbets Field when organist Gladys Gooding played "For He's a Jolly Good Fellow" as the fans serenaded Jake and his wife, Henrietta, as they walked off the field.

8. Heinie Scheer

Bats Right, Throws Right
Philadelphia Athletics, 1922–1923

You can normally count me among those who cast a wary eye upon nostalgia. The world is a more interesting place with the Internet. I enjoy the convenience of cell phones. And on the whole, life is much easier for us without dinosaurs. But is it really a better world without as many baseball players who go by Heinie?

The facts are inarguable. Major League Baseball has 22 Heinies in its illustrious history. But the Heinie phenomenon is a pre-Eisenhower one—none of the 22 played after World War II.

Henry William "Heinie" Scheer made his way to the major leagues early, earning a spot with the Philadelphia Athletics in 1922. "Not in years has [Connie] Mack had a sweeter fielder than this boy," declared Gordon MacKay, sports editor of *The Philadelphia Inquirer* in March of 1922, going on to assert that the unknown part of Scheer's game was his hitting.

But while the A's were powerhouses in 1912 and in 1932, the 1922 vintage finished just 65–89. Scheer hit .170, but it wasn't an empty .170. He added four home runs. Still, he hit .170. The A's brought in Jimmy Dykes, who shared the job with Scheer. The two played to a near-draw—Dykes, 26, hit .252/.318/.353, while Scheer, just 22, hit .238/.301/.314.

But then the A's were presented with an opportunity they couldn't pass up. Scheer was at the center of a trade with Milwaukee of the American Association. In exchange for Scheer, outfielder Wid Matthews, and $40,000, Connie Mack acquired Al Simmons. Scheer went on to a solid career as a minor league second baseman, even forming a Jewish double-play combination with Moe Berg when the latter still played shortstop with the 1926 Reading Keystones of the International League. In November of 1928, when the New Haven Profs—led by a young executive named George Weiss—acquired him, it was front-page news in the *Hartford Courant*, and the paper noted his fielding percentage led the Eastern League.

As for Simmons? He finished with 2,927 hits, a career line of .334/.380/.535. He had three seasons with more than 150 RBIs. In six different seasons, he finished in the top 10 of MVP voting. It was viewed as the fifth best trade ever in Philadelphia baseball history by the esteemed Frank Fitzpatrick of *The Philadelphia Inquirer* in 2006.

But one wonders if Mack, in retrospect, might have been better off holding on to Heinie. After all, they have become quite scarce. And Philly's loss was New Haven's gain—Scheer went on to found the New Haven Little League after retiring from baseball.

9. Al Federoff

Bats Right, Throws Right
Detroit Tigers, 1951–1952

A good-field, light-hitting second baseman, and yet another Jewish player at the position who went on to manage, Al Federoff got ample time to improve his hitting prior to coming to Detroit.

He played for Jamestown in the New York-Penn League but failed to distinguish himself with the bat. He combined bat and glove with Flint of the Class B Interstate League in 1948, batting .291 with a .368 on-base percentage, and led the circuit in stolen bases with 22. But this failed to convince many in baseball of his ability to hit in the majors.

When incumbent second baseman Jerry Priddy broke his leg early in the 1952 season, the Detroit Tigers, running last in the American League, summoned Federoff to hold down the position. To give a sense of the lack of confidence even the Tigers had in Federoff, listen to manager Fred Hutchinson, as quoted by *The Sporting News* in July 30, 1952: "We know from what we saw at Lakeland that the guy can make the plays," Hutchinson said. "His hitting picked up at Buffalo, and he may be ready for the big leagues now. Anyway, he's our second baseman." Can you feel the enthusiasm?

Senators manager Bucky Harris added his thoughts in the same article: "Sure, he's a frail-looking guy, but that isn't necessarily a handicap." Where was Federoff's Jewish mother to fatten him up?

Federoff himself said, "This is the best chance I ever had. They're letting me play regularly, and if I don't make good, I'll have no one to blame but myself."

Unfortunately, he didn't make good, hitting just .242/.294/.277, paltry numbers for even a middle infielder in the early 1950s. He never played major league ball again. But the Tigers employed him as a manager for a decade from 1960 to 1969, and he delivered a pair of league titles.

He also had an impact beyond his own managerial career. A minor league catcher, who played under him, declared him to be the best manager he ever had. That guy ought to know good managers: his name is Jim Leyland.

10. Lou Rosenberg

Bats Right, Throws Right
Chicago White Sox, 1923

Raised playing on "the sandlots of Frisco," Lou Rosenberg was the second youngest player in the American League when he received his four at-bats for the 1923 Chicago White Sox. But reaching the majors that young was not always a blessing, as a poor trial often landed players back in the obscurity of the minors. And with so many minor leagues and so few major league jobs, a player was often better off getting his chance when he was at his peak—a second opportunity, far more often than not, wasn't forthcoming.

He clearly impressed in the spring of 1923 to earn that spot with the White Sox. *The Kansas City Star* wrote of Rosenberg: "His defensive work around shortstop in the Giant-White Sox series has fairly bristled with class." But he only received a solitary plate appearance in May, along with another two in July, and those appearances came with time at second base, not shortstop.

The names on the 1923 American League list of youngest players are littered with players who never saw big league action again. Of the 10 most youthful on the junior circuit, only two players saw action in more than three subsequent seasons. One, George Grant, pitched in eight-and-two-thirds innings in 1923 for the St. Louis Browns, posting a subpar 5.19 ERA (19 percent below league average), but the Browns being the Browns, he pitched another two below-average seasons in St. Louis before being shipped to the Cleveland Indians, where he turned the trick four more times. In other words, even with his relative longevity, it is hard to call Grant a success.

The same cannot be said for the 10th man on the list: Lou Gehrig. Of course, even at age 20, Gehrig made the most of his 26 at-bats, hitting .423/.464/.769. So it is distinctly possible that despite ample ability, Rosenberg never got the chance to show it. But with the White Sox starting Hall of Famer Eddie Collins at second base, Rosenberg would have had to be a Gehrig type of talent to have gotten that chance. Instead, his career lasted through the 1927. He hit .354 while playing shortstop for the Class-C Twin Falls, Idaho, Bruins. But he'd never get another major league chance.

4

Third Base

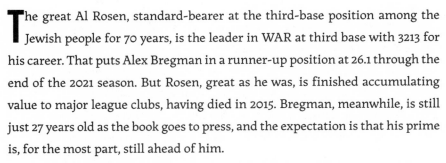

The great Al Rosen, standard-bearer at the third-base position among the Jewish people for 70 years, is the leader in WAR at third base with 32.13 for his career. That puts Alex Bregman in a runner-up position at 26.1 through the end of the 2021 season. But Rosen, great as he was, is finished accumulating value to major league clubs, having died in 2015. Bregman, meanwhile, is still just 27 years old as the book goes to press, and the expectation is that his prime is, for the most part, still ahead of him.

Moreover, Bregman has to date been outperforming Rosen on a rate basis as well. Rosen's career .284/.384/.494 line was good for an OPS+ of 137. Bregman's .281/.377/.507 through 2021 is remarkably similar, incidentally, to Rosen's production and gives him a slight edge with a 138 OPS+. But Bregman had an earlier start because there was no Ken Keltner to block him. Barring injury, there's just not going to be an argument keeping Bregman from this top spot, and it's close enough already that I'm calling it now.

Alex Bregman

1. Alex Bregman

Bats Right, Throws Right

Houston Astros, 2016–present

One of those instances where the great Jewish hope has panned out, Alex Bregman has been on the collective radar of Jewish baseball fans for a long time. Born and raised in Albuquerque, New Mexico, Bregman's history with the game of baseball goes back multiple generations. His father, Sam, and his Uncle Ben both played college baseball at University of New Mexico. His grandfather, Stan, was general counsel for the Washington Senators in the late 1960s, giving the Bregman family access to a clubhouse run by Gil Hodges, then Ted Williams.

So it was only natural that Bregman and his father started having catches at age five. By age 10 his nickname among his coaches was "First Rounder." Upon selection by USA Baseball for the U16 team, Bregman told the *Albuquerque Journal* in 2009: "I just love the game. I could play it every day."

By sophomore year of high school, Bregman had a scholarship offer from Oklahoma State, and the Boston Red Sox picked him in the 29th round of the 2012 draft—an injured finger cost him much of his senior season and dropped his draft stock. So Bregman chose to stick with school a little longer, starred at LSU as the nation's best shortstop as a freshman, and then the Houston Astros selected him second overall in the 2015 draft, planning to fast-track him to the major leagues.

That meant moving him from his preferred position, shortstop, since Houston's 2012 top overall pick, Carlos Correa, had gotten to the big leagues a year ahead of Bregman and played short. But Bregman transitioned naturally to third base, where the defensive metrics place him slightly below average—but nothing tragic in the field—and certainly good enough to play there while accounting for his huge contributions at the plate.

There's not a raw physicality that accounts for Bregman's skills. Just 5'10", he has a rather relentless dedication to the craft. So when he reached the big leagues in 2016, he was ready, hitting .264/.313/.478 as a rookie for an OPS+ of 116 at age 22. By 23 he was a full-fledged star, the Astros were champions of the world, and Bregman's single in the 10th inning of Game Five provided a decisive blow.

Of course, we must consider the Houston cheating scandal in Bregman's legacy—even if, in my view, it is less significant than all the rending of garments made it out to be. The difference—in shades of gray—between stealing signs (a time-honored baseball tradition) and stealing them electronically (against the rules) is far less significant than, say, corking your bat or even taking performance-enhancing drugs. I struggle to find the moral outrage on this truly. Still, Bregman issued an apology in the spring of 2020. "We especially feel remorse for the impact on the fans and the game of baseball, and our team is determined to move forward, to play with intensity, and to bring back a championship to Houston in 2020," he told gathered reporters.

Just how much did the extra edge help Bregman in 2017? It's impossible to say, but I certainly considered it an open question as we moved into 2020 and 2021. Let's take a look at what Bregman's done overlaid with what MLB's timeline was of the cheating. In 2017 it was established that the Astros used video to steal signs, something that continued into part of the 2018 season and then stopped. Bregman's 2017 OPS+ was 125. By 2018 he rose to 152. In 2019, when the investigation found no evidence of cheating, Bregman had his best season to-date: .296/.423/.592, finishing second in the MVP voting. His numbers dropped in 2020, but it also was a partial season, and he missed part of even that—we're talking about 42 games here. I generally dismissed 2020 both as a baseball evaluator and—let's be real—in life terms as well, seeing as how I spent it locked in my house opening packs of baseball cards with my children.

And in 2021 Bregman's line was .270/.355/.422—thanks to a late-season slump from a wrist injury that required surgery following the season. Bregman, true to form, played through it and led his team to the American League pennant. I think the evidence is clear and convincing that Bregman is a great baseball player, full stop.

And director of player development for the Baltimore Orioles Eve Rosenbaum, who we must remember received a membership to SABR for her Bat Mitzvah gift from her parents, making her the intellectual Patient Zero for this work, not only believes Bregman will pass Rosen, but also that he'll have a solid case for best Jewish player ever, especially if the Astros move Bregman back to shortstop at some point in 2022 or beyond. Correa is a free agent as this book goes to press, while Bregman signed an extension with Houston that takes him through 2024.

Even playing in Houston itself has been an advantage for Bregman, Rosenbaum points out. "He's a very smart player," Rosenbaum said of Bregman. "He's very good at making adjustments and he's very good adapting to pitchers. So he's tailored his swings to hit balls into the Crawford Boxes in the left-field seats, giving him an offensive boost."

Dan Szymborski's FanGraphs ZIPS likes him, too. I had him run not just a 2022 projection for Bregman but the remainder of his career. ZIPS has him adding another 27.1 WAR to his career totals, playing through 2031, which added to his 26.1 through 2021, meaning a total of 53.2, just below Koufax and Greenberg. An extended peak or a more gradual decline and Bregman's going to have a legitimate argument to finish ahead of Sandy Koufax and Hank Greenberg among the all-time Jewish players.

2. Al Rosen

Bats Right, Throws Right
Cleveland Indians, 1947–1956

Al Rosen, son of Louis and Rose and pride of Spartansburg, South Carolina, suffered from asthma as a child. A future of athletics seemed unlikely, though his family moved to Miami, Florida, when he was 18 months old for a better breathing climate. Ultimately, doubting Rosen never proved to be a good bet.

Though it is easy to criticize the Cleveland Indians' decision to keep Al Rosen from regular action until he was 26 years old in retrospect, it must've been a hard decision to make even when they did it in 1950. Ken Keltner was enormously popular in Cleveland and had manned third since 1938, when he hit 26 home runs as a 21 year old. Even in 1948 Keltner had put up his finest offensive season, hitting .297/.395/.522 for the last Cleveland world championship team. And Keltner's defensive reputation was stellar—back in 1941 his defensive plays helped to end Joe DiMaggio's 56-game hitting streak.

And let's be clear: Cleveland didn't exactly trumpet Rosen's future impact when they made the move. Here's what manager Lou Boudreau told the El Paso Times on the occasion of releasing Keltner in 1950: "Al Rosen is our No. 1 man for the job. He's looked only fair this spring, but he's known as a late starter." A sportswriter, Leo H. Petersen, said that veteran Bob Kennedy was ready to assume the third base role if "Rosen proves a disappointment again." Stretched over three seasons, Rosen had 65 Major League Baseball plate appearances to his name at that point. He'd missed four years of minor league apprenticeship because he was commanding an assault boat in the taking of Okinawa. So I'm not exactly clear who he was disappointing, Mr. Petersen.

But it just reinforces the point: if Cleveland truly knew what they had in Rosen, they might have cut bait sooner. Rosen homered in each of the first two games in 1950, led the American League in home runs in his first full season with 37, and walked 100 times to boot, putting up a .287/.405/.543 line for the Indians.

Rosen was a fighter—literally, a boxer who won a middleweight state championship in high school, always aware of his role in pushing back against anti-Semitism, but also pushing back on slights from the past. I just love that in June 1950, as he was "slugging the ball in a sensational manner" and battling Ted Williams for the American League lead, he called out Boston Red Sox scout Elmer Yoter by name, telling the AP that Yoter had told him he'd never make it in baseball. "Some day I'll make you eat those words," Rosen recalled replying. He sure did.

By the end of 1950, his hometown of Miami planned a big celebration for his return from Cleveland for the offseason, including a brand new car. Rosen passed on the prizes, asking instead that donations be made to a local children's hospital. That earns him mensch points here, too. Rosen continued his strong play in 1951–1952, while Cleveland struggled in an American League with the New York Yankees. In the days before the wild-card, they finished second both seasons.

The script was similar in 1953, but this time Rosen put up the best season any third baseman has ever had. By now, the baseball world fully understood Rosen's greatness. An April 1953 feature in the *New York Daily News* asserted that only two modern-day sluggers could live up to the greats of the past: Mickey Mantle and Rosen. The latter's line was .336/.422/.613. He hit 43 home runs and knocked in 145 runs. He missed the Triple Crown by .001—Mickey Vernon of the Washington Senators hit .337, and Rosen missed first base with his lead foot on a bid for an infield hit. Another player, knowing what was at stake, might have argued or complained about the umpire, Hank Soar. Not Rosen. "Soar called it right, and I'm glad he did," Rosen said, according to SABR. "I don't want any gifts. Why? I wouldn't sleep at night all winter if I won the batting championship on a call I knew was wrong."

Regardless, Rosen was voted the Most Valuable Player unanimously. According to Adam Darowski of Baseball-Reference, his 10.1 WAR is the best single-season total from any Jewish hitter in major league history, except for Lou Boudreau's 10.4 in 1948.

By the measure of OPS+, which takes on-base percentage plus slugging percentage and adjusts it for era, park, and expresses it relative to average, Rosen had one of the finest offensive seasons of any third baseman ever in 1953. His OPS+ of 180 trails only, among primary third basemen with at least 500 plate appearances, George Brett's in 1980, when he hit .390 for the season, and Miguel Cabrera's 2012, when Miggy won the Triple Crown. That's the kind of company Rosen shared at his best. Brett's a Hall of Famer, and Cabrera clearly will be.

In 1954 Rosen hit .300/.404/.506 in 1954 for an Indians team that won 111 games, though the New York Giants upset them in the World Series. Still,

Rosen missed time, playing in just 137 games after missing a total of six games over the previous four seasons. Back and leg problems had begun to sap Rosen of what should have been the second half of a Hall of Fame career.

After the 1956 season, Rosen retired at the age of 32. He was robbed and so were Jewish fans. He had a long career as a baseball executive. But the "Hebrew Hammer" should have had a place in Cooperstown.

3. Danny Valencia

Bats Right, Throws Right
Minnesota Twins, 2010–2012
Boston Red Sox, 2012
Baltimore Orioles, 2013, 2018
Kansas City Royals, 2014
Toronto Blue Jays, 2014–2015
Oakland Athletics, 2015–2016
Seattle Mariners, 2017

Danny Valencia was the undisputed star of Team Israel's Olympic qualifying tournament in 2019, hitting .375 with three home runs as first baseman and DH a year after he'd last played professional baseball. How did he end up playing for Israel? "I can't lie," he told The Athletic. "My mother was heavily behind this."

Valencia is the pride of Boca Raton, Florida, son of Mindy, who is Jewish and served as Danny's earliest hitting coach, and Michael, who converted to Judaism. But he's always been underestimated. Despite leading his Babe Ruth team to a state title and earning Palm Beach County Offensive Player of the Year honors as a senior at Spanish River High School, the local collegiate powerhouse, University of Miami, did not offer him a scholarship. He spent a year instead at UNC-Greensboro before transferring to Miami as a walk-on before adding 40 pounds of muscle and getting the starting first-base job. "Miami's a good baseball program to be seen at, and I want to play in the pros," Valencia explained in 2005. "I gave up a lot to be a part of it, but hopefully I'll get even more in return."

Added Mindy, of the added financial burden: "Don't remind me."

The other infield corner that year in Miami? Third baseman Ryan Braun, making for the best 50 percent Jewish infield in college baseball history.

Even after starring at Miami, though, Valencia fell all the way to the 19th round of the 2006 draft, getting picked by the Minnesota Twins. Despite the non-prospect level of his selection, Valencia just set about proving everyone wrong again, hitting .311/.365/.505 with Elizabethtown of the Appalachian League in his pro debut and continuing in a similar vein up the Minnesota chain. Power and improving defense at third base were his calling cards. He didn't stop when he reached Minneapolis in June 2010 either, collecting hits in each of his first three games and becoming the team's primary third baseman down the stretch. "Danny Valencia is hardly looking like a rookie for the Minnesota Twins," the Associated Press declared in September 2010.

He hit .311/.351/.448 for a Twins team that won the American League Central and started all three American League Division Series games in the New York Yankees' sweep of Minnesota that October. He finished third in the American League Rookie of the Year voting, and the future looked bright. But Valencia struggled to regain his rookie form, slumping to .246/.294/.383 in 2011 and by 2012 he had lost the third base job to Trevor Plouffe. What's followed has been an itinerant career filled with highlights—a .304/.335/.553 stint as a part timer for the Baltimore Orioles in 2013, for instance—and versatility, as Valencia has played first, second, third, and all three outfield spots in his major league campaigns. He even pitched in 2018 and hit 91 miles per hour on the radar gun.

Valencia starred for Israel again at the 2021 Olympics in Tokyo, displaying his home run power that hadn't dissipated. As the book goes to press, Valencia is 36 years old. If this is it, he's still among the best Jewish infielders in the history of the game with a career line of .268/.317/.426 and aa 103 OPS+ in 3,222 plate appearances. But selfishly, I hope he keeps on playing. He sure looked like he had more left in the tank in Tokyo.

4. Cy Block

Bats Right, Throws Right
Chicago Cubs, 1942, 1945–1946

In the 1940s the Chicago Cubs apparently made a fetish of getting high-average, low-power third basemen. Starting at the hot corner was Stan Hack, a legitimate star player who hit .301 but never managed more than eight home runs in a season. And Hack blocked the way for Cy Block, an eerily similar player.

Block debuted at age 19 with the D-level Paragould Rebels of the Northeast Arkansas League, hitting .323 with seven home runs. As he climbed the minor league ladder, he continued to hit over .300 while reaching the high single-digits in homers—Block's minor league seasons would fit perfectly within Hack's career. But while the man blocking Al Rosen slowed down at age 33, Hack continued producing right through World War II and into 1947. Block got scattered at-bats in 1942 and again after returning from service in 1945–46. He hit remarkably well in 1942, poorly in 1945–46, though in each case he had far too few at-bats to conclude anything from his performance. His career major league line of .302/.383/.358 in 53 at-bats is even Hack-esque.

Block actually split time in '45 and '46 between the Cubs and Nashville of the Southern Association, where he hit .354 and .360. He finished his career in Buffalo of the International League, and his average dropped each season. He hit a combined .276 for Buffalo in 845 at-bats over three seasons—Hack hit .271 in his final year.

There but for the grace of Stan Hack went Cy Block—the Stan Hack doppelganger. And as the noted baseball writer Bill Mazer put it, "It didn't help that the Cubs manager, Charlie Grimm, didn't share Cy's religion."

Block's outspoken nature probably didn't help in a sport that frowns on such things. (That same skillset helped make him a huge success in the insurance business in Great Neck, New York, eventually allowing him to buy a Rolls-Royce, which proudly displayed vanity plates "LBA 325"—his lifetime batting average in the majors and minors.)

He testified before Congress, speaking out against the reserve clause, which bound players to organizations in perpetuity—a reality that kept Block from moving to an organization that might have given him a chance. That happened shortly after he'd hit .298/.398/.476 for Triple A Buffalo in 1950, hardly the stats of a player whose career as a useful contributor was over. In early 1951 Block expressed a desire to keep playing and indeed spent 1951 in the semipro circuit. So this was not a case of a player simply walking away from the game.

Block himself had a different spin on it. Years later, he found himself starting at third base in 1981 for a reunion team of 1945 Cubs managed by Grimm. Block asked his old manager jokingly, "How come after all these years, I finally get to play for you?"

Grimm replied, "Because Hack's dead."

5. Mickey Rutner
Bats Right, Throws Right
Philadelphia Athletics, 1947

Milton "Mickey" Rutner is not the most famous Jewish baseball player to graduate from James Monroe High School. That would be Hank Greenberg. But the multi-sport star there (he also captained the soccer team) enjoyed a solid professional career complete with a brief major league appearance. After hitting over .400 as a freshman at St. John's and attracting some pro attention with the Burlington Cardinals of the Northern League in Vermont, a comparable circuit to today's Cape Cod League, Rutner quickly displayed versatility on the infield.

He was a three-year starter at second in college, and after his single Class-B season at short, the Philadelphia Athletics acquired him from the Detroit Tigers, moving him to third base for their Class-B team in Wilmington,

Delaware. His baseball development was placed on hold during that season, when Rutner was called into the service. World War II kept him from playing again until 1946.

Rutner impressed after coming back, though, hitting .300 or better three consecutive seasons and earning a call-up to Philadelphia in 1947. "Don't underrate Mickey's chances of replacing Henie Mejeskie, the former Baron, at the torrid corner," warned *The Birmingham News* in September 1947. And *The Philadelphia Inquirer* noted Rutner "played adroitly afield" in his debut.

But Rutner hit just .250 in 48 at-bats and, though he earned a spot on the 1948 Opening Day roster, Connie Mack soon shipped him back to Double A Birmingham.

Rutner would have had a tough time breaking into that Philadelphia lineup anyway—Majeskie blocked him at third, and Eddie Joost was in the way at shortstop. In fact, Philadelphia had three straight winning seasons from 1947 to 1949 before losing 102 games in 1950 as the Philadelphia Phillies went to the World Series—a season for on and off-field reasons that helped cost the Athletics the city.

Rutner put up solid batting averages into the early 1950s, hitting no worse than .274 in high-level minor leagues like the Texas League, Southern Association, and International League. Rutner was the inspiration for Eliot Asinof's novel, *Men on Spikes*, the author said. "He never got a shot until it was too late," Asinof said of Rutner.

But Rutner stayed connected to baseball, appearing at Athletics reunion events and even worked as a greeter for the Round Rock Express well into his 80s.

6. Ike Samuels

Bats Right, Throws Right
St. Louis Cardinals, 1895

It would be hard to do less to impress in a brief major league trial than Ike Samuels did when signed off the streets of Chicago to play for the St. Louis Cardinals (then known as the St. Louis Brown Stockings). Samuels hit just .230/.278/.257 in a league that hit .296/.361/.400. He also made 20 errors in 21 games at third base and four in three games at shortstop.

The 1895 Brown Stockings were no attraction, finishing 39–92. The park they played in, Robison Field, was roughly 100 years ahead of its time with a huge amusement park beyond the left-field stands. But the team would not achieve success on the field for another 31 years. Meanwhile, the Browns of the American League, created in 1901, did not win a pennant until 1944. Given the baseball being played in St. Louis, it is safe to say an amusement park was necessary, at least until Branch Rickey arrived on the scene.

7. Eddie Turchin

Bats Right, Throws Right
Cleveland Indians, 1943

Another player given a chance in part due to able-bodied shortages of World War II, Eddie Turchin got his cup of coffee with the Cleveland Indians. Turchin hit .295 with a .443 slugging percentage with the Class D Dominion Hawks of the famous Cape Breton Colliery League in 1937.

He never slugged above .400 again, nor approached his .295 batting average. (It should be noted that the league based in Canada appears to have been a Jewish haven. According to the Encyclopedia of Minor League Baseball, the 1939 circuit leader in batting average and RBIs was Abe Abramowitz, and the wins/ERA leader was Bernie Pearlman.) Turchin drew 86 walks and stole 33 bases for Batavia in the first season of the late, great New York-Penn League in 1939. He played shortstop for the Eastern League champion Wilkes-Barre Barons in 1941 and returned to the infield in 1942 despite hitting .220 with a .246 slugging percentage.

As the March 5, 1942, issue of *The Sporting News* described him, Turchin was "light-hitting, but superlative fielding." It's sad this did not become the common term rather than "good-field, no-hit." The former has a more literary quality to it. Turchin played four games at third and two at shortstop for the 1943 Indians. He committed just one error and hit .231/.375/.231. With the aforementioned Ken Keltner at third base (see Rosen, Al; shortened career due to) and the Jewish shortstop standard-bearer Lou Boudreau at shortstop, the Indians simply had no room for Turchin, not even as an interpreter, though the Brooklyn College-educated Turchin reportedly spoke six languages.

Turchin played for Buffalo in 1943 and Indianapolis in 1946, two high-level minor league teams. He fielded well for both—note that his high error total likely means he got to a lot more balls. In between, he helped the United States win a war—and even hit a double for the Sampson Naval Training Center team in a 4–0 win against Cornell University in September of 1944. After completing his playing career, he managed for one season in the Pittsburgh Pirates' organization, helming the 1947 York Pennsylvania White Roses.

8. Joe Bennett

Bats Right, Throws Right
Philadelphia Phillies, 1923

Bennett had a Moonlight Graham career, getting an assist at third base for the Philadelphia Phillies on July 5, 1923, but never recording an at-bat. The Phillies signed him out of the independent Atlantic League, where he'd been handling third base for Lancaster. By 1924 he was with the Utica Utes but struggled to stick around—even the Utes themselves relocated to Oneonta before the season was out. This was the end of Bennett's organized baseball career—he returned to semipro work back in New Jersey with the Highlands Stars, then started a team of his own (the Red Bank Pirates), but his life was just beginning.

He was a professional boxer. He had his own radio show on WBRB in Red Bank and served on the staff of Harold Hoffman, who was governor of New Jersey in the 1930s. Bennett rose to the rank of lieutenant colonel in the armed forces, earning both a Bronze Star and a Purple Heart while serving in World War II. Much like Moonlight Graham in *Field of Dreams*, Bennett, in his post-playing days, saved plenty of lives.

9. Henry Bostick

Bats Right, Throws Right
Philadelphia Athletics, 1915

Among Jewish players who changed their names, Henry Lipschitz to Henry Bostick has to be the most successful conversion. Henry Bostick could own a manor in Great Britain; Henry Lipschitz can get you that same ring wholesale.

There is little record of Bostick's playing career, though I found record of Bostick playing shortstop for the Boise Irrigators of the Class-D Union Association. And he was valuable enough that when Boise folded on July 20, the team's manager asked the four remaining clubs to take Bostick and seven others temporarily ahead of a return to Boise in 1915.

Sadly, the Irrigators' cashflow ran dry, and instead, according to SABR's minor league database, Bostick played shortstop for Topeka of the Western League, hit .224 with a .295 slugging percentage, and earned a call-up to the Philadelphia A's early in the season. Maybe they wanted to give the British guy a chance.

He played on May 18 and 19, 1915, but Philadelphia lost both games to slip into last place, which is where they finished. There were plenty of reasons why the three-time defending American League champs were slipping—Connie Mack selling off 75 percent of his $100,000 infield for instance—but Bostick was hardly a primary reason.

Though there isn't much official record of his career after that, I found mention of him playing in Casper, Wyoming, as late as 1921 in the Midwest Oil League. *The Casper Herald* even arranged for wire service from the ballpark to keep up with Bostick's exploits.

10. Phil Cooney
Bats Left, Throws Right
New York Highlanders, 1905

Don't let the Cooney fool you—Phil Cooney was actually Phil Cohen from New York. It is certainly an oddity to list Cooney among the third basemen—though he played his one major league game at the position, going 0-for-3. He logged well over 1,700 career games in the minor leagues—roughly 1,000 at shortstop, 700 at second base—and according to the SABR record, not one at third base.

Cooney played for the Paterson (New Jersey) Intruders in 1904, then was loaned to the soon-to-be-New York Yankees at the tail end of the 1905 season after hitting a solid .279 in Paterson. At the start of the year, the Hal Chase-led squad was expected to contend for the American League pennant. But Chase slumped to .249, dissension ran deep within the ballclub, and in a not-unusual result, the New York Highlanders fell 7–2 in Cooney's one game to the St. Louis Browns.

It's worth noting this reported deal in October 1905, which would have sent Cooney to Buffalo because it allows us a sense of how the baseball world viewed Cooney. *The Passaic News* reported "from good authority" that a Buffalo representative had signed Cooney and Harry McArdle, the shortstop and third baseman, respectively, for the Intruders.

"The Silk City club will be weakened by the loss of these two men," the unsigned report read, "as they are considered the best men at their respective positions in the Hudson River League."

After a short trial in Buffalo, Cooney returned to the Intruders in 1906 and batted .191 but evidently contributed enough defensively to help Paterson to the Hudson River League title, narrowly edging out the Poughkeepsie Colts. (If the Hudson River League had existed 100 years later, when I went to school, there would have been nine minor league teams within 50 miles of the Bard College campus, and there's absolutely no chance I'd have gone to class enough to earn my degree.)

Cooney went on to play for mostly A-level minor league teams. The New York boy headed to Portland, Oregon—where he logged 45 steals in one season in 1908—Spokane, Washington; Sioux City, Iowa; Omaha, Nebraska; back east with the Jersey City Skeeters; then finished up out in Sioux City in 1920. Iowans got to see his best season in 1913, when he hit .300 with a .368 slugging percentage while learning a new position, second base. He went on to play five seasons in Sioux City, delighting Packers fans. The *Lincoln Journal Star* even called him "one of the classiest fielders in the minor game." He even turned an unassisted triple play in 1917.

Overall, Cooney was a useful middle infielder for well over a decade. And for a fleeting moment, Cohen, known as Cooney, became a hometown hero for the Highlanders, soon to be known as the Yankees, when the second baseman/shortstop became a third baseman for a day.

11. Steve Hertz

Bats Right, Throws Right
Houston Colt .45s, 1964

A pair of young infielders played sparingly for the Houston Colt .45s in the franchise's third big league season. One of them simply couldn't get at-bats behind Nellie Fox. The other was trapped behind Bob Aspromonte. Still, Houston stuck with the first guy but buried the second guy in the minors.

The first guy was Hall of Famer Joe Morgan. The second guy was Steve Hertz. In hindsight, Houston probably made the right call. Hertz never got a start in his five games with Houston, appearing as part of a double switch twice, as a pinch-hitter twice, and as a pinch-runner once. This pinch-running, during a May 31, 1964, game against the Philadelphia Phillies, was Hertz's moment to shine. After Aspromonte walked, Hertz pinch ran and promptly took second base on a wild pitch. He advanced to third on a walk, then scored on Al Spangler's infield single. He was promptly rewarded with a seat on the bench due to a double-switch.

Hertz provided versatility for the remainder of his minor league career with Houston and the New York Mets, playing second, short, and third. He played three full seasons in Florida and apparently liked it; he went on to coach at Miami Coral Park High School, then Miami-Dade College, where he coached players such as Placido Polanco and Omar Olivares—150 future pros in total—and Hertz won more than 1,200 games.

He did his part to grow the game in the Holy Land as well, managing the Tel Aviv Lightning of the Israel Baseball League. But his real legacy is in Florida, where he earned notice as a Little League pitcher, won Kinloch Junior High's sports award in 1960, and starred in multiple sports at Miami High, where he hit .472 as a senior in 1963. By September the Colt .45s had fended off five other teams to sign him for $50,000. He attended University of Miami for one semester, then it was off to Houston's spring training in—where else?—Cocoa, Florida.

Even in 2021 he's still plugged in on Miami-Dade College's exploits, as the program went to the National Junior College World Series. That's six-plus decades impacting the South Florida baseball community. But his son, Darren, broke his heart when he turned 11—he informed his father that he preferred basketball. Darren's done okay with it—he's an assistant head coach for the Dayton men's team now.

12. Fred Graf

Bats Right, Throws Right
St. Louis Browns, 1913

It was front page news of the *St. Louis Globe Democrat* in February of 1913 when Fred Graf wrote in from his home in Dayton, Ohio, to tell the newspaper that he wasn't enjoying his offseason job very much: "Graf, who will try to make good for the Browns this spring at Waco, apparently doesn't think very highly of his business."

Graf expressed an interest instead in either a rugmaking or a carpet cleaning factory. No context was provided about why Graf wrote to the paper about his off-field frustrations, nor why the *Globe Democrat* printed it. As ever, people are starving for baseball stories in spring training, and almost anything will do.

Graf got that chance on May 14, replacing Jimmy Austin mid-game at third base for the St. Louis Browns and reaching base both times he tried—on a double and a walk—in a game Walter Johnson won 10–5, though it is unclear whether either plate appearance came against Johnson since he only pitched the first six innings. It was a momentous day for the Browns, who ended Johnson's 56-inning scoreless streak, dropping Big Train's numbers on the season all the way down to 8–0 with a 0.30 ERA.

Graf played well in his limited time with St. Louis after his season at Class A Chattanooga ended in September, finishing the totality of his Major League Baseball work at .400/.625/.600 for an OPS+ of 263. That ranks 11th all time among major leaguers ever in OPS+ with a minimum nine plate appearances, which is how many Graf accumulated. That is indeed a small sample size. Then again, maybe with more time and seasoning he'd have gotten even better! We'll never know.

Graf happily returned to Chattanooga, where he played third base clear through the end of the decade and earned a reputation as "generally the best fielding third baseman in the league," according to *The Chattanooga Daily Times*. The fans remembered: in 1936 Chattanooga voted for an all-time Lookout team. Not only was Graf selected as the third baseman, but he also received more votes than any other player—save Baby Doll Jacobson, who went on to a long, successful major league career.

Graf returned the favor, living until 90 in his adopted hometown.

5

Shortstop

Not only is Lou Boudreau the greatest shortstop in Jewish baseball history, but he also is the greatest Jewish manager—and a good argument can be made that he is the greatest player, period. Not Sandy Koufax. Not Hank Greenberg.

There are two reasons, I believe, why this isn't often discussed. For one thing, Koufax and Greenberg's Jewishness were much more well-known than Boudreau's—his mother was Jewish, but Boudreau was raised by his Christian father, following a divorce. For another, Boudreau didn't have the eye-popping home run totals of Greenberg or strikeout totals of Koufax. But according to Baseball-Reference's WAR, Boudreau's career value was at 63.6 due to a combination of strong offense and strong defense at shortstop, arguably the most important defensive position. Greenberg's total? 55. Koufax? 48.9. Ian Kinsler? 54.1.

Lou Boudreau

Now it is worth noting that Greenberg missed roughly four full seasons on the heels of putting up a 9.2 mark in 1940. Take away World War II, and he likely tops Boudreau. And given the unreliable nature of fielding evaluations from that time, it is hard to give Boudreau the ultimate edge. But he certainly should be in the conversation. And he seldom is.

The rest of the shortstops, however, are not in Greenberg territory, unless one is referring to Adam Greenberg, whose major league career consisted of one plate appearance where he was hit by a pitch.

1. Lou Boudreau

Bats Right, Throws Right
Cleveland Indians, 1938–1950
Boston Red Sox, 1951–1952

An interesting aspect of Lou Boudreau's career is that, though the middle of his peak took place during World War II and he played through the war in a weakened American League, he put up his best numbers before and after the war. Adjusted for league, of course, his 1943, 1944, and 1945 seasons were among his strongest. But his only two 100-RBI seasons came in 1940 and 1948, and his three highest home run seasons were 1940, 1941, and 1948.

Boudreau's 1948 is sadly overlooked—it is one of the most impressive seasons in baseball history. Judge it by OPS+, putting his offensive output in park and era context, and he is at 166+ or 66 percent above average. That ranks 11th all time among primary shortstop seasons behind only six of Honus Wagner's seasons (seriously, Wagner might be the best-ever at any position), Arky Vaughn's 1935, Rogers Hornsby's 1917, Rico Petrocelli's 1969, and Robin Yount's 1982. All but Petrocelli are in the Hall of Fame, and Petrocelli is criminally underrated. Alex Rodriguez is one of the great shortstops ever, and Boudreau's OPS+ in 1948 is higher than all but two seasons of A-Rod's career.

But the more one looks at the numbers, the more impressive it is. In baseball hitters fail much more often than they succeed—but Boudreau's 1948 might have been as close to a perfect foil for that truism as any single season. His season line was .355/.453/.534 as a terrific defensive shortstop! He hit 18 home runs, drove in 106 runs, finished second in the league in batting average, second in on-base percentage, and fourth in slugging percentage. He walked 98 times, and—this is my favorite part—he struck out *nine times all season*. Twice as many home runs as strikeouts. To put this in perspective, Rodriguez struck out four times in a single game on seven separate occasions in his career.

It's worth mentioning—as he was doing this on the field—he also managed the Cleveland Indians, leading them to their last World Series title. He hit .273/.333/.455 in the World Series. He drove in a run as starting shortstop in the All-Star Game. He had 16 sacrifice hits, which ranked fifth in the American League. There is no record of how many children he saved from burning buildings in 1948, but it is safe to assume more children saved than strikeouts.

A corollary of Al Rosen's delay coming to the major leagues: the best Jewish third baseman didn't play much alongside the best Jewish shortstop. By 1950 Rosen's first full year at third base, Boudreau lost his job to Ray Boone, logging just 61 games at shortstop. By the next season, Boudreau was in Boston.

Boudreau, like Rosen, did not age well as a player. His all-world 1948 at age 30 was his last Hall of Fame season—he was average in 1949, a part timer in 1950–51, and finished in 1952. Perhaps the toll of also managing from age-26 on dragged down his playing career's latter part. Still, he was elected to the Hall of Fame in 1970, due to both his playing days and his 1,162 wins as "Boy Manager." Amazingly, though he began managing at age 24, his last game as manager came at age 42, and his last top three finish came at age 31. He fit a whole Hall of Fame career into his first 31 years. "He was the greatest shortstop I ever saw," said the remarkable Bob Feller while describing Boudreau to the *Chicago Tribune*. That really says it all.

2. Jim Levey

Bats Both, Throws Right
St. Louis Browns, 1930–1933

One of the easiest mistakes for casual baseball fans to make is believing there is any correlation between errors and fielding prowess. Errors are often assigned by official scorers on balls that are reached but not fielded cleanly. If Shortstop A reaches 100 more balls than Shortstop B but muffs 15 of them, Shortstop A is still immensely more valuable than Shortstop B is.

Well, Jim Levey had an 18-year career as a Shortstop A, making plenty of errors while adding tremendous defensive value to his teams. Levey displayed a fair amount of power as well in his three minor league seasons, putting up slugging percentages of .517, .425 and .440 in three stops before landing with the St. Louis Browns late in the 1930 season.

Levey was quite the athlete. Despite being cautioned by Willis E. Johnson in the November 20, 1930, edition of *The Sporting News* not to "forever mar his baseball career" by taking the injury risk, he went on to play several offseasons with the Pittsburgh Steelers of the NFL, the local football team in the area he'd first drawn notice as a local baseball player as well. His schooling had ended at 16, when he pretended to be 18 and joined the U.S. Marines.

In 1931, though, he hit .209/.264/.285—good for an OPS+ of just 42—and took hold of the shortstop job in St. Louis despite an American League-high 58 errors. Why? Well, consider that of the 11 shortstops with at least 400 plate appearances, seven had an OPS+ below 100 or league average. This includes Rabbit Maranville, who went onto the Hall of Fame. Shortstop was a defensive position at the time, and Levey's "flashy fielding" earned him high marks in *TSN*'s January 1932 Browns season preview. Again—errors are a rotten way to evaluate fielders.

His hitting even took a temporary turn forward, and he appeared ready to become one of the league's top shortstops in 1932. His hot start, which multiple reports at the time credited to his switch-hitting, had him at .346, which ranked third in the American League. "It's the greatest thing that ever happened to me," Levey told the Associated Press in May of 1932. "Here I'd been going along for years thinking I couldn't hit...Boy, I can sock that ball!"

But the average faded—he ended the season at .280, which placed him seventh on his own team. Still, five writers listed Levey on their MVP ballots, and he finished in 19th place, tying Hall of Famer Ted Lyons and ahead of Hall of Famer Joe Sewell.

But it appears the league figured out how to pitch to both the left and right-handed Levey. In 1933 Levey put up a .195/.237/.240 line. The total OPS+ was 24—the lowest single-season mark of 1,659 player seasons by a shortstop in major league history with a minimum of 502 plate appearances. With offensive expectations for shortstops now much higher, that 24 OPS+ is probably as unbreakable a baseball record as Cy Young's 511 career victories.

Levey was traded to the Pacific Coast League's Hollywood Stars, along with two other players, for Alan Strange—his replacement at shortstop. He played for Hollywood for two seasons (alongside a number of major leaguers, such as Vince DiMaggio and Hall of Famer Bobby Doerr), then headed to the Texas League, where he was the circuit's All-Star shortstop for three years running from 1938 to 1940. Levey continued to put up reasonable offense and eye-popping error totals until 1945, missing a season in 1943 to serve the World War II cause.

His baseball IQ lent itself to managing in both the Texas League and for Jamestown, New York, in the New York-Penn League after his playing career ended. He'd find his way to Steelers games, especially when Pittsburgh traveled to Dallas, where he'd settled. He also played in Texas League Old Timers' games. I guess he didn't forever mar his baseball career with football, after all.

3. Eddie Zosky

Bats Right, Throws Right
Toronto Blue Jays, 1991–1992
Florida Marlins, 1995
Milwaukee Brewers, 1999
Houston Astros, 2000

In a just world, Whittier, California, would be known for native son Eddie Zosky, a shortstop with prodigious talent brought low by injuries, and not Richard Nixon, a notorious anti-Semite brought low by his own crimes. Alas, we never truly got to see the full Eddie Zosky experience.

The star at Fresno State spurned a fifth-round selection by the New York Mets out of high school 1986 to go to college, earning Fresno State Hall of Fame honors for his work as a Bulldog. The Toronto Blue Jays then selected him in the first round in 1989 and absolutely planned their future around him.

Zosky actually began his pro career at Double A Knoxville, an incredibly aggressive assignment for a newly pro prospect. After repeating that level in 1990, he posted a respectable .271/.316/.367 line and was promoted to Triple A Syracuse anyway. The Blue Jays also traded away Tony Fernandez, the long-time shortstop mainstay, and gave Zosky his jersey No. 1. "It was a big door that opened," Zosky told *The National Post* in spring training of 1991. "When I heard about it, I was ecstatic."

He was the 22nd best prospect in baseball that year, per *Baseball America*, ahead of guys like Royce Clayton, Jeff Bagwell, and Chipper Jones. He even had an outside shot of making Toronto out of spring training but was ultimately sent to Triple A Syracuse, where he performed similarly in 1991: .264/.315/.350. That was good enough, especially with the best arm in the organization, to earn his call-up—a flop, unfortunately, featuring a .148 average in 28 plate appearances.

Even so, the plan was for Zosky to win that shortstop job in spring training 1992, but he struggled with injuries and performance. Manuel Lee, a stopgap, held on instead. The story continued, unhappily, into 1993. He started slowly, then had a bone spur in his elbow surgically removed in May, costing him a month. So it continued right through 1994, when the new shortstop of the future was Alex Gonzalez, and Zosky was off to the Florida Marlins in a trade.

His career continued in this vein. He wandered the minors, receiving occasional at-bats in the majors. And for his part, Zosky thinks he could have done more with his talent. As he told Adrian Wojnarowski of *The Fresno Bee* in 1997, "The media was writing about me, saying I was going to be the shortstop, so I just chilled and kicked back, telling myself, 'It's going to happen,'" Zosky said. "I did that instead of maybe going out there and working a little harder. It's kind of embarrassing now, when I tell somebody I was a first rounder. I wonder what they're thinking. 'Oh my god, YOU were a first rounder?'"

Zosky had just turned 29 years old when he gave this interview, and it's hard not to have empathy for him. His talent and the realization of what he'd need to do to maximize that talent did not line up in his life. He said he'd play until "someone didn't want me anymore" and he did through 2000. By 2001 his baseball outlet was playing in Fresno State alumni games. He probably wondered what might have been. I do, too.

4. Eddie Feinberg
Bats Both, Throws Right
Philadelphia Phillies, 1938–1939

While the sabermetric movement has taken huge leaps forward in the past 25 years, it is still nearly impossible to prove that a player's performance is affected by God. Think of it like clutch hitting—the battle over existence makes it impossible to quantify.

That said, if such a measurement ever becomes possible, expect sabermetricians to look hard at Eddie "Itzy" Feinberg, a Philadelphia native son of Ukranian Jewish immigrants. After dropping out of high school to play for Centreville in the Eastern Shore League, Feinberg finished with a .334 average,

15 home runs, and 80 RBIs in 1937 and earned a look by the Philadelphia Phillies—and rightly so. Philly sandlot ball was legit with plenty of players, who could have played in the minors, electing for the security of a 9-to-5 job plus sandlot work instead. At age 20 Feinberg's future in baseball seemed bright.

And according to the *Big Book of Jewish Baseball*, Feinberg chose to play on Yom Kippur late in the 1938 season, while Jewish teammates Phil Weintraub and Morrie Arnovich elected to sit out. Feinberg played, went 0-for-8, and "regretted the decision for the rest of his life."

The only problem with this story is that it didn't happen. Yom Kippur in 1938 began at sundown on October 4 after the season ended. The story can't even have been on Rosh Hashanah of 1938—the Phillies were off that day. And while they played a doubleheader on Rosh Hashanah eve in 1938, in the pre-lights days of baseball, sundown, which is when the holiday starts, was also when the games had to end. The Phils did play a doubleheader on Yom Kippur of 1939—but Weintraub was no longer with Philadelphia, and neither was Feinberg—he'd been dealt to the Chicago White Sox, who buried him in the minor leagues.

Incidentally, Howard M. Wasserman studied this issue in detail, running the numbers on all Jewish players who elected to play, or not, on the holiest day of the year. His conclusion in the Fall 2020 edition of SABR's Baseball Research Journal: "At the individual level, the answer appears to be no. As a group, Yom Kippur hitting numbers for nonpitchers match their career batting average and OPS, if limited power and run production, with higher numbers on Kol Nidre than in games during the following afternoon or evening. Pitcher performances have been mixed, with several good starts and relief appearances balanced against some poor games." He did note that teams with Jewish players on them performed worse on Yom Kippur relative to their typical levels.

Feinberg finished his professional career with stints in St. Paul, Minnesota; Scranton, Pennsylvania; and Greenville, South Carolina; among other teams. He was traded to Washington in 1940 but elected to return to Philly instead, playing semipro. "Washington paid lousy, and I knew I could make more money playing semipro," Feinberg told *The Philadelphia Inquirer*. After his playing days were over, he opened a restaurant with his wife, Sally.

In his career in organized baseball, though, he never approached his Centreville numbers. But it does not appear that God, in this case, was to blame.

5. Murray Franklin

Bats Right, Throws Right
Detroit Tigers, 1941–1942

Murray Franklin might have had a fine major league career. But two interruptions, one of his own making, prevented it.

Franklin displayed a plus bat after joining the Detroit Tigers organization in 1937. He had a decent D-level debut for Beckley of the Mountain State League, then dominated in his second season on the circuit—hitting .439 with 26 home runs in 385 at-bats for a .790 slugging percentage. Two seasons in Beaumont followed, where Hank Greenberg had been Texas League MVP earlier in the decade, and Franklin posted .288 and .290 batting averages with slugging percentages of .393 and .396—very good for a shortstop at that time.

By 1941 after a terrific season (.291 average, .428 slugging percentage) for Little Rock of the Southern Association, he debuted for the Tigers. In 13 at-bats he hit .300 and followed with a respectable .260/.301/.344 line for the 1942 Tigers while splitting the shortstop job with Billy Hitchcock, who hit just .211.

But the war called Franklin away. He enlisted in the Navy in September 1942, serving in World War II through the end of the 1945 season. Then, upon his return, he was lured by the higher salaries to the Mexican League in 1946. Organized baseball banned all players who jumped to the Mexican League, and Franklin didn't return to American baseball until 1949, when he joined the Hollywood Stars of the Pacific Coast League.

Franklin was then 35, and no longer covered enough ground to play short. But he played another five seasons in the PCL for three teams, even blasting 13 home runs in 311 at-bats for Hollywood in 1951 at third base.

6. Jonah Goldman

Bats Right, Throws Right
Cleveland Indians, 1928, 1930–1931

All indications are that Jonah Goldman, Syracuse University baseball star, was simply not able to hit major league pitching consistently. His career line was .224/.293/.283, and he was given 306 at-bats in 1930 alone to prove otherwise—his line for the season was .242/.312/.310, which is substandard in any season but particularly 1930, the Year of the Hitter. The league's line was .288/.351/.421.

The following year, 1931, was somehow worse: .129/.182/.145 in 70 plate appearances for an OPS+ of -15. But even by October 1931, Goldman's devotees hadn't given up, though the Cleveland Indians had. "With the exception of Jonah Goldman, the Indians haven't had a shortstop candidate who showed any aptitude for the job," Ed Bang wrote in the October 22, 1931 edition of *The Sporting News*. "Goldman was really a great fielder. His failure to make the grade as a batter upset him so that he did not turn in his customary sparkling defensive performance early last season, and the powers decided they would definitely give up hope of Goldman proving the answer to their greatest need. Jonah has his admirers, however, and they will tell you that the little Jewish lad, if assured the position were his, would become not only a positive sensation as a fielder, but would step to the plate with sufficient confidence to bring him a respectable batting average."

Goldman never got another major league chance but more than acquitted himself in 1932 with Indianapolis, hitting .270, and again in 1933 with Montreal, hitting .254. In between those campaigns, he eloped with the former Rhea Sarnoff. The couple returned to Jonah's native New York, where for 15 cents a ticket, fans could watch the Brooklyn Bushwicks, a semipro outfit, play ball, Goldman holding down shortstop, and big leaguers like Dazzy Vance and Waite Hoyt sometimes showing up as sometime ringers on the mound.

7. Jesse Baker

Bats Right, Throws Right
Washington Senators, 1919

Jesse Baker, real name Michael Myron Silverman, attracted notice with his .278 average and strong fielding with the Richmond Colts of the Virginian League. Following his one game for the 1919 Washington Senators, he headed back to Richmond in 1920, then to the Danville (Virginia) Tobbaconists of the Piedmont League. This was the South less than a decade after a lynch mob had kidnapped and murdered the Jewish businessman Leo Frank over a murder he clearly didn't commit. Half of Georgia's Jews left the state afterward.

You'd have changed your name to Jesse Baker, too.

Not that it helped Baker any with a famous southerner, Ty Cobb, during his one game in the major leagues. On September 14 he got the start at shortstop for Washington against the Detroit Tigers. "Baker, a recruit from the Richmond, Virginia club, was spiked by Cobb and compelled to retire in the second inning," *The Charlotte Observer* reported the next day.

Even so, Baker continued to play well in the minor leagues. He hit .280 for Danville in 1922, and *The Courier-Journal* referred to him as "a whale of a ballplayer."

8. Lou Brower

Bats Right, Throws Right
Detroit Tigers, 1931

While Julio Franco earned acclaim from forever young stories as a 49-year-old pinch-hitter in 2007 for the New York Mets, his ability to play the field was severely compromised. But Lou Brower managed to play second base as a 47 year old.

Granted, it was in the Class-D Sooner State League, but he did so well enough that in conjunction with a .259 batting average and .329 slugging percentage, he was able to play/manage the Lawton Giants to a regular-season title while earning the affectionate nickname "Old Folks" from the fans.

He also received "Lou Brower Appreciation Night" in his honor from the Lawton Giants on August 26, receiving more than $1,000 in cash and gifts while his fiancee, Rita Taylor, watched from the stands. (Incidentally, Brower reportedly was charged with reckless driving that very same night, costing him a $10 fine. All I'm saying is that he came out ahead.)

Brower's career began 22 years earlier with the London Indians of the Michigan Ontario League. His game didn't change much over the two decades. He hit over .300 twice, along with seasons of .296, .291, and .298. He reached double figures in triples eight times, the final time at age 37 for Oklahoma City of the Texas League. He even hit a triple in his age-47 season. Brower managed into his 50s in the Sooner State League, reaching the playoffs six times.

But during his six weeks in the major leagues, the hits didn't fall. Brower took over at shortstop for the Detroit Tigers in June of 1931 to glowing scouting reports. "Brower, a star with Oklahoma City in the Western League last year, has played very impressive baseball since stepping into Double A company," *The Kansas City Times* reported. "His hitting has been rather timely and afield he has played brilliantly at times."

Brower received 62 at-bats but batted just .161. It doesn't appear he was overmatched—eight walks, just five strikeouts—but six weeks was all he got. The younger Billy Rogell took over, hit .303, and held on to the position until 1938, driving in 98 runs in that 1934 pennant-winning season for a Detroit team keyed by Hank Greenberg.

It's hard to say the Tigers got that one wrong. But Brower certainly made up for his brief tenure in the majors with his minor league volume. And "Old

Folks," who was 47 at the time he got that nickname, lived almost another 47 years with Rita at his side for all of them.

9. Allen Richter

Bats Right, Throws Right
Boston Red Sox, 1951, 1953

The pride of Norfolk, Virginia, Allen Richter, the son of Sol, a justice of the peace, and Flora, nee Cohen, never hit much in the minor leagues. That the Boston Red Sox continued to promote him speaks awfully well of his defensive prowess. After serving two years in the Army Air Corps, delaying the start of his pro career, he hit .256 for the D-level Oneonta Red Sox in 1947—and promptly got promoted to Class C Lynn. He hit .238 for Lynn and got ushered up to Scranton, where he hit .273 without a single home run—and was named MVP of the team, winning a brand-new Oldsmobile sedan.

But in 1951 Richter finally hit—to the tune of .321 for Louisville of the Eastern League. He changed his manager's mind about him, too. Pinky Higgins, who'd had an illustrious big league career before managing the Louisville Colonels among other teams, said he hadn't considered Richter big league material at first. "But Rich is making you take serious notice of him this season," Higgins told *The Courier-Journal* in August 1951.

Higgins lamented Richter's lack of footspeed but compared him to another illustrious Jewish shortstop: Lou Boudreau. And Richter noted that he'd gotten stronger, allowing him to use a lighter bat. As he put it: "I can supply my own power now."

It earned him a job in Boston in September 1951. The Red Sox certainly didn't need a shortstop—Johnny Pesky hit .313 with a .417 on-base percentage that season. Richter, light bat and all, logged just a .091 average. He did play three games at short, turning five double plays, made 10 putouts, and added eight assists. Although it is an impossibly small sample, he logged all three categories at a much higher rate than the starter Pesky. That winter Higgins believed he might have to find a new shortstop and that Richter would be in Boston, as the Red Sox pondered making major changes. A December headline in *The Courier-Journal* blared, "Colonels' Problem Is At Shortstop."

Richter thought so, too. When new manager Boudreau sent him back to Louisville, Richter appealed to general manager Joe Cronin, who gave him permission to seek work elsewhere. The San Diego Padres and Bill Starr picked him up, where Richter hit .248 but earned raves from sportswriters on the West Coast as well. "The powerful young star...has made the Padre infield, and has been the big gun on their defense...the Padres haven't had a good shortstop for many years, but it appears as though they have just what the doctor ordered to keep the club in the pennant race," reported United Press International in April 1952.

San Diego finished fifth, but the Red Sox brought him back in 1953, where he logged his final appearance on April 21 as a defensive replacement, then sent him back to Louisville. This time he went willingly. He performed similarly there, along with Triple A Rochester in 1954 and 1955, hitting between .260 and .277 each of the three seasons.

From there, it was back to Norfolk for a successful career in sports broadcasting, business, and real estate, all while staying active in the Jewish community. He lived to 90; his obituary described him as the "oldest living teenager."

10. Reuben Ewing

Bats Right, Throws Right
St. Louis Cardinals, 1921

Would you believe only three major leaguers ever are from Odessa, Ukraine? And all three were Jewish. Ewing, who decided to stick with the Jewish first name but changed to Ewing from Cohen, was one of the three and the only position player. Pitcher Bill Cristall preceded him by 20 years—clearly, he did not look marvelous in his 48⅓ innings of 4.84 ERA pitching. And Isadore

Goldstein came along in 1932, walked 41, struck out just 14, and returned to the minors.

St. Louis Cardinals manager Branch Rickey used Ewing as a defensive replacement late in a June 21 win over the Chicago Cubs, then as a pinch-runner on June 25, and pinch-hitter June 27. Many newspapers at the time referred to him as "Buck," a likely result of the name of the late-19th century baseball great. By June 31st Rickey had sent him on to Waterbury, where he played for a short time near his Hartford, Connecticut, home before a combination of ill health and a reportedly difficult manager ended his season and, it appears, his baseball career.

He went on to a long, successful second career as a realtor back in Hartford while remaining active in B'nai Brith, the American Jewish Committee, and the Hartford Zionist district.

6

Left Field

For the better part of 60 years, Sid Gordon was the undisputed champion among Jewish left fielders. Gordon had five Hall of Fame-caliber seasons along with another few huge years as a part-time player. Gordon's WAR, according to Baseball-Reference, was 38.4, putting him within hailing distance of Hank Greenberg. And like Greenberg, he missed time for the war, though just two seasons to Greenberg's four. But they were his age-26 and age-27 seasons, likely to have been among his finest. He's not the best Jewish player ever—but he isn't that far off.

But Ryan Braun, who just officially retired in September 2021, quickly served notice that he was going to challenge Gordon and ultimately surpassed him. Gordon's best two slugging percentages were .537 and .557—in Braun's rookie year, his slugging was .634, and in 2008 it was .553.

Once adjusting for era, it isn't clear that Braun's 2007 was better than Gordon's best season—Braun's 2007 OPS+ was 154, while Gordon's best mark in

Ryan Braun

1950 was 156. That was simply Braun's rookie year, however. In both 2011 and 2012, Braun exceeded Gordon's best OPS+ season. He's definitely the standard-bearer in left field.

1. Ryan Braun

Bats Right, Throws Right
Milwaukee Brewers, 2007–2021

We have much to discuss here.

Let's start with the statistical. It quickly became clear that Braun's likely outcomes weren't Sid Gordon; they were Hank Greenberg. Greenberg's age-23 season was similar to Braun's rookie season, though in the former's case it was his second full year in the big leagues. He put up a line of .339/.404/.600 with 26 home runs in 593 at-bats. His OPS+ was 156, just above Braun's 2007 of 154.

Add in the belief that Braun would not be forced to fight a World War for the survival of our people—something that turned out to be true—and projecting Braun as the Jewish home run leader of all time was an easy call. He did it, too: 352 ranks ahead of Greenberg's 331, though it took Braun an extra 1,242 plate appearances to amass his total.

Braun actually keeps pace with Greenberg through the two respective age-28 seasons. At that point, which was Braun's 2012 campaign, he'd put up a .313/.374/.568 with 202 home runs. Greenberg, through age 28, checks in at .323/.415/.617 with 206 home runs, including his historic 58-home run spree in 1938.

Just to put Braun in full context through age 28, that 147 OPS+ ranks 43rd in Major League Baseball history among all hitters ever with a minimum 3,000 plate appearances. He was ahead of Jim Thome (146), Darryl Strawberry (145), Eddie Murray (144), Harmon Killebrew (142), and Carl Yastrzemski (139), along with numerous other Hall of Famers who made it to Cooperstown on the strength of their bats.

Then came the Biogenesis scandal. And the way it unfolded in multiple parts did Braun no favors, nor did he help himself. For those unfamiliar: Braun failed a drug test in 2011, then appealed on procedural grounds. He was able to win that appeal, and the wise legal advice would have been to take the win and keep his mouth shut.

But Braun didn't do that. Instead, he held a self-righteous press conference in which he asserted that, "If I had done this intentionally, or unintentionally, I'd be the first one to step up and say, 'I did it.'" He also cast aspersions on the test collector, saying publicly: "What could have possibly happened to it during that 44-hour period [before the collector took the urine sample to FedEx]? There were a lot of things that we learned about the collector, about the collection process, about the way that the entire thing worked that made us very concerned and very suspicious about what could have actually happened." And worst of all, and especially relevant for this book: Jeff Passan reported that Braun privately accused the test collector, Dino Laurenzi Jr., of being anti-Semitic.

All of which made the exposure of Braun as a PED user in the Biogenesis scandal contain another element: the preeminent Jewish player of his generation used a false claim of anti-Semitism to try and avoid responsibility for his own actions.

I turned to Eve Rosenbaum, the director of player development for the Baltimore Orioles, but we quickly realized that this was far more than a simple statistical conversation. Fortunately, she was also a psych major in college with a minor in philosophy. "I'm very used to ethical morality debates where you're trying to prove that you're right, but you don't really know," Rosenbaum said. "Because it is a moral question of: what do you do with someone who was using a substance to improve themselves? How do you weigh that against someone who didn't?"

Ultimately, this is more of a rabbinic question than a sabermetric one, we both agreed. We also came to the joint conclusion that wins are wins, and Braun's WAR, as nearly 10 ahead of Gordon's, gets him the top spot on the list.

To his credit, Braun eventually apologized—both publicly and directly to Laurenzi Jr. The two had dinner together. Braun made a mistake. He also made what has to be considered a good-faith effort to make amends. These kinds of judgements are above my pay grade, and Braun was a truly great player.

My advice to you, if you believe Braun should have an asterisk next to his name, is to put one in your copy of this book. I won't stop you.

2. Sid Gordon

Bats Right, Throws Right
New York Giants, 1941–1949, 1955
Boston Braves, 1950–1952
Milwaukee Braves, 1953
Pittsburgh Pirates, 1954–1955

My favorite aspect of Sid Gordon's career is that he played the majority of his career with the New York Giants, was never a Brooklyn Dodger, and yet was honored at Ebbets Field in 1948. How is this possible? He wasn't a Sal Maglie, who came to the Dodgers late in his career and won the fans over. He wasn't a member of the team.

He was a Brooklyn boy, son of Morris and Rose (nee Meyerson), from the Brownsville section of Brooklyn. His path was nearly to the Dodgers—Casey Stengel, then-Brooklyn manager, liked him, but Stengel was soon fired, and the crosstown Giants swooped in and signed him. By 1941 he was with New York as one of four Jews on the roster. Imagine how that team would have been received in Brooklyn. As Dan Daniel reported in the December 29, 1954, issue of *The Sporting News*: "If the data available in the Brooklyn business office, compiled from the advance sales lists, is reliable, more than 50 percent of the club's patronage is made up of Jewish fans."

This is an astounding fact—if it is even close to true. It also redoubles the tragedy that struck when Walter O'Malley moved the team from Brooklyn, taking the great Sandy Koufax from his Jewish fanbase in New York. But it helps explain why fans were so eager to come to Ebbets Field on July 3, 1948, and give Sid Gordon of the Giants a car. Nor did anyone attempt to take it back after Gordon hit two home runs that day for the visitors.

It took an extra few years to establish himself as a star, though. Gordon posted a solid 1943 line of .251/.315/.373, playing first, second, third, and left. His development stalled, however, thanks to two years in the Coast Guard. Upon his return, Gordon put together a nine-year run of .290/.386/.481 with 186 home runs over that span for an OPS+ of 134. He was nicknamed "The Solid Man," but that really damns him with faint praise.

Consider Gordon's contemporaries. Over that nine-year span, Gordon was one of 43 players with at least 4,000 plate appearances. Among those 43 he ranks seventh in OPS+. The six ahead of him? Ted Williams (193), Stan Musial (172), Ralph Kiner (151), Larry Doby (146), Duke Snider (139), and Jackie Robinson (137). Hall of Famers all. Note also that Snider and Robinson are just ahead of him, too.

And he's ahead of Hall of Famers Yogi Berra (130), Enos Slaughter (122), and Gil Hodges (125), not to mention elite hitters of the day like Ted Kluszewski (124) and Ferris Fain (121). For nearly a decade, Gordon was about as strong an offensive player as there was.

We lost Gordon too soon, at age 57, when he suffered a heart attack playing softball in Central Park. And no wonder that was his final activity. Just after Gordon died, the New York Giants' beat writer Barry Kremenko said: "The proudest thing in his life was that he played baseball."

3. Morrie Arnovich

Bats Right, Throws Right
Philadelphia Phillies, 1936–1940
Cincinnati Reds, 1940
New York Giants, 1941, 1946

It's the age-old dilemma: baseball player or rabbi? Rabbi or baseball player? Morrie Arnovich, born in Superior, Wisconsin, to Orthodox parents Charles and Rosy, was encouraged to become a rabbi by his parents. He chose ballplayer instead. And while Arnovich was not the player either Gordon or Braun was, he certainly provided value to his teams during a career that was cut nearly in half by World War II. He managed a career line of .287/.350/.383 while providing plus defense and had a season in 1939 that landed him on the All-Star team—324/.397/.413 playing some left field, playing some center field, and had an OPS+ of 124.

Arnovich was actually one of three Jews in that 1939 game—the other two were Hank Greenberg and Harry Danning. Arnovich was among the league leaders in hitting all season, finishing fifth behind Hall of Famers Johnny Mize, Paul Waner, Ducky Medwick, as well as Frank McCormick, who would be named National League MVP the following season.

Arnovich missed much of his prime to World War II but still finished with a career batting slash line of .287/.350/.383 for an OPS+ of 100—exactly league average. He never stopped hitting, even in the minor leagues. He finished at .353 with the Class-B Selma Cloverleafs in 1948 while also managing the club. He managed for several years, earning a reputation for getting thrown out of games.

His All-Star season also led the Philadelphia Phillies, who in fairness were en route to finishing 45–106 and needed any distraction, to hold "Morrie Arnovich Day" on July 16, 1939. Arnovich was provided "a complete and up-to-date fishing outfit," according to the July 20, 1939 issue of, *The Sporting News*.

And *TSN* also reported, one Charles Arnovich, father of Morrie, was in the stands, cheerfully supporting his son.

4. Don Taussig

Bats Right, Throws Right
San Francisco Giants, 1958
St. Louis Cardinals, 1961
Houston Colt .45s, 1962

Imagine the surprise of Don Taussig, the pride of Long Beach High School in Long Island who slaved for eight years in the minor leagues so he could play for his relatively local New York Giants. But when the Hofstra grad finally got his chance in 1958, his Giants were clear across the country.

Early on in Class-B Sunbury, the "speedy flychaser" crushed 12 home runs, earning early raves from the local paper, *The Daily Item*. "Don Taussig, who needs only more experience and added the ability to really hit the number 2 pitch to really go up the ladder," the paper said on September 15 in a story about the 19-year-old player enrolling at Hofstra.

Taussig hit .263 with a .396 slugging percentage for Class A Jacksonville in 1952 as a 20 year old, missed a year to serve in Korea, then took a few years to adapt to Double A Texas League pitching. By 1957 he'd made good in Dallas, hitting 22 home runs, batting .281, and slugging .464. To put his performance in perspective, Willie McCovey had nearly identical rate stats, batting .281 and slugging .463. Of course, this was Taussig's third season in Dallas, McCovey's first, and McCovey was six years younger.

Still, one didn't have to hit like McCovey to be a serviceable major leaguer, but Taussig had trouble breaking into San Francisco's outfield of Willie Mays, Leon Wagner, Felipe Alou, McCovey, Willie Kirkland...no easy feat. He was sent to the Portland Beavers of the Pacific Coast League, a high-level minor league, and thrived, hitting .286/.352/.500 with 23 home runs and 101 RBIs.

The St. Louis Cardinals acquired him, and he faced a similar logjam in the outfield with Stan Musial, Curt Flood, and Joe Cunningham. He held his own with the Cardinals, posting a season line of .287/.338/.447...which got him drafted by the Houston Colt .45s in the expansion draft. But Houston gave him just 25 at-bats perhaps because at age 30 he was no longer a prospect. Or as *The Daily Item* put it that spring: "Those who recall Taussig as a Sudbury performer who always did his best, whatever the situation, hope, along with this scribbler, that the third time will be the charm with Don and that he'll earn a regular job with the Texans."

The timing was never quite right for Taussig, an outfielder with power. He did get one measure of revenge against the Cardinals, who'd left him unprotected in the expansion draft, clouting a two-run homer to lift Houston over St. Louis 4–3. Two weeks later it was back to the minors with Oklahoma City.

Not that he was forgotten: along with other Giants from that inaugural year in San Francisco, Taussig was paraded around the grounds of then-AT&T Park in a 1950s-era convertible on April 7, 2008.

5. Alta Cohen

Bats Left, Throws Left
Brooklyn Dodgers, 1931–1932
Philadelphia Phillies, 1933

Had *The Jazz Singer* been written a decade later, it could have been made about a baseball player rather than a jazz singer. You'd probably have had to change the name of the movie, of course. But that ballplayer could have been Alta Cohen. Cohen's father, a Newark, New Jersey, rabbi, renamed him Alta, meaning "old," during the 1918 flu epidemic to protect him, according to Martin Abramowitz, the preeminent Jewish baseball scholar.

Cohen was the Shohei Ohtani of Newark, making all-state in both baseball and basketball and first drawing larger public notice in the *Oakland Tribune* in 1928 when it wrote the 19 year old "weighing 159 pounds, is trying for a pitching job with Rochester. He broke in last fall from the Newark sandlots and in 11 innings allowed six hits and not a run."

But he ultimately found work in 1929 as an outfielder. He posted a .300 batting average with the Class-D Rocky Mount Buccaneers, then improved to a .335 batting average and .460 slugging percentage with the Macon Peaches of the Class A South Atlantic League. "Alta Cohen, young outfielder with the Macon Peaches in 1930, will be a Brooklyn Dodger ere long," declared *The Charlotte News* in June 1931.

Ere long, the newspaper was right. Cohen followed his strong season in Macon with a .316 batting average and .448 slugging for the Hartford Senators of the Eastern League, earning a call-up by the Brooklyn Dodgers.

But by 1932 Cohen had trouble breaking into a very good Dodgers outfield even after Frank O'Doul's injury opened the door to some regular playing time. Cohen didn't help matters with a .156 batting average. He returned to Hartford, hitting .412 in 226 at-bats, though he was only at .249 after being promoted to Triple A Jersey City.

After catching on for a year with the Class B Durham Bulls, Cohen got himself another big league chance by hitting .333 with a .441 slugging for the Double A Toledo Mud Hens. Unfortunately for Cohen, he only hit .188 in 32 at-bats for the Philadelphia Phillies, and the major league portion of his career was complete.

That's when Alta Cohen decided to become a pitcher after all. In 1935 for Toledo, he hit .279 in 452 at-bats—but he also appeared in 11 games on the mound, including six starts, posting a 4–3, 4.58 ERA mark. For comparison of the level, Roxie Lawson, who had a nine-year big league career, posted a 14–8, 3.92 ERA season for Toledo.

Cohen was a full-time pitcher in 1936, posting a 14–12, 5.21 season. He improved on that in 1937 with a 15–7, 4.14 ERA year and earned this praise in the June 17, 1937 issue of *The Sporting News*: "A bright spot for [Manager Fred] Haney is the way his veteran performers are showing up. Alta Cohen, versatile southpaw hurler...Cohen has pitched some magnificent games."

Cohen's transition was complete. He pitched through the 1940 season, finishing up in Jersey City, and stayed in the Garden State, becoming successful in business and serving on the board of Newark Beth Israel Medical Center, among other philanthropic enterprises. And as for his father's wish in naming him Alta? Cohen died in Maplewood, New Jersey—at the ripe *alta* age of 94.

6. Sy Rosenthal

Bats Left, Throws Left
Boston Red Sox, 1925–1926

A trailblazer in many ways, Sy Rosenthal was born to an Orthodox Jewish family. After the couple immigrated from Russia and Austria, respectively, Sy was the youngest of Philip and Anna's five children. By the early 1920s, Sy's playing on the Boston sandlots attracted the attention of Red Sox announcer Stonewall Jackson (no, not that one) who arranged for a tryout for Rosenthal.

The Red Sox farmed him out to Hartford, where he produced headlines like "SI ROSENTHAL ENTERS HARTFORD'S HOMERUN CIRCLE WHILE ON RAMPAGE AT PITTSFIELD." It is delightful to me, incidentally, that both a stadium Rosenthal played in during his first professional season—Wahconah Park in Pittsfield—and his home stadium during his Major League Baseball career—Fenway Park—are still standing and in active use. And *The Boston Globe* noted that in 1923 Rosenthal "connected for one of the longest drives in the history of the park" that day, though it is probably worth noting that this report came in Wahconah Park's fifth year, and the stadium has now been standing for 102 years.

Rosenthal continued crushing the ball at every stop, hitting .376 for San Antonio of the Texas League in 1924 and .331 with 21 home runs in 1925 before the Red Sox finally purchased his contract in September 1925. He thus became one of only two Red Sox players who were both born and passed away in Boston, along with Fenway's first home team Jewish player.

By the end of the month, friends had organized a day in his honor, and Rosenthal received $1,000 on a chilly day at Fenway. This was no small sum in a game where even by 1967 the minimum salary had only reached $6,000.

By the spring of 1926, Rosenthal was in contention for a starting spot in the outfield, working closely with Boston coach Hugh Duffy and drawing notice of the press, as the Red Sox trained that March in New Orleans, while regularly getting time with the first-teamers in right field. Rosenthal won the job and tripled on the day after Opening Day in April, making a fine catch of a Bob Meusel fly ball as well in a 12–11 loss to the New York Yankees at Fenway Park. He soon lost the right-field job to Roy Carlyle, though later in the season, he supplanted Ira Flagstead in left. But it proved a disappointing season for Rosenthal, who hit just .267/.317/.372, a far cry from his minor league production.

Rosenthal's major league career was over, but he never stopped hitting, routinely topping .300 in stops like Chattanooga, Dallas, Atlanta, and Galveston. Just compare him to those who got future major league opportunities to get a sense of his talent. For the 1929 Dallas Steers, Rosenthal hit .339 with a .475 slugging percentage. His teammate Milt Stock, a longtime major league infielder, checked in that same year at .307 and .401. Or look at 1930, when Rosenthal hit .355 with a .498 slugging for the Atlanta Crackers. A young shortstop in the same lineup, Luke Appling, hit .326 with a .508 slugging percentage ahead of beginning his long, Hall of Fame career that same season.

By 1933 Rosenthal was crushing it with the Quincy Indians of the Class B Mississippi Valley League, finishing second in hitting with a .388 mark while leading the league with 39 doubles. He played until 1935 and never stopped hitting.

As with many other players of the time, Rosenthal retired from organized baseball but continued on back home in Dorchester while beginning his next career, manufacturing tin cans. But when World War II arrived, both he and his son Buddy enlisted. Buddy became a Marine and was killed in action; Sy suffered injuries that left him a paraplegic on D-Day.

The Red Sox held another day for Sy Rosenthal in 1947, but the circumstances couldn't have been more different. Even so, Rosenthal lived another 22 years, throwing himself into charitable work, raising money for everything from Black churches to local Little Leagues. "We wouldn't have to set up a Brotherhood Week if we observed the basic tenets of our faith, whatever it may be," Rosenthal said, according to SABR, after leading the effort to raise money for a gymnasium at a St. Augustine seminary in Mississippi. "If you have good will in your heart, you don't need a special week."

7. Brian Horwitz
Bats Right, Throws Right
San Francisco Giants, 2008

Very little had been expected of Brian Horwitz, who exceeded those expectations after signing with the San Francisco Giants as an undrafted free agent in 2004. After getting his history degree at Cal-Berkeley, he'd been ready to head to chiropractic school, but he put that plan on hold, signed for $1,000, and took his chances.

Undrafted free agents don't usually win batting titles, but Horwitz hit .347 in his first season to win the Northwest League crown. He hit .349 in 2005 for Augusta of the South Atlantic League. By 2007 he put up a .320/.379/.418 line between Double A and Triple A. But he didn't have the power to earn a call up to the majors. So he went out in 2008 and hit for power. After a career-high of four home runs in any season, Horwitz hit five in his first 136 minor league at-bats. When Dan Ortmeier got injured, the Giants brought up Horwitz at the end of May 2008.

He earned a start against the New York Mets on June 2, 2008, and New York announcer Gary Cohen pointed out that Horwitz was a line drive hitter with little power. Horwitz hit his first major league home run on the very next pitch. "I just put my head down and ran," Horwitz told reporters after the game. "I know this isn't a home run park and I don't have as much power as everybody...it's an out-of-body experience. I'm really enjoying it."

He'd hit just one more home run in the big leagues, finishing with a .222/.310/.389 mark in 42 plate appearances with the Giants. Now he lives in Phoenix with his wife, Krysti. The couple cofounded Online Visibility Pros, an online advertising agency for home improvement companies.

Still, by 2010, as he concluded his pro career in the Cleveland system, he'd found a following among Jewish fans. "Of my fan mail, about one-third to one-half is from Jewish fans," Horwitz said in the spring of 2010. "They've been following my career and they're really proud to see me up in the big leagues or just to see the success I'm having."

8. Al Silvera

Bats Right, Throws Right
Cincinnati Red Legs, 1955–1956

For those Jewish parents who wish to use bedtime stories for instruction, allow me to present a ready-to-use "stay in school" cautionary tale: Al Silvera. Once upon a time, there was a big right-handed slugger named Al Silvera. He was a high school star at Fairfax High in Los Angeles—the Los Angeles Player of the Year in 1953 and 1954—and made his parents very happy by not only going to college, but also choosing University of Southern California, which was very close and allowed him to visit his parents every chance he got.

But after his freshman year, the big, bad Cincinnati Red Legs came along and offered him $50,000 and a car to leave school without his degree. Silvera decided to take the money, not realizing that time with his family is priceless. The car came in handy since he was running over his mother's shattered dreams.

Due to the size of his bonus, according to major league rules at that time, Silvera had to spend the whole year in Cincinnati, which is bad enough, but he only got 13 at-bats, which is even worse. He returned to the minors in 1956 but hit only .197 in Port Arthur and Abilene after Cincinnati granted him an unconditional release.

By 1958 Silvera hit just .212 for the Albany Senators of the Eastern League and got released. He came back to California with his money and tried to buy back the time he'd lost with his family. But that time was all gone. Then he tried to buy some precious memories from college. But those, too, were beyond his reach.

If only Silvera had stayed in school and gotten his degree, not only would he have lived the life of a famous professional baseball player due to a more normal development curve...but he'd also have made his mother happy.

7

Center Field

Of all the positions, center field is the hardest to rank the Jewish players. Many players have good claims on the top spot, each from different eras, and each with different strengths.

Let's start with one who didn't play in Major League Baseball, but we must pay attention to: speed demon Thelma Eisen of the All-American Girls Professional Baseball League. In 1946 Eisen, who was raised Orthodox, stole 128 bases in just 99 games, earning all-league honors. Her defense was elite, and she was the ignition key to the Peoria Red Wings' offense. She went on to manage as well. Mark my words: there will be women in the major leagues, and eventually Jewish women will make it into future editions of this book. In a more just world of baseball opportunities for women, it would have happened long ago.

Lipman Pike was the very first Jewish player in professional baseball and performed admirably in the National Association, the National League, and the American Association. He put up tremendous offensive numbers and certainly would be a fine choice at the position.

Goody Rosen had arguably the best single season of any Jewish center fielder in 1945 and combined stellar defense and plate discipline in a 14-year major and minor league career.

Gabe Kapler played a pivotal super-sub role for the 2004 World Series champion Boston Red Sox but appeared headed to an even bigger major league career when he had three double-digit home run seasons for the Texas Rangers by age 25. And after a year as minor league manager, Kapler came out of retirement in 2008, put together a fine career that concluded in 2010, and went on to manage the Philadelphia Phillies and now the San Francisco Giants, who reached the postseason in 2021.

Elliott Maddox, a mid-career Jewish convert like Rosen, had terrific defense and plate discipline. He played for a World Series team, the 1976 New York Yankees. His 14.9 WAR and defensive chops make him the choice if what you need is a traditional leadoff hitter.

1. Goody Rosen

Bats Left, Throws Left
Brooklyn Dodgers, 1937–1939, 1944–1946
New York Giants, 1946

A close reading of his career makes it clear that Goody Rosen deserved more of an opportunity to play regularly in the major leagues. But that same close read reveals that Rosen probably has the best case for top Jewish center fielder anyway.

Rosen started his career in 1932 with the Stroudsburg Poconos of the Interstate League (Class D) and quickly earned a promotion to Double A Eastern League. He then languished with Louisville for five long years, hitting between .293 and .314, showing tremendous plate discipline and slugging between .377 and .444 while fielding his position extremely well—drawing notices for "a stunning catch" in the local paper by 1933. In one three-day stretch in May 1937, Rosen reached base five times apiece in two separate games. Yet it wasn't until the tail end of 1937 that Rosen got a chance in the major leagues.

Unlike some others profiled in this book, Rosen took immediate advantage of his opportunity. He hit .312/.361/.403 in 1937 and should have cemented his role with the Brooklyn Dodgers with his 1938 season. In his first full season in the majors, Rosen hit .281/.368/.389 with 65 walks against just 43 strikeouts. His offensive numbers were good for an OPS+ of 106—better than 15 of the 23 National League starting outfielders.

Given that he could play all three outfield positions and excelled at all of them, it is hard to believe that in 1939, the Dodgers benched Rosen in favor of Ernie Koy (OPS+ 105), Art Parks (OPS+ 86), and Gene Moore (OPS+ 72). Rosen's production came down a bit, but as a young player coming off of a solid season, how was he not given more of a chance to straighten out? Instead, he spent much of the year at Triple A Montreal, where, surprise, surprise, he hit .302 with a .426 slugging percentage.

Rosen returned his contract to Larry MacPhail in the winter of 1940 unsigned, and MacPhail, in fairly typical Larry MacPhail fashion, sold his contract to Columbus of the American Association in a fit of pique. He remained buried in the minors for four years. Rosen had typical Rosen years with Triple A Syracuse, posting .282, .290, .263, and .276 averages with decent pop and plus defense.

Finally, with the war taking a toll on players, Rosen got another chance to play with Brooklyn. He had a middling 1944 but took off in 1945. Rosen's line was .325/.379/.460. He finished third in batting average, sixth in slugging percentage, 10th in on-base percentage. A rarity for a player that draws a fair amount of walks, Rosen finished second in the league in hits. He made the All-Star team and finished 10th in the league in MVP voting for a third-place team. This probably undersells his value, too: among those who received MVP votes, Rosen's 5.5 WAR ranked fifth in the National League. It is the best single season of WAR by any Jewish center fielder in Major League Baseball history.

According to the June 14, 1945, edition of *The Sporting News*, he even had two hits to defeat the archrival New York Giants—a two-run homer on June 5 and a game-winning single on April 28.

The Dodgers, however, had a surplus of outfielders, so Rosen was dealt to the rival Giants. He put up terrific numbers, hitting .281/.377/.390, which in the offense-starved 1946 season was good for a 117 OPS+. He was a bright spot for the disappointing Giants, who, perhaps aware that they weren't going to draw fans with wins, put together a team with five Jewish players: Rosen, Morrie Arnovich, Harry Feldman, Mike Schemer, and Sid Gordon. Rosen also deployed his clutch abilities against Brooklyn—on July 5 he hit a game-winning single to beat his former team.

Rosen ended his pro career in 1947 with a victory lap in Toronto, his hometown, putting up a .274 average and .369 slugging percentage with the Triple A Maple Leafs. He was 35 and had lost his best seasons to the minors. His career OPS+ was 111 in 2,163 career plate appearances. To put that in current context, there are 21 players active in MLB today with at least 2,000 plate appearances and a majority of their time in the field playing center. Only four of them have a higher OPS+ than Rosen's 111: Mike Trout, Andrew McCutchen, AJ Pollock, and Charlie Blackmon.

Overall, his career WAR is just 11.8, but I believe that is misleading not only due to the years he missed, but also because when by all accounts he was an elite defensive player, we simply did not have the tools to properly measure and account for that at the time.

So yes, Kevin Pillar has him beat in career WAR with 16.5 through 2021. But between the years he missed, thanks to asking his employers to pay him what he was worth and a lack of full defensive value within those numbers, I'm putting him atop this list.

2. Kevin Pillar

Bats Right, Throws Right
Toronto Blue Jays, 2013–2019
San Francisco Giants, 2019
Boston Red Sox, 2020
Colorado Rockies, 2020
New York Mets, 2021

Kevin Pillar, a multi-sport star out of West Hills, California, and son of Mike and Wendy, was called to the Torah and earned all-league honors in basketball, baseball, and football all before turning 18. He and his family grew up Los Angeles Dodgers fans, though Pillar's hero on the field was Cal Ripken Jr.

After a dominant career at Cal-State Dominguez, a Division-II school, Pillar was selected in the 32nd round of the 2011 Major League Baseball Draft by the Toronto Blue Jays, hardly the hallmark of a future regular in the big leagues. But Pillar set about proving his doubters wrong immediately, leading the Appalachian League in hitting at .347.

It continued in 2012. Pillar earned Midwest League All-Star honors and collected six hits in a game for the Lansing Lugnuts. Still, he hadn't cracked any public lists of top Toronto prospects, even after tearing up the Arizona Fall League, a haven for baseball's brightest future stars. Finally, once he did it again in 2013 at Double A New Hampshire (.313/.361/.441) and Triple A Buffalo (.299/.341/.493), the Jays bowed to reality and called him up. On the day it happened, Toronto general manager Alex Anthopoulos, rather than pretend his scouting acumen was somehow otherworldly, admitted the obvious: no one expected Pillar to reach the major leagues. Pillar pointed out the imperfection to the draft system on that August day he debuted, discounting the value of players from smaller schools.

He struggled as a rookie, hitting just .206/.250/.302 in his first 102 at-bats, improved somewhat in part-time duty in 2014, but by 2015 he'd established himself as the regular center fielder in Toronto. His batting line of .278/.314/.399 tells just part of the story. To get the rest, my best advice is to Google "Kevin Pillar diving catch."

Pillar had a five-year run from 2015 to 2019, in which he averaged 152 games a year—not quite all the games but certainly Ripken-esque—with 14 home runs and 16 stolen bases a season and an OPS+ of 88. That's solid enough once accounting for his speed and defense.

How good was his defense? Well, by both Ultimate Zone Rating and DEF (Fangraphs' catch-all defensive stat), Pillar ranked sixth in all of baseball among center fielders in 2015, just ahead of some guy named Mike Trout. In 2016 both his UZR and DEF rated the best of any center fielder in the game. And he was seventh in both 2017 and 2018 in DEF. That's an extended run of elite defensive play, backed up by those who watched him.

By the time Toronto—in the midst of a rebuild—traded him to the San Francisco Giants in early 2019, he'd become the longest-tenured Blue Jay.

He's made friends in every clubhouse since, earning the respect of his teammates on the New York Mets, for instance, for returning in just two weeks from a pitch that hit him flush on the nose, leading to multiple nasal fractures, a gory injury to witness.

Pillar is the kind of player who seldom gets additional chances to start at this point—his .231/.277/.415 line in 2021 for the Mets won't lead teams to bang down his door with regular playing time in 2022. Dan Szymborski, creator of FanGraphs' projection system ZIPS, estimates Pillar's 2022 expected production to be .241/.277/.399 with 15 home runs. But he is precisely the type of player who can stick around until he's 40 if he wants, adding to his lead in most WAR by a Jewish center fielder.

3. Joc Pederson

Bats Left, Throws Left
Los Angeles Dodgers, 2014–2020
Chicago Cubs, 2021
Atlanta Braves, 2021

Joc Pederson is another data point in the performance-enhancing qualities of having a Jewish mother. Pederson's father, Stu Pederson, played briefly in the big leagues but isn't Jewish. Joc's mother, Shelly, is, and Joc has already bested Stu in every major offensive category, including a lead in career home runs, as of 2021, of 148–0. The proof is undeniable.

Pederson, another California boy made good, played baseball and football at Palo Alto High School and quickly impressed after the Los Angeles Dodgers selected him in the 11th round of the 2010 draft. By 2011 he was slashing .353/.429/.568 for the Ogden Raptors of the Pioneer League, then in 2012 managed a .313/.396/.516 mark for the Rancho Cucamonga Quakes, adding 26 stolen bases for good measure. His walk rate steadily increased as well. Note the high batting averages, which didn't stick around—but the total package was enough to put him on *Baseball America*'s top 100 prospects list in the spring of 2013, checking in at 85th overall.

But by 2013 the flaw in his game preventing true stardom began to manifest itself. His numbers were still excellent as he reached Double A, then Triple A. But note the splits: an OPS of 1.029 against right-handed pitching. Against lefties? .568.

Even so, he was the 34th best prospect, per *Baseball America*, entering 2014 and eighth overall by 2015 when he took over as Los Angeles' everyday center fielder and topped *USA TODAY*'s "100 Names To Know" in their 2015 baseball preview. Pederson didn't intend to miss out on that opportunity either, calling veteran Justin Turner all winter to talk about one thing: hitting. "We want him to play well when he gets up here," Turner explained to Dylan Hernandez of the *Los Angeles Times* that spring.

Pederson did well enough, making an All-Star team and finishing sixth in Rookie of the Year balloting, though his overall season line of .210/.346/417 wasn't quite the immediate stardom many envisioned. But everyday center fielder for a division-winning club is a pretty strong start to one's career.

Pederson provided more of the same for the Dodgers in 2016, but those devastating righty/lefty splits limited him from getting all the starts—a .469 OPS vs. lefties compared to .918 against righties. By 2017 the emergence of young Cody Bellinger—a fellow lefty swinger, but one who reached the big leagues hitting pitchers of all stripes—turned Pederson into a part timer.

Even so, he played a critical part on Los Angeles division winners throughout the decade of the 2010s and again on the World Series-winning team in 2020. In 170 postseason plate appearances for the Dodgers, Pederson's line was .272/.349/.503 with nine home runs, including three in the 2017 World Series alone. Had Los Angeles prevailed that year, he might well have joined Steve Yeager as a Jewish World Series MVP.

The Dodgers farm system has more talent now than a *shiva* has potato salad, and so the Dodgers let Pederson sign with the Chicago Cubs after the World Series win. He played regularly in Chicago and well enough that the Atlanta Braves acquired him at the trade deadline. Once again, a Pederson-led team reached the postseason, and the Braves won it all in a month many came to call "Joctober." Not only did Pederson hit another three postseason home runs during Atlanta's rampage, but he also did it in style—by wearing a pearl necklace that quickly caught on. Fans, other players, even admirers in the Arizona Fall League began playing with the Pederson pearls.

Still just 29, with a career line of .232/.332/.462 through the 2021 season in 2,998 plate appearances, there's a real opportunity for Pederson to age gracefully into his 30s and hold the top spot among Jewish center fielders by the time he's finished playing. Dan Szymborski of Fangraphs has a ZIPS projection for him at .238/.322/.467 in 2022.

4. Elliott Maddox

Bats Right, Throws Right

Detroit Tigers, 1970

Washington Senators, 1971

Texas Rangers, 1972–1973

New York Yankees, 1974–1976

Baltimore Orioles, 1977

New York Mets, 1978–1980

It is important to note that Elliott Maddox's career line was most negatively affected by his era and parks of any Jewish center fielder. His career line was .261/.358/.334—unimpressive in raw total but good for a career OPS+ of 100. By contrast, .259/.296/.408—a .705 raw OPS compared to Maddox's 692—is 12 percent less valuable at an OPS+ of 88. Context matters here. And contemporary reports regarded Maddox as the best defensive center fielder in the American League during his time with the Texas Rangers and New York Yankees. And he had an excellent batting eye, walking more than he struck out in his career.

A couple of interesting notes on Maddox: for one thing Maddox was a decent base stealer for much of his career, succeeding 54 of 86 times he took off through 1977. That is a success rate of 63 percent, a bit below ideal but not terrible. But during his three seasons with the New York Mets, he managed just six of 22 times to make it safely, an inexcusably poor 27 percent success rate. It is hard to understand such a decline or why manager Joe Torre didn't give him a stop sign. But it lowered his career rate to under 53 percent.

Another fun fact: Maddox converted to Judaism for the 1974 season on the heels of a .238/.356/.262 season. His line jumped to .303/.395/.386 in 1974 and continued through 55 games of .307/.382/.394 in 1975 before Maddox injured his knee at Shea Stadium.

This begs the question: does converting to Judaism mid-career improve one's line by 69 points of average, 26 points of on-base, and 132 points of slugging? Here is a look at some other players and their improvement had they converted mid-career to Judaism: Value-Added Judaism

Babe Ruth, 1927: .425/.512/.904

Ted Williams, 1941: .475/.579/.867

Mario Mendoza, 1979: .267/.242/.381

Ruth and Williams become video-game good, and even Mendoza becomes a pretty decent option at shortstop. MLB players always look for an edge, and organizations are always pushing the new frontiers of developmental tools. Might I suggest: a synagogue?

5. Lipman Pike

Bats Left, Throws Left

Troy Haymakers, 1871

Baltimore Canaries, 1872–1873

Hartford Dark Blues, 1874

St. Louis Brown Stockings, 1875–1876

Cincinnati Reds, 1877-1878

Providence Grays, 1878

Worcester Ruby Legs, 1881

New York Metropolitans, 1887

If you base evaluation of Lipman Pike against the other center fielders on reputation of the time, Pike clearly would have to be the No. 1 choice. According to the SABR biography of Pike by Robert H. Schafer, Pike was named one of the three best outfielders of 1870–1880 by *Sporting Life* in 1911, 18 years after his death. And 25 years after that, he even received a Hall of Fame vote on the very first Cooperstown ballots of 1936.

Pike led his leagues (first National Association, then National League) in home runs four times. But context matters here, too: his season-high was seven. His total games played: 70 was his season-high, and he had just five years with more than 50.

Then there are the questions about his honesty. Pike was accused by his team in 1881 of throwing games and suspended by organized baseball for a time. Earlier in his career, he was accused of disloyalty to his Philadelphia club, though it was assigned to his being a foreigner (from New York). Whatever concerns history will raise about, say, Ryan Braun and PEDs or Alex Bregman and sign-stealing, no one ever questioned their efforts to win.

Even things like Pike's reputation as a power hitter come with all kinds of caveats. He hit four home runs for Cincinnati in 1877—but the Reds' Lakefront Park was 180 feet down the left-field line, 196 to right field—in a park that had smaller dimensions than my Little League field.

Even so, let's not lose sight of his power. As baseball authority of the time O.P. Caylor recalled: "I remember Pike's ball playing best through a hit I once saw him make in Cincinnati...Pike was the first man up in the game. He hit the first ball pitched, and none who saw that ball sail out over the right fielder's head will ever forget it. It went not only over the right field fence, but also continued to sail until it cleared the brick kiln beyond and dropped into the high weeds bordering on Mill Creek. I am impressed with the belief that if the distance could be measured, that hit of Pike's would go on record as the longest fly ball hit ever made."

If only Statcast had been around in 1877.

Pike's primary argument for supremacy comes down to contemporary acclaim—his death at 48 of heart disease (watch out, everybody: corned beef and knishes are not easy on our arteries) led to a massive outpouring of grief and appreciation in the baseball and Jewish communities. As *The Boston Globe* wrote of Pike in October 1893 on the occasion of his death: "Lip Pike, who died at his old home in Brooklyn last week, was one of the finest batsmen the game of baseball ever produced. His long drives on the Boston Common while a member of the old Atlantics of Brooklyn and Athletics of Philadelphia were never equaled."

Added *The Pittsburgh Press* a week later: "The late Lip Pike was a very fast runner, and few could compete with him in a sprint race."

His contemporary, Jimmy Hallinan, summarized it this way in 1921 at the height of Babe Ruth's rise: "Lip Pike was one of the hardest hitters that the game ever saw. Ruth hasn't got a thing on him."

6. Gabe Kapler

Bats Right, Throws Right
Detroit Tigers, 1998–1999
Texas Rangers, 2000–2002
Colorado Rockies, 2002–2003
Boston Red Sox, 2003–2006
Milwaukee Brewers, 2008
Tampa Bay Rays, 2009–2010

Like Fred Sington, Gabe Kapler was able to translate his strength—he is a bodybuilder—into monumental minor league numbers but only sporadic power in the major leagues. His finest minor league season came with Double A Jacksonville of the Southern League, when he hit .322/.393/.583 with 28 home runs and 146 RBIs. This was no anomaly—Kapler has a career slugging percentage of .432 in 2,042 minor league at-bats. But in the major leagues, despite playing the lion's share of his games in hitter-friendly parks in Texas and Boston, Kapler's slugging percentage was just .420—respectable, but not prodigious.

Even so, the Woodland Hills, California, native exceeded any reasonable expectation for a 57th-round pick in the 1995 draft, crushing minor league pitching and forcing himself onto the Detroit Tigers roster in 1999. "He's going to will himself into being a big leaguer," Mr. Tiger himself, Al Kaline, told the *Detroit Free Press* that spring.

That's precisely what Kapler did, putting up a respectable .245/.315/.447 line as a rookie with 18 home runs and 11 stolen bases in 1999. But when the Texas

Rangers needed a young centerpiece in return for dealing 1998 MVP Juan Gonzalez, Detroit offered Kapler. "No problem. My first year, I'll hit 40 home runs, drive in 150 runs," Kapler joked to T.R. Sullivan, the dean of Rangers beat writers, about filling Gonzalez's shoes.

Kapler did post his finest season with a .302/.360/.473 line and 14 home runs in 116 games, including a Texas team record 28-game hitting streak, and bigger things seemed possible in September, when he finished the campaign with a .395/.455/.618 month. The Rangers signed him to a three-year, $5.6 million extension the following spring. But a pulled muscle delayed his season's start, and he ended up regressing some with a .267/.348/.437 batting line. After a difficult first half in 2002, the Rangers decided to trade him to the Colorado Rockies at the deadline for Todd Hollandsworth. "Gabe Kapler turned out to be one of the Rangers' best defensive outfielders," Sullivan said. "He also won the admiration and respect of his teammates with his hustle and hard-nosed style of play. But he never fulfilled the power potential expected from him."

Kapler found similar results in part-time work with Colorado, then Boston, winning a ring with the Red Sox as a fifth outfielder in 2004. He took a one-year sabbatical from playing in 2007, getting an early start in his next career as a minor league manager before deciding to return to the game in 2008.

Kapler did get off to a huge start, hitting .283/.304/.566 in April 2008 for the Milwaukee Brewers, finishing the season at .301/.340/.498, a resounding endorsement of his decision to return to the field. After two seasons with the Tampa Bay Rays and a spring training with his hometown Los Angeles Dodgers in 2011 before ultimately failing to make the team, Kapler coached for Team Israel, moved into the front office with Los Angeles, and then to the manager's chair with the Philadelphia Phillies. When the Phillies moved on from Kapler after a disappointing 2019, the San Francisco Giants swooped in and hired him. The Giants finished with the best regular-season record in baseball in 2021, and he was named National League Manager of the Year.

7. Harry Rosenberg

Bats Right, Throws Right
New York Giants, 1930

Just like Joc Pederson and Kevin Pillar in the current game, I often think Sy Rosenthal and Harry Rosenberg would have made the perfect platoon and almost certainly would have been excellent additions to a major league club given their minor league records. It is eerie how much the two mirror one another.

Rosenthal was five years older and made his major league debut five seasons sooner. He was a lefty but was born and raised on the right coast and collected the lion's share of his minor league hits in the east. And he had 10 seasons with a batting average .324 or higher but maxed out at just 21 home runs. Rosenberg was five pounds lighter. He was a righty but made his name on the left coast. And he had 11 full seasons with a batting average .314 or higher but maxed out at just 11 home runs.

Rosenthal got a brief look at age 21–22 but never returned to the big leagues despite his minor league success. Rosenberg got just nine at-bats at age 22 but never returned to the big leagues despite his minor league success. Rosenberg had more games played and a higher career average. But Rosenthal compiled his stats in more hitting-unfriendly leagues. And neither hitter got to show what he could do at the highest level when they reached their primes.

In his age-27 season, Rosenberg out-hit teammate and future major league All-Star Max West .354 to .266 and outslugged him .511 to .379. Granted, West was just 18, but even when West was 20 and Rosenberg was 29, each man hit .330 for the Mission Reds of the Pacific Coast League. A year later West had an everyday job with the Boston Braves, while Rosenberg continued on in the PCL. He routinely outperformed former and future major leaguers as teammates, too.

Ah, Rosenthal and Rosenberg—the platoon that might have been.

8. Ed Mensor

Bats Both, Throws Right
Pittsburgh Pirates, 1912–1914

According to *The Big Book of Jewish Baseball*, Ed Mensor was one of 17 children, and Mensor's father started a family baseball team. One can only imagine how psychologically damaging it would have been for a player on this team to get benched or even platooned.

Mensor logged a majority of his big league time in the field playing center, though he spent most of the rest of the 1910s playing infield for outposts like Columbus, Spokane, and Oakland, concluding his pro career in 1921 with the Calgary Bronchos of the Western Canada League. He slugged a pair of doubles in his very first game with Calgary to beat the Moose Jaw Millers, finishing the season with a respectable .270 average. By 1922 he was back in Astoria, Oregon, playing for a Standard Oil company team—part of an extended second career he enjoyed on the semipro circuit in outposts throughout the American West.

Mensor's nickname was "Midget," and he was listed at 5'6". Of course, that still places him nearly two feet taller than the only midget to ever play Major League Baseball, the 3'7" Eddie Gaedel. Amazingly, the three players nicknamed "Midget" nearly all overlapped their short careers with Bill "Midget" Jones playing from 1911 to 1912 and Duke "Midget" Reilley playing in 1909.

Both Mensor and Jones took full advantage of their limited strike zone—Mensor's career batting average was .221, but his on-base percentage was .367. Jones put up a career .226 batting average and a .397 on-base percentage. But Reilley had just a .258 on-base percentage to go with his .210 batting average and drew just four walks. My suspicion is that Reilley was neither a midget, nor legally, a Duke. His full name was Alexander Aloysius Reilley, and as anyone would, he was looking for any nickname he could get.

9. Mark Gilbert

Bats Both, Throws Right
Chicago White Sox, 1985

It's fair to say that Mark Gilbert's 26 plate appearances for the 1985 Chicago White Sox won't be the lead item in his obituary someday. Gilbert was an early fund-raiser for a 2008 presidential candidate named Barack Obama and ultimately served President Obama as ambassador to New Zealand from 2015 to 2017.

Gilbert starred at Florida State, also playing basketball and earning a degree in finance, before embarking on a long minor league career in search, he told the great Jerome Holtzman, of a line in the *Baseball Encyclopedia*. He changed positions from pitcher to outfielder after wowing his Seminoles coach, former major leaguer Woody Woodward, with his speed going up the line to first base.

Woodward had it right: Gilbert logged a career minor league line of .282/.382/.361 with 242 stolen bases.

I do take issue with the decision to give Gilbert only a week of regular playing time. With everyday center fielder Darryl Boston out of the lineup, the White Sox called up the 28-year-old Gilbert to play all three outfield positions in July 1985, which he did in the course of a single week, logging time in left, center, and right. Gilbert had hits in five of the six games he started and scored runs in three of them. He had a hit and a walk July 25, a double on July 26, and a two-hit game on July 27 in the leadoff position.

So what does then-White Sox manager Tony La Russa do? He plugs Luis Salazar, he of the .267 on-base percentage, into the leadoff position. Gilbert had four walks in his week in the big leagues. Salazar had 12 all year in 327 at-bats.

It worked out for everybody, I suppose. Gilbert hurt his knee, retired the following year, went into finance, and became an ambassador. He even went on the Lou Limmer career path, serving as president of his synagogue, B'nai

Torah, in Boca Raton, Florida. La Russa is a Hall of Famer, and his White Sox won the 2021 American League Central. Still, I'd like to know how it all turns out if Gilbert had gotten more time to play.

10. Adam Greenberg

Bats Left, Throws Right
Chicago Cubs, 2005
Miami Marlins, 2012

A top-flight collegiate center fielder at University of North Carolina, Adam Greenberg was drafted in the ninth round of the 2002 draft by the Chicago Cubs. Greenberg quickly climbed the ladder, showing above-average plate discipline everywhere he went and stealing bases at a very high percentage. His career minor league batting average is .268, but he has a .372 on-base percentage and stole 128 bases in 174 attempts.

But on July 9, 2005, in his first major league at-bat, on the first pitch, he was hit in the back of the head by a fastball. He didn't even get to run to first base. He suffered from post-concussive syndrome, and his 2005 season was lost. After a poor 2006 start in the minor leagues, the Cubs released him.

He had a solid 2007 with the Double A Wichita Wranglers of the Kansas City Royals organization, hitting .266/.373/.428, but the Royals didn't keep him in 2008, and he moved on to the Arkansas Travelers of the Los Angeles Angels' organization.

Incredibly, Greenberg got another major league at-bat. The Guilford, Connecticut, star simply never gave up, playing season after season for the indy league Bridgeport Bluefish, a long way from the major leagues. He stayed on pro baseball's radar with his play for Team Israel as well.

And in the waning moments of the 2012 season, the Miami Marlins signed him after a protracted social media campaign run by Matt Liston, and before a crowd of 29,709, Greenberg got his chance to hit again in the major leagues—facing the 2012 Cy Young Award winner R.A. Dickey.

I'd like to tell you he homered. Sadly, he struck out. But he did earn a spring training invite from the Baltimore Orioles out of it, nearly made the club in 2013, and then finished up his career with one more season in Bridgeport—crucially, on his own terms.

8

Right Field

Right field is the Jewish people's deepest position. If a baseball diamond were America, right field would be New York City. If a baseball team's roles were professional organizations, right field would be the American Bar Association. If all of baseball's positions were supermarkets, right field would be Zabar's.

Nineteen of baseball's Jews patrolled right field. And a large number of them excelled at the major league level. Cal Abrams and Art Shamsky were critical parts of championship teams, while Richie Scheinblum, in his one full season as a starter, was an All-Star. Even the lesser right fielders like Moses Solomon and Micah Franklin put up huge home run totals. And one of the earliest right fielders, Jacob Pike, was one of baseball's first Jews.

But far above the rest of the field is Shawn Green, one of the finest players in Jewish baseball history, though a premature decline kept him from seriously challenging for a spot in the Hall of Fame. Green put up three 40-home run seasons, second among Jewish players to Hank Greenberg's four. But

Shawn Green

Green also had four seasons with 20 or more steals with a season high of 35—Greenberg's season-high in steals was just nine.

Unfortunately for Green, his last great season was at age 29, and he didn't reach New York until age 33. So while Green's acquisition ended a 25-year Jewish player drought for the New York Mets, the dream of a true Jewish megastar playing in New York, one that dates back to John McGraw, remains elusive.

1. Shawn Green

Bats Left, Throws Left
Toronto Blue Jays, 1993–1999
Los Angeles Dodgers, 2000–2004
Arizona Diamondbacks, 2005–2006
New York Mets, 2006–2007

It is impossible to consider Shawn Green's career a disappointment. The first-round pick of the Toronto Blue Jays in the 1991 draft hit 328 career home runs—third most of any Jewish player—made two All-Star teams, won a Gold Glove and a Silver Slugger award, and even earned a pair of Hall of Fame votes when he reached the Cooperstown ballot in 2013.

But compare Green's numbers through age 29 to other Hall of Famers, and it is easy to see why so many people thought Green would be right there among the Hank Greenberg/Sandy Koufax canon. But for health, he could have surpassed them.

Let's take one such example: Shawn Green vs. Hall of Famer and Red Sox legend Carl Yastrzemski. Yaz vs. Green is particularly instructive. Through age 29, Green had 234 home runs in 4,324 at-bats; Yaz had 202 home runs in 5,175 at-bats. Each had three 40-home run seasons, Green had four 100-RBI seasons; Yaz had five. Green's best adjusted OPS+ seasons were 154, 154, 144—Yaz's were 193, 177, 171. But Green's three best had come in his previous four seasons—Yaz had a 135 and a 119 mixed in.

Through age 29 Yaz's OPS+ was 139; Green's was 127. But it is remarkably close, considering that Yaz was a first-ballot Hall of Famer—and Green likely won't come close to enshrinement. To get a further sense of the company he was keeping: Dave Winfield checks in at 135, Al Kaline 133, Tony Gwynn 132, Rusty Staub 129, Larry Walker 128, Harold Baines 115, among primary right fielders with at least 4,000 plate appearances by age 29.

Green wrote *The Way of Baseball*, one of the finest memoirs of any baseball player, Jewish or otherwise, in 2011. His ability to crystalize the key moments of his career—when he squeezed the final out of the New York Mets' National League Division Series win against the Los Angeles Dodgers in 2006, even understanding when it was time to walk away because he knew he wouldn't be there for his daughter's first day of kindergarten if he continued—it all speaks to a deeper understanding of life he's taken into his post-baseball pursuits.

In 2013 Green got one last chance to play—for Team Israel. A player who found his connection to Judaism through his interactions with the fans, he told me, when I had a chance to speak with him at the St. Louis Jewish Book Festival, the most prominent Jewish player of his generation getting a chance to suit up for Israel felt just right.

But a true measure of Green's spiritual connection to Judaism came back in 2001. Sitting on 49 home runs with a consecutive games streak of 415, Green chose not to play on Yom Kippur. He put it this way in the book: "I wanted to show respect for the customs of my heritage. Additionally, sitting out the game further severed connections to my ego, allowing me to let go of my label as Major League Baseball's current Ironman. I was grateful it came along just when it did, as my public observance furthered my pursuit of 'at-one-ment,' being at one with the present moment."

2. Cal Abrams

Bats Left, Throws Left

Brooklyn Dodgers, 1949–1952

Cincinnati Reds, 1952

Pittsburgh Pirates, 1953–1954

Baltimore Orioles, 1954–1955

Chicago White Sox, 1956

Another player whose career was delayed by World War II, Flatbush's own began in the minors in 1942, hit .327, then it was off to war. Cal Abrams returned in 1946, but those crucial early years missed may have cost him his chance to shine as a prospect in the eyes of talent evaluators across baseball. He deserved better.

Abrams finished with a career batting average of .269 but an on-base percentage of .386. In a more enlightened statistical time, Abrams would have had regular outfield work even with a below-average slugging percentage of .392. Really, as long as Billy Beane had a job, so would Cal Abrams. But Abrams never got 500 at-bats in a season—in fact, while getting 448 in 1953, Abrams was traded mid-year.

In fairness to the Brooklyn Dodgers, Abrams happened to come along at a time when Brooklyn simply didn't need outfielders. Who would Abrams replace in Dodgerland circa 1951—Duke Snider? Carl Furillo? Even the underrated Andy Pafko put up a .255/.347/.501 line with 30 home runs that season. Abrams had the misfortune of playing for Charlie Dressen, who somehow managed the following feat: after Abrams hit .371/.477/.539 through the end of May, he started him just 13 games the rest of the season. Pafko took most of his playing time, and Dressen lacked the good sense to work Abrams into a rotation with his three everyday outfielders to keep everybody fresh. Fortunately for Dressen, this did not turn out to be the biggest error in judgement he'd make and be remembered for with the 1951 Dodgers.

But the Pittsburgh Pirates and Baltimore Orioles simply had no excuse not to play Abrams. If he'd gotten out of Brooklyn sooner, perhaps he'd have been viewed as a prospect. But there is little doubt Abrams was a better outfielder than many who got the chance to play every day.

For the 1954 Orioles, Abrams put up a line of .293/.400/.421 in 506 plate appearances. No other Orioles player topped 106 OPS+ that year. In 1955 his 118 OPS+ trailed only Dave Philley among Baltimore hitters. Yet the Orioles traded him for a past-his-prime infielder, Bobby Adams, and he barely played for the 1956 Chicago White Sox. With his Major League Baseball career over, he was sold to the International League's Miami Marlins. He hit .278/.422/.394 there—vintage Abrams—and won team MVP honors. He returned in 1957 with his sights set on the big leagues. But his phone didn't ring.

Abrams also clearly identified with his Jewish roots—he wore No. 18 or "Chai" for the lion's share of his career—and his Dodgers experience. According to his Associated Press obit, Abrams was buried in his Brooklyn Dodgers uniform. No word on whether or not Dodger Dogs were served at the shiva.

3. Art Shamsky

Bats Left, Throws Left
Cincinnati Reds, 1965–1967
New York Mets, 1968–1971
Chicago Cubs, 1972
Oakland Athletics, 1972

Art Shamsky, son of William and Sadie, pride of St. Louis, provides a window into what a superstar Jewish baseball player would experience in New York. He played four seasons with the New York Mets, never getting more than 403 at-bats in any season while part of an outfield platoon. Yet both Ray Romano and Jon Stewart named dogs after him. One can only speculate how many dogs Shamsky would have inspired had he played every day.

Shamsky grew up a St. Louis Cardinals fan, attending the same high school that fellow Jewish standout Ken Holtzman would, before signing with the Cincinnati Reds in September 1959. By 1965, after battering pitchers at a series of minor league stops along the way, he debuted at Busch Stadium in front of family and friends, playing for the Reds. By 1966 he was putting up a season line of .231/.321/.521, which is even more impressive in the pitcher-friendly context of the time. That's an OPS+ of 121. For reference, in-prime Pete Rose's OPS+ that year was 115, Vada Pinson's just 103. Shamsky even hit four straight home runs, and the bat that he used to do so now lives in Coopertown. But after a down year in 1967, Cincinnati sent him to New York, where immortality followed.

What is interesting about Shamsky's career is that he would have been an extremely useful everyday player even with a tremendous platoon split. Shamsky's overall line looks ordinary by today's standards—253/.330/.427—but he played in the most difficult hitting period since the Dead Ball Era, and 75 percent of his career at-bats came in Shea Stadium, a pitcher's park. Shamsky's career OPS+ was 110—better than 12 of 18 outfielders in his own division in 1970, for instance.

Another quick point on Shamsky: Ron Swoboda is remembered as *the* right fielder on the 1969 Mets due in large part to his game-saving catch in Game Three of the 1969 World Series. But Shamsky got 61 starts to Swoboda's 70 and outhit Swoboda .300/.375/.488 to .235/.326/.361. In WAR Shamsky laps Swoboda, 1.9 to 0.5—Shamsky actually rated fifth among all 1969 Mets hitters in WAR. Pretty clearly, Shamsky was the team's best right fielder. Not a bad legacy for a team that won 100 games.

4. Richie Scheinblum

Bats Both, Throws Right

Cleveland Indians, 1965, 1967–1969

Washington Senators, 1971

Kansas City Royals, 1972, 1974

Cincinnati Reds, 1973

California Angels, 1973–1974

St. Louis Cardinals, 1974

Like Art Shamsky, Richie Scheinblum, pride of Englewood, New Jersey—where as a high schooler he played for the trailblazing women's baseball player and coach, Janet Murk, who taught him to switch-hit—was another above-average hitter whose raw totals were depressed by late-1960s run environments. His final career line of .263/.343/.352 was good for a career OPS+ of 104.

But two things appear to have held Scheinblum back. For one thing, he did not excel in short trials when the Cleveland Indians desperately wanted to give him the right-field job. With limited competition like Chuck Hinton and Vic Davalillo, Scheinblum hit .218 in 1968 and routinely hit "something like .180" in spring training each year, according to the March 29, 1969, issue of *The Sporting News*. "For four years, I've been overawed," Scheinblum said in the same issue, "but not anymore."

Then he went out and hit .186 in 199 at-bats.

Much of the time, something mental is used as an excuse by a player who simply can't hit big league pitching. But clearly, that wasn't the case for Scheinblum, who was a talented hitter. He went to the Triple A Wichita Aeros of the American Association and hit .337/.424/.576 with 24 home runs in 1970. He improved on that star line with Wichita in 1971, hitting .388/.490/.725—725!—with another 25 home runs and just 26 strikeouts. He then returned to the majors with the Washington Senators in 1971 and hit .143.

But he finally got a full season in the major leagues in 1972 at age 29 and took full advantage. He flirted with a batting title all season, trailing eventual winner Rod Carew .317 to .316 as late as September 11 before a late-season slump dragged his season line down to .300/.383/.418—good for sixth in the American League. He struck out just 40 times, made the All-Star team, and was named AL Player of the Month in August.

Beneath a seven-column headline in *The Kansas City Star* in June 1972, Scheinblum described himself as "a doubles hitter, not a home run hitter or a singles hitter." However, Kansas City made him the main piece of a two-for-two trade that winter to bring in Hal McRae. And Scheinblum, whose fielding made him a prime candidate to play DH, found himself in the National League for the debut of the new rule in 1973.

Scheinblum struggled with the Cincinnati Reds, hitting .222, and got shipped back to the American League, where he posted a .328/.417/.428 line for the California Angels over 77 games in 1973. But he struggled through a 1974 for three teams and headed to Japan, where he hit .33 home runs in two seasons for the Hiroshima Karp.

Anytime Scheinblum got the chance to settle into a full-time role, he hit. Unfortunately, teams often make player evaluations on small samples. They are statistically unreliable, and in Scheinblum's case, it probably cost him a career as a regular.

5. Norm Miller

Bats Left, Throws Right
Houston Astros, 1965–1973
Atlanta Braves, 1973–1974

Add Norm Miller to the list of hitters who were hurt by the late 1960s and the Astrodome—his OPS+ was 95, a far better representation of his hitting than his raw career line of .238/.323/.356.

But Miller also was denied much development time. A Los Angeles kid, the Angels grabbed him in 1964, and he excelled at Quad Cities in the A-level Midwest League, posting a .301/.446/.525 line. That was good enough to get plucked away by the Houston Astros, who promoted him late in 1965 after a .289/.406/.492 season for Double A Amarillo of the Texas League.

Miller was 19, while teammates Larry Dierker (18), Rusty Staub and Joe Morgan, (both 21) all got the chance to play Major League Baseball. But Miller never got the chance to play regularly—his season high in at-bats was 409. But it must have felt to Miller like he got the majority of his career at-bats on April 15, 1968. He played all 24 innings in Houston's 1–0 win against the New York Mets and led off the bottom of the 24th with a single, coming around to score the winning run. It was his first hit in 10 plate appearances.

Miller did tell a story to the baseball journalist Dan Epstein that I found concerning, and relevant to this book: "Well, I played for a manager named Harry Walker for five years, and Harry was a bad guy. At 23 there was no doubt that I had the chance to be a pretty good ballplayer. I was playing every day in 1969 and hitting .300, and then all of a sudden, I was benched for a week for no reason. Finally, I went up to Harry and I said, 'Why aren't I playing?' He said, 'None of your goddamn business.' And, because this is before free agency, I was stuck playing for him for several more years.

"I found out 25 years later exactly what it was about. For years after I retired from baseball, I used to stop by the Astrodome and pitch batting practice. One night, I was in the press club afterward, eating dinner, and a fellow came in who was a retired Astros executive from the days when I was on the team. I don't want to tell you his name—he's dead now, anyway—but he walked up to me and said, 'I've had something on my mind and I just want to tell you. I was never a huge fan of yours—I thought you were pretty cocky—but I always thought you should have been in our lineup every night. The reason you didn't play [regularly] was, Harry said to me one night, 'There ain't no Jew gonna play on my team like that.'"

Read Jim Bouton's *Ball Four*, and you'll find more about what "a bad guy" Walker was; Bouton was Miller's roommate. I think I've identified when it happened. Miller did not play between June 12—when he started in right field, got a hit, and improved his season line to .290/.387/.414—and June 29. On June 17 *The Atlanta Constitution* reported he was on military duty, but by June 22 he was telling a reporter with the *Kilgore News Herald* that "what has helped me the most is playing every day."

Still, he sat until June 29, when he made his return to the lineup and doubled. Miller had started 49 of Houston's first 60 games and played extremely well. Despite this he started just 56 of their final 102 contests, and his post-benching line dropped to .242/.313/.323. No doubt, that can serve as an ex post facto justification for Walker. But there's simply no reason he should have done it in the first place. And according to Miller, we know the rationale behind Walker's decision.

6. Fred Sington

Bats Right, Throws Right
Washington Senators, 1934–1937
Brooklyn Dodgers, 1938–1939

Fred Sington is another example of the rule that it is harder to hit major league pitching than to do nearly anything else in sports. A member of the college football Hall of Fame, Sington likely would have been a top draft pick of the NFL had the league been as prominent as it is today. He was such an impressive lineman at Alabama that Rudy Vallee recorded a song about him entitled "Football Freddy." For the record, a contemporary of Sington's, Taylor Smith, said he was better at baseball in high school, and furthermore, while "Football Freddy" in the song is "not so good in school," Sington was Phi Beta Kappa at Alabama.

The man known as "Moose" found his way to baseball professionally and used his power-hitting prowess to reach the major leagues. In 1932 he hit 35 home runs over 524 minor-league at-bats and in 1934 posted totals of 29 home runs, a .327 batting average, and a .575 slugging percentage for the Albany Crackers of the International League. "I'm just beginning to wonder what it takes for a man to get an opportunity in the big leagues," Sington asked reporter Fred Russell of the *Nashville Banner* in January 1938.

However, in 611 major league plate appearances over six seasons, Sington totaled seven home runs. The 6'2", 215-pound Sington certainly had the strength to drive pitches out of the park. And a career line of .271/.382/.401 simply reads like a superstar's productivity, if only he'd hit more home runs in his opportunities to play.

Sington became a fixture in Alabama civic life after his career ended, and Bill Robinson, writing in the *Montgomery Advertiser* in 1998 said this of Sington: "He is not only Mr. Birmingham, but in many ways, he is Mr. Alabama."

7. Ruben Amaro Jr.

Bats Right, Throws Right
California Angels, 1991
Philadelphia Phillies, 1992–1993, 1996–1998
Cleveland Indians, 1994–1995

Is it possible to quantify how much value is added to a baseball player's career to have a Jewish mother? Ruben Amaro Jr., the product of a Jewish mother and a non-Jewish Major League Baseball player, may provide a window into this idea. Amaro Jr. and his father, Ruben Amaro Sr., both played in the major leagues. Both were similar hitters, though Amaro Sr. played shortstop, and Amaro Jr. was an outfielder. Amaro Sr. had 2,155 at-bats of .234/.309/.292 for an OPS+ of 71. Amaro Jr. hit .235/.310/.353 for an OPS+ of 80. So pretty clearly, a Jewish mother added a significant amount of offense to Amaro Jr., primarily in power production.

Nine points of OPS+ is far from trivial. It is the difference between Willie Mays and Willie Stargell or between Mike Piazza and John Kruk. Let's hope, for his sake, that Amaro Jr. reliably called his mother to thank her for this gift. Joc and Stu Pederson offered a second data point about the value of a Jewish mother.

So I ran the theory by the man himself, Ruben Amaro Jr., during a phone interview in May 2021. "I think that is absolute bullshit," Amaro Jr. said before dissolving into laughter. "I'm sorry, but that's how I feel."

Seriously, respect to you, Ruben, for being so blunt two minutes into our interview.

But what is clear in Amaro Jr.'s history is that the connection he has with his mother's side—his Jewish heritage—is very special to him. It's a Philadelphia kind of Jewish history he shares, dating back to his father's time as first-base coach for the Philadelphia Phillies who won the World Series in 1980 and the National League pennant in 1983—Amaro Jr. was the bat boy—and back further still to Amaro Sr.'s time playing with the Phillies in the 1960s.

Every bit as important in understanding Amaro Jr.'s background, though, is his mother's mother, Dorothy Herman, known as the proprietor of Dorothy Herman's Gourmey Cheese, a staple of the Reading Terminal Market. That's where Ruben Amaro Sr. and Judy Herman met at the cheese shop owned by Dorothy. Marlene, Judy's sister, taught Ruben Sr.'s teammates, Tony Taylor and Pancho Herrera, English.

Talking to Amaro Jr., a third-generation baseball great (his grandfather, Santos Amaro, likely would have been a big leaguer himself if not for the color barrier), I could feel the very idea of America coming through the phone. On Sunday mornings in Northeast Philly, it was Amaro Sr., the Mexican American side of Amaro's family, who spearheaded the brunch procuring, heading to Bustleton Avenue in Northeast Philly. "And we would get bagels and we would get lox and whitefish and we would kill it," Amaro Jr. recalled. "That was a big delicacy on the weekends when my dad was around. And we would add whatever cheeses and whatever stuff that my grandma would send home from her shop. So that was part of the process as well."

Amaro Jr., who rose to the level of general manager with the Phillies, is still part of the broadcasts for Phillies games and he's still carrying on the traditions of his family, including namechecking Moishe and Itzy's, a local Jewish food outpost. I came away from our conversation without a confirmation of one of my grand theories, but more than that, I came away from our conversation hungry.

8. Dick Sharon

Bats Right, Throws Right
Detroit Tigers, 1973–1974
San Diego Padres, 1975

It is easy in retrospect to question the Pittsburgh Pirates' decision to draft Dick Sharon with the ninth overall pick in the 1968 draft, just two picks ahead of Greg Luzinski. Of course, Luzinski went on to hit 307 home runs, including 19 against the Pirates. Sharon fell 294 short of that total and never played for Pittsburgh.

From Redwood City and Sequoia High School, where he also played basketball, Sharon is another California boy turned Jewish major leaguer. Upon arrival in the Pittsburgh system, both his batting average and power didn't show up in games, though his defense in center field drew rave reviews. He broke through in 1970, though, hitting .254/.336/.457 for the Salem Rebels of the Class A Carolina League on a team featuring big leaguers like Kent Tekulve and Rennie Stennett. The power dipped at Double A Waterbury in 1971, but he increased his stolen base proclivity, nabbing 26 in 32 attempts, and by 1972 the full package came together with Triple A Charleston: .268/.325/.452, 14 homers, 15 steals, plus defense in center.

The problem, of course, was the system he was in. The great Al Oliver played center field and was then in his mid-20s prime. Oh, no problem, you say, just move him to a corner, right? Well, I'll let you decide who to bench: left fielder Willie Stargell or right fielder Roberto Clemente.

So it was off to Detroit, then San Diego, where over three seasons, Sharon played all three outfield positions. Sharon's average, however, never made him a compelling choice for major league playing time—even in the minors, his average climbed above .255 once. In the big leagues, he struggled to even reach that—.218/.293/.355 for a career OPS+ of 79. Batting average is overrated as a stat, but if you also cannot reach base enough or hit for power, regular opportunities will prove elusive.

9. Milt Galatzer
Bats Left, Throws Left
Cleveland Indians, 1933–1936
Cincinnati Reds, 1939

Milt Galatzer, product of the Chicago sandlots like Phil Weintraub, was a skilled batter, though the extent to which his offensive value was tied to his batting average meant a couple of low averages in major league trials kept him from establishing a regular role in the big leagues.

Galatzer did not hit for power—he had one home run in 717 big league at-bats, and his season high in any minor league season was seven while with the Class D Frederick Warriors in 1930. But he nearly never struck out—after 21 strikeouts in his first big league season and 160 at-bats, he fanned just 25 times over the next 557 at-bats. So while his career line was just .268/.354/.326, clearly Galatzer was not overwhelmed by big league pitching.

Nine times in the minor leagues, Galatzer hit over .300 in a full season, and seven of those years his average was above .320! He hit for the Terre Haute Tots, he hit for the Toledo Mud Hens, he hit for the New Orleans Pelicans, he hit for the Indianapolis Indians. Had he gotten to play every day in the major leagues, chances are he'd have hit there, too.

But chances are his use would have been limited as an everyday player. Galatzer did not steal bases (just 10 career steals in 22 attempts) and he really didn't hit extra-base hits, either—only once did he accumulate 10 doubles in a season. But he'd have been a fine fourth outfielder—instead, he played until 1946 with the obvious interruption to serve his country.

He was also part of the rare pregame ejection in 1942. *The Indianapolis News* reported on July 9, 1942, that Galatzer was called out on strikes by umpire Bill Kelley with the bases loaded in a game against the Toledo Mud Hens on July 7. He argued it but clearly hadn't finished speaking his piece. *The News* wrote: "Just before Wednesday's conflict began, there was an outburst from the Indians' dugout. It was Galatzer, renewing the argument about that third strike with Kelley, who had just taken his place near first base. The start of the game was delayed several minutes as Milt shouted his ideas of that strike at Kelley. Finally he was fired out of the ball park."

So as you can see, Galatzer took the strike zone extremely seriously.

10. Mose Solomon

Bats Left, Throws Left
New York Giants, 1923

Nobody had a better nickname in major league history than Mose "The Rabbi of Swat" Solomon. And he earned it with one of the finest individual seasons any minor leaguer had.

In 1923, playing for the Hutchinson, Kansas, Wheat Shockers of the Class C Southwestern League, Solomon hit .421 with 49 home runs, slugging .833 in the process. And it should have been more. Reported *The Hutchinson News* in September 1923: "He hit one home run here and one at Salina which never counted because the games were called because of rain before five innings had been played."

It's a long way from Class C to the majors, but the New York Giants snapped him up, earning front-page stories on *The Sporting News* in consecutive weeks.

On September 6, 1923 under a headline of "Dick Kinsella Finds That $100,000 Jew," *TSN* touted Solomon, who was found by the scout Kinsella, as a player who will "become as popular at the Polo Grounds as Babe Ruth has been with followers of the Yankees in New York." Rest assured, the Giants didn't pay $100,000 for Solomon—they merely thought he'd be worth that much to the team.

Any investment that increases ten-fold in value is pretty impressive, so the September 13, 1923 headline—"Worth Million to Giants?"—simply reinforced the Solomon hype. Given that there are "more Jews in New York than in all of Palestine," John McGraw indicated this was Solomon's new worth to the Giants. Solomon was also touted for his fighting skills, which likely came in handy as a Jew playing baseball in 1923 Kansas. Indeed, *TSN* reported that word soon went around the league to "Lay off the big Jew," which is respectful in some ways—certainly the best he could have hoped for from opponents. He was also known as the "Hutchinson Jew"—a revealing look at the size of Hutchinson's Jewish community at the time.

Solomon managed a .375 average in eight at-bats with the 1923 Giants, but his primary position of first base was manned by the Hall of Famer George Kelly with fellow Hall of Famer Bill Terry in wait. He was sent to the minors for more seasoning, but at higher levels, his power disappeared. In 1925, playing for the Hartford/Albany Senators of the Double A Eastern League, he hit just two home runs in 511 at-bats. That was a far cry from 49!

A closer examination of Hutchinson's totals indicates that the Wheat Shockers might have played in a tremendous hitter's park. Solomon led the team with 49 home runs, but he had teammates with 35 and 21, while his 15 triples made him one of four Hutchinson players to reach double figures in three-baggers.

But during that magical season of 1923, Solomon even pitched two games for the Wheat Shockers. He allowed nine runs in 11 innings—and went 2–0. Hutchinson was no place for pitchers' duels.

Solomon was a multi-sport star, also excelling as a triple-threat quarterback in the early days of the NFL. After injuries ended his career in both sports by 1928, he moved his family to Miami and became a critical part of the Royal Castle hamburger chain, an empire that reached 200 strong. Those who want a taste of Solomon's legacy can visit the one Royal Castle left. It's in Miami on NW 79th Street.

11. Brian Kowitz

Bats Left, Throws Left
Atlanta Braves, 1995

Brian Kowitz, pride of Baltimore—where he grew up with fellow Jewish major leaguer Brian Bark, eventually rooming together as the two progressed in the Atlanta Braves organization—was a legitimately great college player for Clemson University. He hit .403, had a 37-game hitting streak, and made the all-ACC first team, as well as *Baseball America*'s second team All-America.

With Kowitz a bit on the small side at 5'10", 180 pounds, Atlanta made him its ninth-round pick in the 1990 draft, nabbing him ahead of players like Fernando Vina, Tony Graffinino, and Rusty Greer. Kowitz started slowly in professional ball, largely due to a promotion from rookie ball straight to Double A, but when repeating the high A Carolina League, he hit .301 with a .429 on-base percentage for the Durham Bulls, earning him promotions to Double A and then Triple A in rapid succession.

He reached his apex as a prospect in 1994, putting up a .300/.357/.444 line for Triple A Richmond, stealing 22 bases, and leading his team to the International League title. He capped the year with an appearance as "utility player/coach" in *Major League II*. I like to think he comes in to replace Pedro Serrano for defense in a bunch of double-switch scenes that got cut out of the final version, though this is pure speculation on my part.

Kowitz's average dropped to .280, and his slugging fell to .365 for Richmond in 1995, though he did get a shot to replace the injured David Justice mid-year.

But he hit just .167/.259/.208 in 24 at-bats and never saw big league action again. He's spending plenty of time with big leaguers, though, as a partner in Heller-Kowitz Insurance Advisors specializing in high net worth clients, particularly professional athletes.

12. Adam Stern

Bats Left, Throws Right
Boston Red Sox, 2005–2006
Baltimore Orioles, 2007
Milwaukee Brewers, 2010

It was Ontario's own Adam Stern's rotten luck to play for the Boston Red Sox in the two seasons between their two World Series victories. Fellow Jewish player Gabe Kapler got to experience one—Kevin Youkilis got to experience both. But Stern was left out in the cold.

Stern was drafted by the Atlanta Braves in the third round of the 2001 draft with the 105th overall pick—Ryan Howard went 140th. Stern never played for Atlanta, as he was a Rule 5 draft pick by Boston after Stern posted a stellar Double A season for Greenville, hitting .322 with a .480 slugging percentage. Described as "a speedy runner and a good defensive outfielder" by the Associated Press in the spring of 2005, Red Sox manager Terry Francona added that "we already like what we see." Stern then fractured his thumb, allowing Boston to keep him through a loophole—injured Rule 5 players don't need to be offered back to their original teams if they are on the injured list.

After Stern returned to the minors, he had another superlative season, posting a .321/.385/.494 line. But in 2006 that line came way down to .258/.300/.388. Dealt to Baltimore, he hit .270/.326/.360, leaving this one-time prospect with the likelihood of never reaching the big leagues again.

But a hot start at Triple A Nashville in 2010—.349 average through early May—led to one more call to the majors, this time for the Milwaukee Brewers. He finished his Major League Baseball career with an 0-for-8 stretch, though his overall season in Nashville—.325/.399/.462—was impressive. For comparison, his teammate that season, 24-year-old Lorenzo Cain, hit .299/.384/.425 ahead of a terrific major league career. Stern then headed to the Pan American Games as a member of Team Canada.

13. Max Rosenfeld

Bats Right, Throws Right
Brooklyn Dodgers, 1931–1933

Max Rosenfeld was a New York boy who made himself a beloved member of the Alabama community first by playing baseball and football in Tuscaloosa, then spending multiple seasons after college starring for the Birmingham Barons of the Class A Southern Association. "Max had two of his greatest years as a Baron," *The Birmingham News* recalled in 1953. "He hit .302 in 1927 and drove in 98 runs. He hit .344 in 1928 and drove in 97 runs."

By January 1931 Rosenfeld found himself in *The Sporting News'* "A Team of All Nations" in a page one headline. Max Rosenfeld and Alta Cohen made up the Jewish contingent, while "Frank O'Doul in left is very Irish."

Sadly for the Jews, neither Rosenfeld nor Cohen stuck—though Rosenfeld did have a strong 1932—.359/.359/.590 in 39 at-bats. Instead, Rosenfeld settled into a long career in the high minors, hitting .260 to .280, slugging .360 to .380, and eventually landing the player/manager's job with the Miami Beach Flamingos.

Rosenfeld endeared himself to the people of Miami, too—he hit .341 in 1940 and in the winter of 1945, as the Florida International League prepared to resume for the 1946 season, he even served as temporary chairman of the circuit. He stayed active in baseball even as he went into the real estate business and at the time of his death in 1967 was part of the Miami chapter of the Old Timers Professional Baseball Association.

14. Micah Franklin

Bats Right, Throws Right
St. Louis Cardinals, 1997

The New York Mets have a storied tradition of poor drafting from Steve Chilcott over Reggie Jackson to Shawn Abner over everyone else. Micah Franklin, sadly, falls into the miss category as well—Franklin was selected by New York in the third round of the 1990 draft ahead of fourth rounder Garret Anderson and fifth rounders Bret Boone and Ray Durham.

For his part Franklin thought it took too long. "I was extremely excited to be drafted to be picked by the Mets, but at the same time, I felt disrespected to go so late. So, I had a chip on my shoulder," Franklin told journalist Andrew Martin in 2020.

The Mets gave up on Franklin after just two seasons, though he could have been useful in the organization. Franklin hit for power immediately upon leaving the Mets (at this point, virtually a cliché), putting up a .335 average and .534 slugging for Cincinnati's Pioneer League team. He went on to hit double figures in home runs 10 times in the minor leagues and hit 30 bombs for the Nippon Ham Fighters in 1999, which may be a violation of Jewish law.

Franklin even hit in his time with the St. Louis Cardinals, posting a .324/.378/.500 line and a pair of home runs. But St. Louis elected not to bring him back, and he signed with the Chicago Cubs. He led the Iowa Cubs—and even the whole Pacific Coast League—in slugging percentage, putting up a .329/.437/.655 line. Unfortunately for Franklin, the Cubs had a right fielder that year named Sammy Sosa, who put up a major league line of .308/.377/.647. Left fielder Henry Rodriguez added 31 home runs himself, and Franklin gave up on America and headed to Japan.

His totals in the minors are impressive: 268/.375/.491 with 200 home runs. It's hard to imagine he couldn't have enjoyed a solid big league career with more opportunity. The man knows hitting and now he's paid to provide that knowledge to others. Franklin is the hitting coach for the Class A Visalia Rawhide, an affiliate of the Arizona Diamondbacks.

15. Sam Mayer
Bats Right, Throws Right
Washington Senators, 1915

Sam Mayer played well in his September 1915 call-up with the Washington Senators, posting a .241/.333/.345 line, which was good enough in 1915 terms for an OPS+ of 101. And, certainly, one can look favorably upon his 18-year minor league career. He hit early and late, posting a .307 batting average and .467 slugging percentage for the Fulton Colonels of the Kentucky-Illinois-Tennessee League and a .319 batting average and .398 slugging percentage for the Pittsfield Hillies of the Eastern League, playing in beautiful Wahconah Park.

But I am most intrigued that the brother of Erskine Mayer, the hugely successful pitcher, tried his hand at the craft himself. For Savannah of the South Atlantic League in 1913–1914, he pitched a total of 87⅔ innings, allowed 29 runs, and walked just 37. If all the runs were earned, his ERA was still just 2.97.

He even got a pair of batters faced in his time in D.C., walking them both. "Griff [Washington manager Clark Griffith] is evidently determined to find out whether in Sam Mayer he possesses either an outfielder, infielder or pitcher, for he has tried the kid in all three positions since Mayer first joined the club," *The Washington Herald* reported in September 1915.

Shortly thereafter, Griffith chose none of the above—he'd promised the Kansas City Blues $2,500 for Mayer's contract if he kept him past October 1 and determined he wasn't worth it.

But Mayer's pitching stopped for everyone. He returned to Atlanta, where he and Erskine lived in the offseason, but as an outfielder. Five years later he pitched another seven innings for the Atlanta Crackers, allowed just one run, and picked up the victory in 1920. A man of many talents, he'd become assistant manager and financial secretary for the club that year as well.

In all, he was 7–3 in his minor league pitching career. So what stopped him from pitching? Did he not want to be caught in his brother's shadow? Was his hitting so good that teams didn't want to merely use him on the mound? There's a story in that career stat line, one I hope to someday find out. But it's a remarkable talent, and Sam Mayer was capable of pitching and hitting at an elite level years before Babe Ruth and a century ahead of Shohei Ohtani.

16. Sam Fuld

Bats Left, Throws Left
Chicago Cubs, 2007, 2009–2010
Tampa Bay Rays, 2011–2013
Oakland Athletics, 2014–2015 (two different stints with A's in 2014)
Minnesota Twins, 2014

A very similar player to Max Rosenfeld, Sam Fuld was the New Hampshire High School Player of the Year in 2000 and a standout outfielder for Stanford. He has continued to hit for a high average, steal some bases, and field his position well at every level for the Chicago Cubs. But he received very little chance to play early in his career. He repeated Triple A in 2008 after posting a .287/.376/.395 line between Double and Triple A in 2007.

John Sickels, the dean of all prospect evaluators, wrote of Fuld in his 2008 book: "He would be an excellent fourth outfielder, due to his speed, defense, on-base ability, and hustle."

Fortunately, Fuld got the call from the Cubs after putting up a .286/.358/.399 line in Triple A Iowa and he kept on producing—two hits, plus an outfield assist to nail Jack Wilson at the plate in a Chicago win against the Pittsburgh Pirates. By July 4 Lou Piniella plugged him into the leadoff slot. "He's a good defensive player and he gives you what you would classify as a prototype leadoff [hitter], where he takes a lot of pitches, works the count."

Sweet Lou had that one right. Fuld finished his rookie season at .299/.409/.412. He entered 2010 spring training as the expected center fielder for Chicago. But he hit just .143 and got sent down to Triple A, only resurfacing late in the season before getting traded in an eight-player deal that winter to the Tampa Bay Rays, who knew just what to do with him.

Fuld's three-year run as an unconventional player for baseball's most unconventional manager, Joe Maddon, yielded a .230/.301/.326 line for only a 78 OPS+. But his defense and versatility helped Tampa Bay reach a pair of post-seasons and still win 90 games the season it fell short in 2012.

Sadly, Fuld became that most-expendable kind of player to the Rays after 2013—arbitration-eligible. They non-tendered Fuld, and he finished out his career with the Oakland A's and Minnesota Twins, then as the starting center fielder for Team Israel at the 2017 World Baseball Classic.

His career totals are unimpressive in purely offensive terms—.227/.307/.325 in 1,535 plate appearances—yet he was treasured by all of his employers for baseball acumen. So it should come as no surprise that the only player I've ever approached for an interview, who was reading The *New Yorker* at his locker, got a job in the Philadelphia Phillies front office the day he retired. The Phillies hired him as major league player information coordinator, a bridge between analytics and the players. "I think there's a little more credibility," Fuld said.

By 2021 he was the Phillies' general manager. His career as an executive is just beginning.

17. Herb Gorman

Bats Left, Throws Left
St. Louis Cardinals, 1952

Tragically, the record is incomplete for Herb Gorman. He was a masterful hitter, batting .351, .341, .310, and .305 from 1947 to 1950 in the Western and Pacific Coast Leagues while posting slugging percentages of .516, .576, .473, and .470. His biggest years came for the Hollywood Stars of the Pacific Coast League. By spring training 1952, he'd been purchased by the St. Louis Cardinals before collecting 10 hits in his first 26 at-bats, drawing notice of baseball writers. "Herb Gorman has been doing such a fine job with his bat that observers wondered how he could be omitted from the first base picture," Red Byrd wrote in *The Sporting News* in March 1952.

He made the club and was touted by the Associated Press as a rookie to watch, while *The Wisconsin Jewish Chronicle* noted he was one of six Jews in the major leagues that season, along with Sid Gordon, Al Rosen, Saul Rogovin, Joe Ginsberg, and Cal Abrams. But he received a solitary pinch-hitting assignment, grounding out to second against Chicago's Turk Lown in an 8–1 Cubs win on April 19 before Bill Starr's San Diego Padres of the PCL bought him from the Cardinals for $7,500. "San Diego's purchase of Herb Gorman from the Cardinals was a shrewd move—the ex-Hollywood Star can hit all kinds of pitching," the *Mirror News* reported in May 1952. Gorman put up a respectable .261/.326/.389 for the Padres.

But after getting off to a 3-for-4 start in the 1953 season, Gorman suffered a heart attack on the field in the fourth game of the season, summoning help from his left-field spot, losing consciousness by the time he reached the clubhouse. Fittingly, he'd hit two doubles in what turned out to be his final game. "Herb Gorman had learned to play the game of life equally as well as he had learned to play the game of his profession," Rabbi Morton J. Kohn said at Gorman's funeral later that week.

18. Nate Berkenstock

Bats Unknown, Throws Unknown
Philadelphia Athletics, 1871

Don't let all the hype around George Wright fool you, kids: it was Nate Berkenstock, Jewish haberdasher and baseball pioneer, who was the oldest professional player in the game's history. Berkenstock's tombstone says that he was born in 1832, a spring chicken, and Hall of Famer Wright wasn't born until 1835, a virtual millennial in National Association terms.

Berkenstock did come to the title in a backhanded way, to be sure. His peak came prior to the game turning professional—by the time of the National Association, he'd moved to the front office, serving as treasurer for his hometown Philadelphia Athletics. But a run of injuries opened a spot for a right fielder and in stepped Berkenstock, playing under the name Pratt for unexplained reasons.

Berkenstock was 0-for-4 with three strikeouts, but he also made three putouts in right, including the final one, as the Philadelphia Athletics defeated the Chicago Cubs 4–1 to win the National Association title. "Certainly, a word of commendation should be given to 'Pratt' [not Tommy] who played right field for the Athletics. He used to play baseball years ago, and he handled the ash and ran after the balls with all the uncouth rusticity of a bygone age," wrote *The New York World* in its game story the next day.

So the answer to the question of how long Jews have been in professional baseball is an easy one: always.

19. Israel Pike

Bats Left, Throws Left
Hartford Dark Blues, 1877

The younger brother of early baseball star Lipman Pike, accounts vary on such things as whether his name was Jacob or Israel—either way, that's a name for a Jewish ballplayer.

Regardless, according to Peter Morris of the SABR Biography Project, we know for sure that Pike became a haberdasher. We are reasonably sure that he is the same Pike who earned one hit in four at-bats for the National League's Hartford Dark Blues in 1877.

The best evidence of this Pike being the Israel Pike, who is Lipman Pike's little brother, is a box score from an Old Timers' Game in 1885. And I choose to believe the brothers, now retired, got to enjoy a beautiful afternoon of baseball in Washington Square Park. "How the people cheered when the Atlantics took the field," *The Brooklyn Daily Eagle* reported the next day. "And what a rare lot of old boys they were."

9

Left-Handed Starters

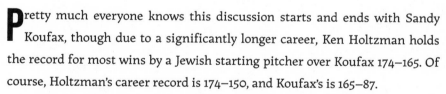

Pretty much everyone knows this discussion starts and ends with Sandy Koufax, though due to a significantly longer career, Ken Holtzman holds the record for most wins by a Jewish starting pitcher over Koufax 174–165. Of course, Holtzman's career record is 174–150, and Koufax's is 165–87.

Based on WAR, Koufax tops Holtzman 48.9 to 27.3, meaning that despite more than 500 more innings pitched for Holtzman, Koufax's career was about twice as valuable. This is not a knock on Holtzman, a very good pitcher—Koufax was simply that incredible.

To me, the saddest part about Sandy Koufax, who retired after his age-30 season due to arthritis in his elbow, is that though the injury ended his career, it hadn't ended his effectiveness—in fact, he'd become a better pitcher as he aged, and 1966, his final season, was by most metrics his best. It's been reported that his problem could have been easily fixed with minor surgery today.

Keep in mind also that pitching numbers only got better in 1967–1968. Merely by pitching to age 32, Koufax was a near-lock for over 200 wins. Bob Gibson, who was the same age as Koufax, pitched to a 2.44 ERA in 1966 but 1.12 in 1968. Would Koufax have put up a sub-1.00 ERA in 1968? It certainly seems possible.

1. Sandy Koufax

Bats Right, Throws Left
Brooklyn Dodgers, 1955–1957
Los Angeles Dodgers, 1958–1966

In his updated *Historical Baseball Abstract*, Bill James argues correctly that Sandy Koufax posted an ERA roughly twice as high on the road as he did at Dodger Stadium, a notorious pitchers' park—57–15, 1.37 ERA at home, 54–19, 2.57 ERA on the road.

But what is missed in this analysis is that Koufax got better as he aged away from Dodger Stadium—indeed, he became nearly as elite a pitcher on the road as at home by age 30. His home ERAs were static and ridiculous—1.75, 1.38, 0.85, 1.38, 1.52. But on the road, watch the progression: 3.53, 2.31, 2.93, 2.72, 1.96. By 1966 his road ERA was within half a run of his home ERA. Batting average against was .202 at home, .207 on the road, a negligible difference. And his strikeout rate was actually higher on the road (157 in 151⅔ innings) than at home (160 in 171⅓ innings).

So while James doesn't argue that Koufax was a Dodger Stadium creation, others have—and incorrectly. Let's stack up Koufax's 1966 against the 2007 Cy Young winners, for instance, but give Koufax the benefit of just his road work. Road Koufax, 1966: 151⅔ IP, 14–4 record, 1.96 ERA, 32 BB, 157 K; Jake Peavy, 2007: 223⅓ IP, 19–6 record, 2.54 ERA, 68 BB, 240 K; C.C. Sabathia, 2007: 241 IP, 19–7 record, 3.21 ERA, 37 BB, 209 K. Although Koufax's win total might have hurt him, voters would have been hard-pressed to vote for either Peavy or Sabathia over Road Koufax. Now this obviously fails to take era into account. But even era adjustments have their limits.

Obviously, fewer runs were scored in the 1962–66 era than, for instance, the five-year period of dominance by Pedro Martinez from 1999 to 2003. But beyond a certain point, I believe it is impossible for pitchers to avoid giving up runs. Defense, no matter the offensive period, is ultimately finite, and grounders will find holes, fly balls will find gaps or leave the park entirely. Unless a pitcher is striking out 600 men a season with a minimum of walks— and Koufax came as close as anyone since 1900 to doing so, striking out 382 in 1965 against just 71 walks—there is a floor for a pitcher's ERA, and it isn't 0.00. Adjusting ERA for era and park, as the terrific stat ERA+ does, is a fine shorthand for pitcher evaluation. I simply suspect it fails on the extreme here to evaluate the difference between Koufax's 190 in 1966 and Martinez's 291 in 2000.

One other note—Koufax won an MVP in 1963 but finished second in 1965 and 1966. A win both seasons would have made him the only pitcher to be a three-time winner, and even one would have elevated him alongside Hank Greenberg as another Jewish player with multiple MVPs. Willie Mays is the clear winner in 1965. Evaluating this through WAR, his 11.2 led the absolutely stacked National League field, and Koufax's 8.6 checks in at fourth after Mays, Juan Marichal, and Jim Maloney.

The 1966 season is a different story. Roberto Clemente won the MVP with a WAR of 8.2. Koufax was 1.5 wins ahead of him at 9.7, tied for first with Marichal. And the Los Angeles Dodgers finished first that season; the Pittsburgh Pirates were third. Even head-to-head, Koufax won the battle, holding Clemente to a .231 batting average in 13 at-bats. Clemente was an inner-circle Hall of Famer. But Koufax should have won this award.

And then there's this: the 1966 Dodgers finished 95–67. The 1967 Dodgers, sans Koufax, came in at 73–89. Beyond his pitching, though, I don't think anyone other than Greenberg has meant as much to a broad cross section of the Jewish people. It's fascinating the way the two have left an indelible mark on the Jewish culture—Greenberg as a portrait of strength, Koufax a tribute to intellect, though in both cases, the true picture of the man is much more complicated.

I'd like to think a Jewish star in today's game would matter as much. Is baseball as resonant as it was in 1934 or 1965? Perhaps not. But it could be as simple as this: there was only one Hank Greenberg and one Sandy Koufax. And that goes well beyond home runs and strikeouts.

2. Ken Holtzman

Bats Right, Throws Left
Chicago Cubs, 1965–1971, 1978–1979
Oakland Athletics, 1972–1975
Baltimore Orioles, 1976
New York Yankees, 1976–1978

Ken Holtzman was a very good major league pitcher. There are conventional ways of measuring this—the 174 wins, the career ERA+ of 105, the pair of no-hitters. But what is striking about Holtzman is the way he seemed to raise his game, hit another level of ability. Although it is hard to quantify clutch performance due to sample size, there are plenty of exhibits in Holtzman's career.

Take 1969, when he was serving in the military yet still could return to the Chicago Cubs to pitch weekend games. A disruption in routine like that would adversely affect most pitchers. But Holtzman pitched 261⅓ innings of 113 ERA+ baseball, winning 17 games. His postseason numbers also far surpass his regular-season stats—in 13 postseason games, 12 starts, he went 6–4 with a 2.30 ERA in 70 innings. But it doesn't even end there—a career .163 hitter, Holtzman hit .308/.357/.769 in 13 postseason at-bats with three doubles.

And there's more. His second lowest ERA by month was September. In his career, hitters had a batting average against of .255—but with runners in scoring position, it dropped to .244 (usually, this number goes up), and even with the bases loaded, the number stood at .256 with just two grand slams given up in 184 plate appearances—a home run rate half of his overall career mark.

And take September 25, 1966, in a late-season game between the Cubs and Los Angeles Dodgers. It meant nothing in the standings—the Cubs were firmly ensconced in eighth place—but for Holtzman, going up against Sandy Koufax, the game had to have extra meaning. It was also Holtzman's penultimate start of the season before returning to University of Illinois, where he was still an undergraduate.

Holtzman took a no-hitter into the ninth and bested Koufax 2–1. It was Sandy's final loss in the major leagues, and he allowed just four hits, striking out five. But Holtzman allowed two hits, struck out eight, and got the better of the Jewish duel.

After it was over, his girlfriend Roberta and her friend Stephanie were waiting for him to change so he could drive them back to campus. Holtzman told *The Daily Times*: "Stephanie is president of the Sandy Koufax Fan Club in Champaign."

3. Dave Roberts

Bats Left, Throws Left
San Diego Padres, 1969–1971
Houston Astros, 1972–1975
Detroit Tigers, 1976–1977
Chicago Cubs, 1977–1978
Pittsburgh Pirates, 1979–1980
Seattle Mariners, 1980
New York Mets, 1981

A far better pitcher than his career record of 103–125 showed, Dave Roberts simply couldn't stay healthy. But he still piled up 2,099 innings of 3.78 ERA pitching for a career mark of 97, which is just about average for a starter (100 is true average, but relievers tend to have higher ERA+ marks).

When Roberts was healthy, however, he was much better than average—in his five seasons from 1970 to 1974, his average ERA+ was around 113. For context, Nolan Ryan's career ERA+ was 112.

A mark of how good a healthy Roberts was came in 1979, when the Pittsburgh Pirates acquired him mid-year to use him as a swingman. Roberts pitched 38⅔ innings of 121 ERA+ ball for Pittsburgh as the Pirates won the World Series. But this understates his versatility. In his very first appearance with Pittsburgh following the trade, he pitched two innings. He started three games down the stretch. And he finally proved to the Pirates, who'd kept him in the minors for much of the 1960s, that he belonged.

It was the only time Roberts pitched for a team that won more than 84 games. Five times his teams lost 97 games or more—and his final team, the 1981 New York Mets, were on pace to reach 97 losses if not for the strike. A little better luck with his rosters, and Roberts, who trails Steve Stone for third place among wins by Jewish pitchers, would have finished considerably ahead of him.

4. Max Fried

Bats Left, Throws Left
Atlanta Braves, 2017–present

Although Alex Bregman is the top performer among current Jewish everyday performers, Max Fried is the clear standard-bearer as pitcher. It's hard to compare him to Sandy Koufax in part because he's simply had a much better start to his career than Koufax did. Fried even recorded a victory in the deciding Game Six of the 2021 World Series.

Notably, Fried had to switch high schools unexpectedly when Van Nuys Montclair Prep discontinued its sports program. But he moved to Harvard-Westlake, a haven for current major leaguers including his high school teammates, Lucas Giolito and Jack Flaherty, and continued his upward trajectory, getting selected seventh overall in the 2012 draft by the San Diego Padres and becoming a *Baseball America* top 100 prospect in both 2013 and 2014. But the Padres flipped him to the Atlanta Braves in 2014 as part of a Justin Upton deal. Upton was an All-Star for San Diego in 2015, but Atlanta won that trade.

Fried had Tommy John surgery in 2014 and missed most of that year and all of the following season. But by 2016 he was steadily progressing up the Atlanta minor league ladder, not posting flashy stats—his walk rate too high, strikeout rate a bit too low—but doing enough to get promoted.

Signs that the Fried, who'd merited a seventh-overall pick, had returned first showed up in the spring of 2017. "The pitching prospect generating the most buzz is left-hander Max Fried, a 23 year old," MLB.com wrote. "He was impressive for [Class A] Rome."

He made his first appearance with the Braves later that year, pitched to a 3.81 ERA over 26 innings but didn't rate anywhere in *Baseball America*'s top 100 prospects. Finally, by the start of 2018, he cracked MLB.com's list at 83 but beneath some other teammates like Ian Anderson. He put up a similar season in 2018, mostly at Triple A Gwinnett, and in 33⅔ innings with the Braves, there was little indication stardom was imminent.

But it was. Fried's 2019 was a revelation. He went 17–6 with a 4.02 ERA and a significant cutting down of walks. And in 2020, despite everything that made the year difficult, he was dominant—7–0 with a National League-best 2.25 ERA. For those wondering if a small 2020 sample was a fluke, his 2021 was far closer to his 2020 than anything that came before: 14–7, 3.04 ERA, and the control issues now three years in his rearview mirror.

He dominated the Milwaukee Brewers in the NLDS. Fried's complete season included a world championship, the Silver Slugger award at the position of pitcher potentially the last we'll ever see—if the National League makes the catastrophic mistake of adopting the designated hitter—and even a Gold Glove. Better still, Fried managed to win the most Jewish battle in World Series history. Facing Bregman in Game Two, he induced Bregman to fly out to right field, in a ball caught by...Joc Pederson.

Fried doesn't turn 28 until January of 2022, but he's at 11 WAR and halfway to Dave Roberts, who pitched until he was 36. Dan Szymborski of FanGraphs has Fried's 2022 ZIPS at 12–7. 3.96 ERA, another 2.6 WAR, and, if anything, that feels low, considering he's topped 2.6 WAR in each of the past three seasons, including 2.9 in the 2020 campaign that lasted just 60 games.

Through age 27, Holtzman's WAR was 23.3, but remember he got an early start and was in the big leagues by 19. And Koufax, by age 27, checks in at 27.5 WAR, but 20.8 of that came from age 25–27 as he ascended into the paragon of dominance.

Holtzman only put up a 3.8 WAR from age-28 on, meaning that we're coming up on the period in Fried's career where a typical peak will help him erase Holtzman's lead. I think Fried has a real chance, when he's finished, of leading Holtzman and trailing only Koufax among Jewish lefties in career value. Considering the top righty starter in WAR among the Jewish people, Barney Pelty, accumulated only 21.7, that'll make Fried the No. 2 overall starter in the Jewish rotation as well.

5. Ross Baumgarten

Bats Left, Throws Left
Chicago White Sox, 1978–1981
Pittsburgh Pirates, 1982

There are few better examples of how meaningless won-loss records are for a pitcher than Ross Baumgarten's 1980 season. Baumgarten, pride of Highland Park, Illinois, who grew up rooting for Chicago Cubs left-hander, Ken Holtzman, shot through the Chicago White Sox system after being taken in the 20th round of the 1977 draft. His minor league career included a 9–1, 1.82 ERA stop at Appleton of the Midwest League, but he pitched very well at each level. After 23 innings at the major league level in 1978, he earned a rotation spot in 1979 and went 13–8 with a 3.54 ERA. His future seemed secure.

But in 1980 Baumgarten went 2–12. His ERA of 3.44 was actually lower than in 1978. His walk rate went down, his strikeout rate went up. He lost games 1–0, 3–1, 3–2, and 3–2 again. He got no-decisions in another five games where he threw quality starts, pitching 34⅔ innings of 1.81 ERA baseball in those five games. Teammate Lamarr Hoyt had an ERA more than a run higher—and his record was 9–3.

A side note: he pitched a one-hitter in one of his only two victories that season—on July 2. His team only got him one run. And Rod Carew, supposed friend to the Jews because he married a Jewish woman and raised his kids in the faith, got the hit off of Baumgarten. Thanks a lot, Rod. I guess your admirable Jewish charitable work didn't include the Ross Baumgarten No-Hitter Foundation.

But that was his final win of the season. A few weeks later he hit the disabled list with a sore shoulder and missed a month. Even though he went 0–7 in his final 11 starts, his ERA over that span was a respectable 3.90. "I've always said a little adversity is good for everyone," Baumgarten told the *Chicago Tribune*'s David Israel in July 1980. "But this whole year has been a study in adversity for me with the exception of getting engaged." That part worked out—he and his wife Nancy, live in Naples, Florida, where Ross is a financial advisor.

The loss total undoubtedly put Baumgarten on a short leash, and after a difficult 1981, he was traded to the Pittsburgh Pirates, where a more deserved 0–5 start ended his major league career. But his career 22–36 mark is unjustified. His career ERA+ is exactly 100—for current context that's right in line with Hyun-Jin Ryu's 2021 and ahead of Yu Darvish's 2021.

Had he posted a second double-digit win season, he'd likely have gotten plenty of chances to keep pitching instead of being viewed, unfairly, as a fluke. In reality that win number with a luckier 1980 would have been a lot higher.

6. Lefty Weinert

Bats Left, Throws Left
Philadelphia Phillies, 1919–1924
Chicago Cubs, 1927–1928
New York Yankees, 1931

Lefty Weinert began his career as an outlaw. After a handful of innings as a teenager over three seasons with the Philadelphia Phillies—his first outing coming in 1919, when he was 17—Philadelphia attempted to option him to Syracuse. He declined and was ousted from organized baseball, instead spending most of 1921 pitching in semipro games around Philly.

He returned to the Phillies in 1922, but the run of poor Philadelphia baseball teams continued around him. The 1920 Phils went 62–9—and that was their high-water mark while Weinert was a Phillie. He spent 1922 in the rotation with a respectable 8–11, 3.40 ERA showing for an ERA+ of 136. The ERA placed him seventh in the National League—adjusting for park and era pushed him to second in the NL that year. That he did this at age 20 was remarkable.

The next year, 1923, did not go as well. He had a record of 4–17 and a 5.42 ERA. In May of 1924, Weinert was optioned to Los Angeles of the Pacific Coast League, where he posted a 2–3 record with a 5.29 ERA. At that point the Phillies released their rights to him, and he elected to spend most of the next two years pitching more semipro ball for outfits like the Ben Franklin Club of Philadelphia, the Oaklyn (New Jersey) Oaks, and the Strawbridge and Clothier team after asking for a release from the Vernon Tigers in May 1925.

Rumors would pop up in the press—he's headed to the New York Giants in one, the Chicago White Sox in another—but nothing ever came of it. And it was reported late in 1926 that while playing for that Strawbridge and Clothier team, he'd done so alongside ineligible players, leading baseball commissioner Kenesaw Mountain Landis to suspend him for the 1926 season.

I thought that was odd—why is Landis making rules about semipro play, and if a semipro team used ineligible players, how is that Weinert's fault? The great baseball historians John Thorn (MLB's official historian) and Jacob Pomrenke (of SABR) theorized that he may have played with players from, for instance, the Black Sox, and thus ran afoul of MLB in that way. As Pomrenke put it to me in an email: "That said, Landis ignored his own rule far more often than he followed through with the threat. And if an ineligible player quickly groveled and apologized to his satisfaction, they'd almost always get reinstated."

Quite a long arm of the law on this one, however you feel about Shoeless Joe Jackson and company.

But after getting reinstated in December 1926, Weinert headed back out west to play for the Mission Bells of the PCL and manager Harry Hooper. He excelled with a 17–12 record and a 3.14 ERA in the notoriously hitter-friendly PCL. It was the best ERA of any of Mission's starters, and five of them, including Weinert, were former or future major leaguers.

The performance earned him 15 games, including another four starts for the 1927–1928 Chicago Cubs, with middling results—ERAs of 4.58 and 5.29 in those two seasons. An 18-win, 3.00 ERA season for the Class A Memphis Chickasaws in 1929 and a 16-win, 3.63 ERA campaign for Double A Louisville Colonels in 1930 earned Weinert a third shot with the 1931 New York Yankees, who selected his contract at the end of the 1930 season.

Now 29, Weinert struck out a hitter per inning. But his ERA in those 24 frames was 6.20, and by July, according to the July 9, 1931 issue of *The Sporting News*, "[Yankees Manager Joe] McCarthy clung to him, always hoping that he would flash big league stuff but finally decided that he would help Louisville more than [New York owner] Colonel Ruppert's club." *TSN* did note that Weinert "seemed to be pursued by considerable hard luck."

Still, three chances to make good in the major leagues is pretty lucky, especially at that time. Weinert posted another three double-digit win totals in the minor leagues from 1932 to 1934. He went on to coach baseball at Villanova University and scout for the Brooklyn Dodgers and Cleveland Indians before dying in a car accident in Florida in 1973.

7. Harry Kane

Bats Left, Throws Left
St. Louis Browns, 1902
Detroit Tigers, 1903
Philadelphia Phillies, 1905–1906

Although Harry Kane pitched for 13 years—for the Wichita Falls Drillers to the Hugo Hugoites, the Williamsport Millionaires, to the Springfield Midgets— he had his greatest success with Savannah of the Southern Association in 1905–1906, winning 22 games in 1905 and 17 the following year. Between those successful minor league seasons, Kane packed 86 innings of 63 ERA+ pitching into stints with the St. Louis Browns, Detroit Tigers, and Philadelphia Phillies.

That is not to say his major league career didn't include some high points. In September 28, 1905, *The Philadelphia Inquirer* reported beneath a headline "Kane Raises Cain With St. Louis, 6–0," Kane "turns out a crackerjack" and "his twirling at times is spectacular." Kane's real name was Cohen, and *The Inquirer* claimed he was known as "Klondike Bill." However, with apologies to a great newspaper, I can find no other instance of Kane being known as Klondike Bill, and a contemporary of his in baseball, minor league outfielder Bill Douglass, is widely referred to as "Klondike Bill," a more intuitive leap given his name is, you know, Bill.

Klondike or not, Kane went on to umpire in many leagues for nearly two decades from the Texas League to the Pacific Coast League. At work in the latter, he died at a hotel on the road in 1932.

8. Bill Cristall

Bats Left, Throws Left
Cleveland Blues, 1901

Don't get me started on Bill Cristall, the Buddy Young Jr. of Ukranian base-ball players, who had a simply marvelous 13-year career in the minor leagues. Analyze this: he won 25 games in 1902 alone for Los Angeles and Oakland of the California League.

But for the 1901 Cleveland Blues, Cristall was not the Candyman. (That was, clearly, their first baseman, Candy LaChance.) He pitched to a 4.84 ERA and 1–5 record for an ERA+ was 74—he was no Miracle Max.

The Blues threw Cristall from the train, but he won 10 or more games six times in the next 16 minor league seasons and, despite standing just 5'7", played "My Giant" in the New York state capital region, logging seasons for Albany, Schenectady, and Troy.

After 700 Sundays as a player, Cristall moved on to managing. But after starting 1919 in charge of the Bay City Wolves of the Michigan-Ontario League, he was replaced mid-year. I guess nobody told Wolves management that if you rush a miracle man, you get rotten miracles.

10

Right-Handed Starters

Although the stars among Jewish starting pitchers are all southpaws, a majority of the righties would be a good fit in nearly any rotation. What is astounding is how close the top few are to one another. Check out the top righties as ranked by ERA+:

Barney Pelty, 100

Erskine Mayer, 99

Steve Stone, 98

Saul Rogovin, 96

Barry Latman, 94

Jason Marquis, 93

Ultimately, Pelty gets the edge for a number of reasons that extend beyond the tiny edge in ERA+. Pelty holds the innings edge over his rivals for the

Steve Stone

top spot with 1,908 innings pitched. But while this is an imperfect means of judging him against his more modern rivals, it allows us to see a 25 percent cushion over Erskine Mayer, who pitched in a similar time. Pelty had four full seasons with an ERA+ of better than 100—including a 161, 122, and 119. Marquis' top season was 128, though six of his seasons were 100 or better. For Steve Stone, his top season was a 123—his Cy Young year of 1980—with only two other seasons above 100.

It doesn't hurt that Pelty had the finest Jewish-themed baseball nickname this side of the "Rabbi of Swat"—Pelty was known as "The Yiddish Curver." Figure also that Pelty's poor teams—until his final half-season with the Washington Senators, none of his teams finished higher than fourth place—and it is fair to surmise that his won-loss record would have been much better than his actual mark of 92–117 for most other teams. Moreover, teams that poor usually have below-average fielding teams. Such fielding doesn't get fully captured by ERA, as the plays fielders don't come close to are just as rough on pitchers as those they boot away. Through all of that, Barney Pelty still stands as the finest Jewish right-handed pitcher of all time.

1. Barney Pelty

Bats Right, Throws Right
St. Louis Browns, 1902–1912
Washington Senators, 1912

Due to the gaudy won-loss total in his finest season, Steve Stone generally gets the edge when people name the finest Jewish right-handed pitcher. But a close comparison between Stone's 1980 and Pelty's 1906 show Pelty's to be the far superior season.

Stone did register a 25–7 mark, while Pelty came in at 16–11. But Stone pitched for a 100–62 Baltimore Orioles team—Pelty for the 76–73 St. Louis Browns (who went on to become the Orioles, incidentally). Stone received slightly more than 5.5 runs per game in his starts, 204 runs over 37 starts.

Pelty, it is safe to say, received far less than that—he started 30 of St. Louis' 149 games, but the Browns scored 558 runs all season. Pelty's ERA was 1.59; Stone's was 3.25. And even once accounting for park and era, Pelty's ERA+ was 163, and Stone's was 123. Stone had a great season. But Pelty had a far greater season—and a better career around it, too.

Incidentally, had Pelty's neutralized 125–84 record stood, he'd have had a .598 career winning percentage—good for 117th all time and just ahead of Warren Spahn and Curt Schilling.

To get a sense of Pelty's regard around the league, here's how Washington Senators manager Clark Griffith described it to *The Washington Times* when the Senators acquired him in the middle of the 1912 season: "All we needed was one more seasoned twirler, and Pelty should win a lot of games for us."

Story of Pelty's career, though: he won only one for Washington despite a solid 103 ERA+ over 43⅔ innings for the Senators.

Pelty's nickname, "The Yiddish Curver," reflected his curveball as a true out pitch, and he also added plus fielding capabilities to his overall skillset. This was a truly fine pitcher.

Pelty returned to his hometown of Farmington, Missouri, after he finished playing, where he ran a general store with plenty of books that his parents had started, later serving as an inspector for the Missouri Food and Drug Department. Accordingly, the road leading into Farmington's sports complex is named "Barney Pelty Drive."

2. Erskine Mayer

Bats Right, Throws Right
Philadelphia Phillies, 1912–1918
Pittsburgh Pirates, 1918–1919
Chicago White Sox, 1919

Erskine Mayer was a very capable No. 2 starter on the 1915 Philadelphia Phillies, a team that went to the World Series. But keep in mind, he had a season that would have made him an ace on many other pennant winners. And the No. 2 starter was the great Grover Cleveland Alexander, who had his finest season— 31–10, 1.22 ERA.

Mayer, from Atlanta, Georgia, and the son of a musician, drew the attention of scouts with a 15–2 record for the Fayetteville Highlanders of the Class D Eastern Carolina League. The Phillies snapped him up in 1912, and by 1913 he was a fixture on the Philadelphia staff, posting a 9–9 record in 170⅓ innings of 3.11 ERA (107 ERA+) pitching. The sidearm curveball specialist was so slick on the mound that Brooklyn manager Wilbert Robinson called him "Eelskin."

In 1914 he was nearly the equal of the great Alexander. Mayer posted a 21–19 record, 2.58 ERA, while Alexander was at 27–15, 2.38 ERA. Then came his huge season. It appears injuries slowed Mayer over the remainder of his career. He'd be effective but in shorter and shorter bursts. By 1919 he posted an 8.37 ERA for the Chicago White Sox. This was a peculiar irony since he was one of the White Sox who *wasn't* throwing games.

Added to Mayer's ledger, incidentally, is his hitting—a career line of .185/.234/.252 with a pair of home runs, which is good for a pitcher in any time, but Mayer was hitting in the Dead Ball Era.

In all, Mayer is unjustly forgotten by most baseball fans, apparently not a new experience for him. As the September 9, 1915, issue of *The Sporting News* reports of Mayer: "It may be he thought he should have more credit for it and that there should be a little more said about Mayer and less about Alexander. Looking over that record, we incline to think along the same lines."

Hollywood disagreed—and Ronald Reagan played Alexander, not Mayer, in 1952's *The Winning Team*.

3. Steve Stone

Bats Right, Throws Right
San Francisco Giants, 1971–1972
Chicago White Sox, 1973, 1977–1978
Chicago Cubs, 1974–1976
Baltimore Orioles, 1979–1981

Steve Stone's career started and ended with his curveball. Stone was born and raised in Euclid, Ohio; the son of Orthodox parents Paul and Dorothy; a three-sport athlete (baseball, tennis, and golf) in high school who was called to the Torah in 1960.

According to *The Big Book of Jewish Baseball*, Stone decided to throw mostly curveballs in 1980, though he knew such a choice would ruin his arm, which had been sore for the better part of eight years. The results were huge—a 25–7 record, 3.25 ERA. It was easily the best season of his career, winning percentage-wise, and many point to it as a fluke season.

But this severely underrates how good a healthy Stone could be. Back in 1971, when he was a rookie starter for the San Francisco Giants, he was heralded as "the most promising young pitcher we've had since Juan Marichal came up" in the May 1, 1971, edition of *The Sporting News*. The one speaking was Giants coach Larry Jansen, an excellent pitcher in his own right.

In that same article, what did Stone credit his success to? "I began getting my curve over the plate last year," he said. "That's the main reason I improved enough to merit a chance up here."

By 1972 he posted just a 6–8 record—but a 2.98 ERA for an ERA+ of 117. "He has good command of all of his pitches," Giants pitching coach Don McMahon said in June of 1972. "His fastball is major league, and so is his curve."

Injuries—most notably, a rotator cuff tear—took their toll in between, but Stone and his curveball were no fluke.

Stone's worked as a broadcaster for both the Chicago Cubs and Chicago White Sox. He currently announces White Sox games with Jason Benetti, and they represent one of the best booths in the major leagues.

4. Scott Feldman

Bats Left, Throws Right
Texas Rangers, 2005–2012
Chicago Cubs, 2013
Baltimore Orioles, 2013
Houston Astros, 2014–2016
Toronto Blue Jays, 2016
Cincinnati Reds, 2017

This book is filled with stories of players who, if for this and but for that, would have had a better career. I don't think you can argue Scott Feldman did anything other than max out reasonable expectations for his accomplishments on the field.

Feldman, who grew up in Burlingame, California, was not a star in college, nor did he attend a big-time program: the College of San Mateo. The Texas Rangers selected him in the 30th round as a favor to his agent, according to Feldman. He had Tommy John surgery that September, but once he returned in late 2004, he rocketed through the system—by August of 2005, he reached the major leagues, striking out two in a scoreless inning in his debut. "He's pounding the strike zone, and that's impressive," his manager, Buck Showalter, told the *Fort Worth Star-Telegram* in early September. "I'm not going to tell him that most guys don't do that when they first get here."

Feldman's 0.96 ERA sure made a great first impression. Still, even in 2006, Feldman split time between Texas and Triple A Oklahoma City, getting sent down five times. Moreover, he did not make a start—the ceiling everybody seemed to have for him was a middle reliever. His 3.92 ERA was solid that season, but it ballooned to 5.77 in 2007, and his customary control all but disappeared.

By 2008, the question was whether he could secure the final bullpen spot in the spring. But he didn't curse his luck; he took responsibility. "If I get guys out, I wouldn't have been sent down," he told Rangers writer T.R. Sullivan.

It's astonishing, really, that following a spring he worked out of the bullpen, then got sent down on March 22—instructed to make the switch from reliever to starter—and that by April 13, he was back in Texas, starting in May. "Scott Feldman is looking like a permanent member of the starting rotation," Jeff Wilson of the *Star-Telegram* wrote.

Feldman finished with a 5.29 ERA—this is 2008, though, so that was good for a respectable ERA+ of 84—and broke out in 2009, winning 17, pitching to an ERA of 4.08, an ERA+ of 114 given park and era. His offseason work clearly had improved his command of on his change-up. He was here to stay.

That was Feldman for the next decade. His WAR of 8.2 undersells what he meant to his teams—a classic innings-eater, occasionally more, with 1,386⅓ innings of 97 ERA+ pitching.

In a February 26, 2008, interview with *The Dallas Morning News*, when asked what his long-term financial goals are, Feldman included in his desired luxuries, "I'd like to get a car for my mom."

Scott Feldman was well-trained. Feldman, according to Baseball-Reference. com, made more than $52 million in his major league career. Feldman's an investor now with his company, Feldman Enterprises. I'd imagine his mom drives anything she wants.

5. Jason Marquis

Bats Right, Throws Right

Atlanta Braves, 2000–2003

St. Louis Cardinals, 2004–2006

Chicago Cubs, 2007–2008

Colorado Rockies, 2009

Washington Nationals, 2010–2011

Arizona Diamondbacks, 2011–2012

Minnesota Twins, 2012

San Diego Padres, 2012–2013

Cincinnati Reds, 2015

What I love most about the turbulent, roller coaster career of Jason Marquis is how he calmly set about reinventing himself again and again. Marquis did not throw hard—92.7 miles per hour with his fastball as a rookie, and his velocity dipped from there, and Marquis spent most of his career topping out in the upper 80s. But he was a tinkerer—more curves one season, slider-heavier the next, a cutter at different periods featured, then discarded. He was a pitcher in the truest sense of the word. "For me, it's about the delivery," Marquis said to me when we caught up prior to a game in Baltimore back in 2013, standing at his locker, talking about his latest reinvention. "When my delivery's right, there's so much more movement. The life on my ball, there's so much more quality on it when things are going right. To me, life and movement on the ball—you can ask hitters, a guy throwing 93, his ball could look 89. A guy throwing 89, his ball could look 93. And that's life on the ball, perceived velocity, whatever you want to call it."

Marquis was selected in the first round of the 1996 draft by the Atlanta Braves ahead of Jacque Jones, Milton Bradley, and Jimmy Rollins. Marquis headed to the St. Louis Cardinals along with Adam Wainwright and Ray King for J.D. Drew and Eli Marrero after the 2003 season. It's worth noting that, even though Wainwright was a top prospect at the time, reports of the deal referred to Marquis first.

Marquis put up two strong seasons for St. Louis in 2004 and 2005, then a disaster of a 2006—14–16, 6.02 ERA. Those who wrote him off were mistaken—his ERA of 4.57 over two campaigns in 2007–08 was good for an ERA+ of 101. He figured it out.

The Chicago Cubs traded him to the Colorado Rockies for Luis Vizcaino. Marquis went out and made an All-Star team. He signed with the Washington Nationals, and his ERA cratered to 6.60 in 2010. He recovered to 3.95 in 2011. He figured it out. The same thing happened with the Minnesota Twins in 2012, when his ERA ballooned to 8.47. The San Diego Padres picked him up off the scrap heap, and he put up an ERA of 4.04 in 2012 for them, then 4.05 in 2013. He figured it out. I talked to his catcher, Nick Hundley, and his manager, Bud Black. No one was surprised.

A bonus with Marquis—the 2005 Silver Slugger winner posted two of the top 11 single season batting averages by starting pitchers from 2000 to 2007 with a .292 mark in 2004 and a .310 mark in 2005. His career line of .196/.214/.278 with five home runs in 721 plate appearances isn't Ohtani-esque, but it was good for an OPS+ of 28 or eighth among the 36 primary pitchers with at least 500 plate appearances since 2000.

6. Saul Rogovin

Bats Right, Throws Right
Detroit Tigers, 1949–1951
Chicago White Sox, 1951–1953
Baltimore Orioles, 1955
Philadelphia Phillies, 1955–1957

Saul Rogovin, son of Jacob and Bessie, was a product of the New York public school system before drawing the attention of Mel Ott at a New York Giants' tryout camp as an outfielder in 1941. By 1945, struggling to make headway in his career as a hitter, he switched to pitching and took off quickly. It helped that the great Paul Richards, as astute an observer of baseball talent as ever lived, took an interest in Rogovin and brought him to the Buffalo Bisons. "Paul taught me all I know about pitching, and I learned quite a bit," Rogovin told the *Port Huron Times Herald*.

By 1948 he was the Bisons' best pitcher, and the *Pottsville Republican* reported that Rogovin "stands an excellent chance to make the big time as a pitcher."

The *Pottsville Republican* was right. But an ear infection delayed his season, and after his big league debut, it was back to Buffalo, where he dominated—16–6, 3.65 ERA. By 1951 he was taking regular starts and won the American League ERA crown after posting 12–8, 2.78 ERA marks for the Detroit Tigers and Chicago White Sox. Chicago traded for him, having given up Bob Cain. Chicago's manager? That's right: Richards.

By the time he was celebrating that at his Brooklyn home in the winter of 1951, calling it "a miracle" after his sore arm in 1950 almost ended his career, it looked as if Rogovin was poised to become an elite AL pitcher. But arm troubles and a sleep disorder limited him for the duration of his career even with Richards' support, first in Chicago, then with the Baltimore Orioles.

Living up to the idea that we are the people of the book, Rogovin went on to a successful career as a New York City high school English teacher, returning to school in his '50s and earning a literature degree from City College. But the Brooklyn-born Rogovin prefaced his time teaching Hemingway with a solid, occasionally spectacular baseball career, finishing with an ERA+ of 96 and 7 career WAR.

7. Barry Latman

Bats Right, Throws Right
Chicago White Sox, 1957–1959
Cleveland Indians, 1960–1963
Los Angeles Angels, 1964–1965
Houston Astros, 1966–1967

While questions about the extent of Ty Cobb's racism continue to be debated with compelling arguments on both sides, there is little evidence that Cobb was anti-Semitic. In fact, as unlikely as it may seem given Cobb's background and reputation, it would not be a stretch to call Cobb a friend to the Jews.

Well, maybe not a friend. Cobb did, according to Al Stump's biography of Cobb, start an on-field brawl by telling Philadelphia A's player Claude Rossman that a member of the Detroit Tigers had called him "a Jew bastard." These apparently being fighting words, Rossman and the Tigers got into a fight, getting Rossman ejected. This isn't likely to win Cobb any B'nai Brith awards—but as anti-Semitism goes, it's pretty tame by 1909 standards.

But by the 1950s, Cobb had become a friend to young Barry Latman, pride of Los Angeles, son of Elsie and Nathan, who, unlike Rossman, actually was Jewish. Latman was a star at Fairfax High School in Los Angeles—teammates with fellow Jew and future major leaguer Larry Sherry. Latman's father, according to the April 2, 1958, issue of *The Sporting News*, got Latman an audience with Cobb. "I was feeling pretty cocky," Latman told *TSN*. "I had just pitched a perfect game and was on top of the world. A friend of my father knew Mr. Cobb and took me to see him at Palo Alto. This was in 1953, and Mr. Cobb really brought me down to earth. I'll always be grateful for his interest."

According to Latman, five years after that conversation, the two still corresponded, including an eight-page letter from Cobb that spring. Will this get him a statue in Boca Raton, Florida? Probably not. But I'd think twice before putting Cobb's portrait on the sidewalk so that all the Jewish ladies can run over him with their walkers.

As for the recipient of Cobb's advice, Latman turned into a pretty solid major league pitcher. He was a swingman, a starter/reliever hybrid—between 1959 and 1964, Latman started between 18 and 21 games, while relieving in 16 to 27 games each season, save one year when he relieved in 11 contests. All this after taking a three-year break in his development from ages 10 to 13 at his parents' behest, so he could study for his Bar Mitzvah.

After brief moments in Chicago in 1957 and a truly dominant 1958—47⅔ innings with a 0.76 ERA and just one home run allowed—he was promoted to stay for the 1959 American League champion Chicago White Sox, posting an 8–5, 3.75 ERA season. "Barry Latman—chief hope for the future of the aging pitching corps," the *Chicago Tribune*, still making predictions 11 years after Dewey Defeats Truman, wrote in April 1959. "Latman, only 22, gave hint of potential when he won three late-season decisions for the White Sox... Strapping 6–3 right-hander, Latman is beating control troubles." Sadly, for Fairfax High School, while his schoolmate Sherry won World Series MVP honors, Latman did not get into a Fall Classic game.

The following April, the White Sox traded him for Herb Score, the once-great phenom who'd faltered after getting hit by Gil McDougald's line drive. Despite Score's early-career heroics, Cleveland Indians fans, who called *The Plain-Dealer*, supported the acquisition of Latman by a reported rate of 3-to-1. Unfortunately, his record ran to just 7–7 in 1960, though a respectable 4.03 ERA kept his team in games all season.

In 1961 he went 13–5, 4.02 ERA for Cleveland, mostly out of the pen, earning an All-Star Game berth in the process. Given how relievers were not held in high esteem at the time, this is fairly remarkable. But his first half numbers— 8–0, 2.90 ERA—could not be overlooked. Latman's career continued in an up-and-down manner through his final season at age 31 in 1967. Even in 1966 his 2–7 record doesn't capture his excellence—a 2.71 ERA in 103 innings for an

ERA+ of 127. "You know he lost a couple of heartbreakers," his manager, Grady Hatton, said, defending him the *Orlando Sentinel* the following spring.

An off-field note about Latman—he was a professional singer before coming to baseball, singing with the Bob Mitchell Boys Choir, which appeared in numerous films and recorded with Bing Crosby and Frank Sinatra.

8. Harry Feldman

Bats Right, Throws Right
New York Giants, 1941–1946

Harry Feldman grew up in the Bronx, threw for Clark Junior High School and Textile High, and signed with his hometown New York Giants, who assigned him to Class D Blytheville of the Northeast Arkansas League, where he was an instant star in 1938. "Harry Feldman was on the firing line for the Giants and turned in the season's most outstanding pitching performance," the *Blytheville Courier News* reported in May.

By July he'd run up a 13–1, 2.02 ERA mark and earned a promotion to Class C Fort Smith of the Western Association. In 1939 he posted a 25–9 mark. After a pair of seasons with Jersey City of the International League, New York's top farm team, Feldman got the call in September 1941, the same day as fellow Semite Sid Gordon, incidentally.

Feldman did a bit of everything for those war-years Giants, starting 78 games, finishing 28 others with six shutouts and three saves. For a 1945 team that featured Phil Weintraub, Ernie Lombardi, and Mel Ott, he ran a 12–13 record and a 3.27 ERA for an ERA+ of 119. Dick Young called him "Hard Luck Harry Feldman" in a column that year, noting on July 25 that all three times the Giants had been shut out, Feldman had been on the mound. "He's a very patient fellow, this Feldman," Young wrote. "But how much can a guy stand?"

Feldman finished with a 35–35 mark, along with a 3.80 ERA, for an ERA+ of 96. But his combination of walks (91 in 1944, eighth highest in the league) and home runs (a top five finish in both 1944 and 1945) meant that when soldiers returned from World War II, there wasn't a major league place for Feldman. He added to that likelihood by jumping to the Mexican League—when it folded, baseball was reluctant to find places for the players that left.

Feldman returned to Fort Smith after retirement, opened a record store but only lived to 42, dying of a heart attack on a fishing trip.

9. Jason Hirsh

Bats Right, Throws Right
Houston Astros, 2006
Colorado Rockies, 2007–2008

Jason Hirsh had the talent to blow the other right-handed Jewish starters away. Hirsh stands 6'8", which is impressive in and of itself. The tallest Jewish player in history, he is someone who could look Eddie Gaedel in the eye if he was standing on the shoulders of a second Eddie Gaedel.

But Hirsh's combination of strikeout ability and control is what makes him such an appealing prospect. Despite playing in hitter-friendly minor leagues for the lion's share of his apprenticeship time, Hirsh still posted a 2.95 ERA in 484⅓ minor league innings with 419 walks and 161 strikeouts. This success came despite a jump from Division-II California Lutheran, which took a chance on the mammoth high schooler, hoping for and getting a jump in velocity as he grew into his body. The Houston Astros picked him in the second round of the 2003 draft, and he proved that a wise move—he was named Texas League Pitcher of the Year in 2005 and then Pacific Coast League Pitcher of the Year in 2006. "If the Astros had a young hurler who established himself as something more than back-of-the-rotation filler, it was Hirsh," *Baseball Prospectus* wrote in its 2007 annual.

Hirsh was unlucky on the injury front, however, breaking a leg to lose out on the chance to pitch in Colorado's improbable playoff march in 2007 and missing the first third of the 2008 season with rotator cuff soreness. He pitched well in 2009 and 2010 for Scranton/Wilkes-Barre, the top farm team for the New York Yankees, but didn't get another shot at the major leagues.

Let no one, however, doubt his toughness. He broke his leg in the first inning of his final 2007 start—but he went on to pitch six innings, allowing just two earned runs. A quality start is tough enough to come by—let alone from a pitcher with a fracture.

10. Eli Morgan

Bats Right, Throws Right
Cleveland Guardians, 2021–present

A rocky Major League Baseball beginning for Eli Morgan—8.44 ERA through his first five starts—gave way to a stretch run of solid pitching for the Cleveland Indians. His season ERA ultimately dropping all the way to 4.37 in 13 starts after the All-Star break.

Morgan reached the big leagues on the strength of his change-up, a slow pitch that averages around 75 miles per hour, and one he embraced after discarding a splitter over concerns about what that would do to his arm over the long term. "When I got to [Gonzaga University], they told me that if I wanted to pitch, let alone be a starter, I needed to have a good change-up," Morgan told Fangraphs' David Lauria in September 2021. "That was a big thing up there, so I started throwing it a lot more and got comfortable with it. Because I throw a four-seam fastball, I throw a four-seam change-up. That's something one of my pitching coaches mentioned: 'Make sure it comes out with the same seams as your fastball.' That's what I went with, and I had pretty good command of it right from the start. Over time, I began getting more movement on it, getting more fade."

It worked for him—opposing hitters managed just a .174/.257/.376 line against the pitch in 2021. Now he needs to find similar success with at least two of his other pitches. Dan Szymborski's ZIPS has Morgan at 6–7 with a 5.14

ERA in his 2022 projection. But Cleveland pitchers have been regularly outperforming expectations, and Morgan is one to watch for sure.

11. Dean Kremer

Bats Right, Throws Right
Baltimore Orioles, 2020–present

The 2021 Baltimore Orioles were deep within a rebuild. And so Dean Kremer, 25, first Israeli citizen to reach the major leagues, Bar Mitzvahed in the Holy Land, had a real opportunity to prove himself.

It didn't go all that well, to be honest. His season line was 0–7, and this was not your hard-luck 0–7—his ERA was 7.55. Even during the part of the season he spent in Triple A Norfolk, his ERA was 4.91. This kind of production at age 25 doesn't usually presage a long major league career.

Even so, Kremer's an easy pitcher to root for, and his ability to miss bats—8.6 strikeouts-per-nine-innings through his first two major league seasons with double-digit strikeouts-per-nine innings numbers at every minor league stop—means it isn't time to give up hope just yet.

Despite his trailblazing role—if Kremer never appeared in another major league game, he'd still be a significant figure in Jewish baseball history—Kremer said he came late to the idea that his being Jewish mattered in a baseball context. "I've always been just a Jewish kid playing baseball. They've never really coincided," Kremer told me in a May 2021 Zoom interview. "They've always been pretty much separate. But I guess when I started playing for the national team, I want to say back in 2014, that's when it really like—right, I'm Israeli and I play baseball, linking them together."

There are reasons for hope in his repertoire, too—he threw his cutter more in 2021, finding success with it, and the curveball has served him well in both seasons. But he threw that four-seam fastball much more in 2021 than in 2020, and hitters teed off on it. He talked about wanting to throw his change-up more when we spoke, but it was not a useful pitch this season.

The Orioles have great talent coming, like Grayson Rodriguez and D.L. Hall, but everyone needs more arms. Dan Szymborski has Kremer's ZIPS projection at 6–8. 5.64 ERA. Baltimore is hoping for something better from Kremer in 2022. So am I.

12. Richard Conger

Bats Right, Throws Right
Detroit Tigers, 1940
Pittsburgh Pirates, 1941–1942
Philadelphia Phillies, 1943

Richard Conger was the UCLA bookend to the USC story of Al Silvera. Conger signed with the Detroit Tigers after just one year of college, and the Tigers threw him right into the major league fire. "Baseball scouts nowadays believe in getting them young," Charles P. Ward of the *Detroit Free Press* wrote from Tigers spring training in Lakeland, Florida, in February 1940. As Conger put it, he left UCLA early "because the call of baseball was too strong."

Conger actually did pretty well, allowing one run over three innings for the Tigers, who then sent him to Beaumont of the Texas League, where he posted an 8–10 mark and a 4.28 ERA—pretty good for someone nearly nine years younger than the league average age.

The Pirates grabbed him in the Rule V draft, and Conger put up ERAs of 3.34 in 1941 and 3.39 in 1942 for the Pittsburgh Pirates' minor league affiliates in Albany and Toronto but got just 12⅓ innings with the big league club. It is hard to figure—Conger allowed just two earned runs in those innings for an ERA over the two seasons of 1.46.

Once Conger posted an 11–6, 1.96 ERA for Toronto in 1943, the major leagues could ignore him no longer. Unfortunately, he bombed in his trial with the Philadelphia Phillies in 1943, putting up a 6.09 ERA over 13 games, including 10 starts. At the end of the season, Philly sold him to Los Angeles of the Pacific Coast League. He pitched well for them in 1944, posting a 13–7 record, 2.88 ERA with just 35 walks in 169 innings. That's the type of line that normally gets a player another big league shot, but instead Conger headed into the Marines for the tail end of World War II. Upon returning, he simply wasn't the same pitcher. He pitched until 1950 but never again with his pre-war effectiveness.

After he retired from the game, Conger, according to *The Big Book of Jewish Baseball*, worked in the *Los Angeles Times'* stereotyping department and then died at just 48.

13. Mike Saipe
Bats Right, Throws Right
Colorado Rockies, 1998

Mike Saipe was so close to a storybook debut. Pitching at home for the Colorado Rockies on June 25, 1998, he'd allowed just three runs over six innings at the pre-humidor offensive cauldron that was Coors Field. With one out in the ninth, the Rockies led 5–3. "I know anything can happen in this game, but when there was one out in the ninth, I sort of smelled it that I could come out with a W," Saipe told *The Denver Post* that evening.

But then destiny met Dave Veres, who served up a game-tying home run to Derek Bell. It was as close as Saipe would come to a victory in the big leagues. Saipe was crushed in his second start at Seattle, allowing home runs to Mariners sluggers Edgar Martinez, Ken Griffey Jr., and two to David Segui.

But let's not focus on the negatives. Here's Saipe, to *The Denver Post* back when he got the call-up, on June 25, 1998. "I'm not going to be able to express the way I feel," he said. "I've never had this feeling before. It's obviously the high point in my life. This is reaching the top of my profession. This is what everybody's goal is. So, am I excited? Yeah, I'm really excited. But I haven't thought too deep about it because I'm living it."

No sympathy necessary for Saipe, who also, it should be noted, won 67 games in the minor leagues. He briefly got to live out his dream. Veres may have taken away his victory—and Veres, who blew 36 saves, was no stranger to the feeling—but Saipe knows he succeeded for one night on the highest level.

14. Leo Fishel

Bats Right, Throws Right
New York Giants, 1899

According to the excellent SABR biography by Jane Jacobs, Leo Fishel, son of Leopold and Theresa and the pride of Babylon, New York, gave up his youthful dreams of major league success in order to pursue a career as a lawyer. It is hard to argue with the idea that in a different financial time for baseball, Fishel might have chosen differently. According to the Jacobs bio, Fishel was once offered $20 to pitch a single semi-pro game for a White Plains, New York, team against (presumably) archrival Tarrytown—at the time he was renting his law office for $7 a month.

He received a mixed review for his one professional starting effort, which took place on May 3, 1899. *The Sporting News* said the following of Fishel in the May 6, edition: "He has good curves but was a bit unsteady in the second and fourth innings. Fishel gave the locals several chances to score by his wildness, but the team could not make hits when they were needed." The New York Giants lost 7–3 that day.

No such reviews would be possible for Fishel's law practice, which expanded, moved to Mineola, and allowed for Fishel to become town counsel for the town of Hempstead.

Fishel didn't let his baseball connections drop, according to Jacobs. In 1905 he coached Freeport High School. His shortstop, George Morton Levy, went on to become his law partner. I think it is safe to assume there was a dominant entry in any Long Island legal softball leagues for quite some time.

15. Jeff Stember

Bats Right, Throws Right
San Francisco Giants, 1980

Eighty-one years after one Jewish pitcher, Leo Fishel, made his major league debut for the Giants, another did so, this time for the San Francisco version of the franchise in the Astrodome. This time it was Jeff Stember, pride of Westfield, New Jersey, whom the Giants selected in the 26th round of the 1976 draft. He struggled with control—his evident talent and 6'5" frame masked by walks—until he had a breakthrough in 1980 with the Double A Shreveport Captains. "Big Jeff Stember, a hard-throwing 6-foot-5 right-hander, brought the Captains' woes to a quick end, silencing the red-hot bats of the Jackson Mets," Rick Thomas wrote in *The Shreveport Times*. "It was the fourth shutout for Stember, including his third against Jackson."

With future big league bats like Ron Gardenhire, Brian Giles, and Mike Howard, Jackson was no pushover team.

After performing similarly with Triple A Fresno, Stember got the call on August 5, starting against the Houston Astros. Stember struggled through the first three innings, walking a pair but had only allowed one earned run, thanks to a first-inning home run by Terry Puhl. The Giants trailed 3–1, however, as a Rennie Stennett error in the third had led to two more Houston runs.

With manager Dave Bristol managing for his job, he pinch hit for Stember, hoping Max Venable could come through with the bases loaded. Venable did, and the Giants went on to win the game, but Stember did not get the victory. Would Stember have been allowed to hit in a 1–1 game in the fourth? As Joaquin Andujar once infamously said, "There is one word in America that says it all, and that one word is, 'You never know.'"

Ten days later Stember was optioned back to Phoenix. His performances dipped in Triple A in 1981, and by the spring of 1982, he still hadn't found himself as a pitcher. "He's got a good arm but no consistent release point,"

Giants pitching coach Don McMahon told the *San Francisco Examiner*. "One ball may go way high, and the other ball may go way low."

McMahon knew what he was seeing—in Stember's final season in Triple A, he pitched to a 7.43 ERA with more walks than strikeouts.

11

Left-Handed Relievers

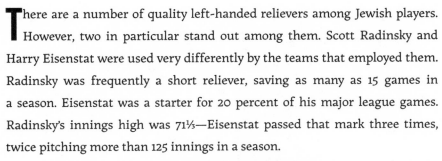

There are a number of quality left-handed relievers among Jewish players. However, two in particular stand out among them. Scott Radinsky and Harry Eisenstat were used very differently by the teams that employed them. Radinsky was frequently a short reliever, saving as many as 15 games in a season. Eisenstat was a starter for 20 percent of his major league games. Radinsky's innings high was 71⅓—Eisenstat passed that mark three times, twice pitching more than 125 innings in a season.

But both pitchers were extremely effective. Radinsky's ERA+ over his 481⅔ innings was 118; Eisenstat's ERA+ over 478⅔ innings was 116. I give Eisenstat the edge for three reasons. 1) Because 20 percent of Eisenstat's games, and well over 20 percent of his innings, came as a starting pitcher, his ERA is certainly higher than if he'd simply been just relieving.

2) Eisenstat was traded straight-up for Earl Averill, a Hall of Famer. Although Radinsky was quite valuable, no one was ever trading a Hall of

Famer for Radinsky. So that gives us a sense of his perceived value during his career. 3) At the end of his career, Radinsky went on to sing lead for Pulley, a punk band. At the end of his career, Eisenstat fought in World War II, rising to the level of second lieutenant to help defeat the Nazis. Now, this may be my anti-punk music bias showing, but I am hard-pressed to think of a single punk album that rises to the level of defeating the Nazis. I can even expand it further to any album ever made. Though I think Frank Sinatra's concept albums were transcendent, I still believe defeating the Nazis was a larger accomplishment than "Come Dance with Me." So the edge goes to Eisenstat there, too.

1. Harry Eisenstat

Bats Left, Throws Left
Brooklyn Dodgers, 1935–1937
Detroit Tigers, 1938–1939
Cleveland Indians, 1939–1942

On the final day of the 1938 season, with America's Jews riveted on Hank Greenberg's pursuit of Babe Ruth's single-season home run record, Harry Eisenstat, pride of James Madison High School (where he also excelled in basketball) in Brooklyn, New York, almost made history of his own.

Greenberg stood at 58 home runs, two short of the Babe's 60, entering the final day of the season, which called for a game against the Cleveland Indians. Greenberg was facing Bob Feller, who was kryptonite to his home run hitting. And Feller was on, striking out 18 Detroit Tigers on the afternoon.

Harry Eisenstat was better. Eisenstat beat the great Feller 4–1. It was not the type of game conducive to a home run chase—Greenberg finished with 58. But had Eisenstat turned the trick, he'd have produced the first no-hitter in Jewish baseball history. Instead it was—who else?—Sandy Koufax who notched Judaism's first no-no on June 30, 1962—though if we're being literal, Judaism's first no-no was "Do Not Have Any Other Gods Before Me."

Eisenstat lost likely more than half of his total career to World War II. He had a fantastic season for Cleveland in 1942, posting a 2.45 ERA over 47⅔ innings for an ERA+ of 140 before entering military service.

It's also worth pointing out that while Greenberg sat out Yom Kippur to honor his faith, Eisenstat did, too. "We felt there might be some resentment from the fans, but there wasn't," Eisenstat recalled years later to the *Orlando Sentinel*. "They understood."

By 1945, according to the Utah Historic Quarterly, he was still in the service, playing for a Provo, Utah, semipro team between deployments and displaying such control that his catcher, Don Overly, described even "his bad pitches are so close to being good that they could be called the other way." But a disastrous exhibition outing against the New York Giants late in spring training 1946 led to Cleveland releasing Eisenstat.

Eisenstat had a rewarding post-baseball life, moving to Shaker Heights, Ohio, and opening a hardware store. His wife, Evelyn, was married to him for 64 years when he died in 2003.

2. Scott Radinsky

Bats Left, Throws Left
Chicago White Sox, 1990–1993, 1995
Los Angeles Dodgers, 1996–1998
St. Louis Cardinals, 1999–2000
Cleveland Indians, 2001

Given the medical hurdles Scott Radinsky faced, his career is nothing short of a modern miracle. Radinsky was highly regarded coming out of Simi Valley High School in California, striking out 180 hitters in just 100⅔ innings, then selected as a third-round pick in the 1986 draft by the Chicago White Sox, 30 slots ahead of Bo Jackson. As the *Los Angeles Times* put it in June 1986: "Most major league scouts on the West Coast knew as much about him as they did about their wives and children."

Radinsky eventually excelled in the minors after his first two years were marked by control issues. During his 1989 in A ball, he had a 1.75 ERA, 83 strikeouts in 61⅔ innings for South Bend of the Midwest League, earning him a shot at making the 1990 White Sox out of spring training, and he did just that—riding his skateboard to the ballpark from his Chicago apartment much to the amazement of observers.

Radinsky had a solid rookie year, though his first half was far better than his second half—his ERA jumped from 2.12 prior to the break to 9.82 afterward. But in 1991 Radinsky was effective all season long, putting up a 2.02 ERA in 71⅓ innings for an ERA+ of 198. No less an authority than the baseball writer Peter Gammons said Radinsky would be the next great closer in baseball.

He followed with a similarly effective 1992—2.73 ERA in 59⅓ innings—but his performance dropped off in 1993.

Although it can't be known what role it played, a likely reason for Radinsky's reduced effectiveness could well have been that he had Hodgkin's disease, which cost Radinsky the 1994 season. "Rad was a guarantee," White Sox pitching coach Jackie Brown told the *Chicago Tribune* while pondering how the White Sox would replace him in the spring of 1994. "He was for sure."

He returned in 1995 but posted a 5.45 ERA and struck out just 14 in 38 innings, well off his career norms. He took a pay cut of nearly 50 percent and returned to his hometown Los Angeles Dodgers in 1996, and there his early-career effectiveness returned. Radinsky posted three fantastic relief seasons in a row, pitching in an average of 65 games per season with ERAs of 2.41, 2.89, and 2.63. Even in pitcher-friendly Dodger Stadium, that was good for ERA+ marks of 163, 135, and 154. Three seasons of elite relief pitching would be impressive enough—to do so as a cancer survivor only multiplies the impact of his performance.

Radinsky finished his career with the St. Louis Cardinals and Cleveland Indians and even battled back from Tommy John surgery to play a final season with Calgary of the Pacific Coast League. And while he has continued in baseball, serving as a pitching coach for numerous minor league teams and major league coaching stops in Cleveland and Los Angeles, his musical career may have eclipsed his pitching one. Here's how Peter Gammons described Radinsky in a March 10, 2008 post on his blog: "Scott Radinsky's band, Pulley, has released its ninth CD, available online. Radinsky, now a pitching coach in the Indians organization, is one of the sport's most interesting people and likely a very good future major league pitching coach. He had a successful major league pitching career and earned more than $11 million. He has a very successful musical career. He owns a popular skate park in Los Angeles as well as a skate equipment company. He doesn't need baseball; he loves it and especially enjoys working with young pitchers."

Relief pitchers, lefties especially, have a reputation for being complicated. But this isn't Sparky-Lyle-sit-naked-on-a-birthday-cake complicated. Radinsky is, by any standards, a renaissance man.

3. Craig Breslow

Bats Left, Throws Left
San Diego Padres, 2005
Boston Red Sox, 2006
Cleveland Indians, 2008, 2017
Minnesota Twins, 2008–2009, 2017
Oakland Athletics, 2009–2011
Arizona Diamondbacks, 2012
Boston Red Sox, 2012–2015
Miami Marlins, 2016

Craig Breslow took the clichéd double-major-in-molecular-physics-and-biochemistry-at-Yale path to the major leagues. (In my companion book, *The Molecular Physician Baseball Talmud*, Breslow ranks at the top of virtually every list.) He was the first Eli to make the major leagues since Ron Darling.

As you can tell from his majors, Breslow was going to live the Jewish mother's dream and become a doctor. But as he told Baseball Prospectus in a December 18, 2006, interview, "That was the contingency plan if baseball didn't work out, but it kind of gets tucked further away as I have more success. I guess it still is, but hopefully I'll have 15 years in the game and I won't have to think about it for awhile. That said, I've always felt strongly about medicine, and it's something I'll keep as an option. We'll see when the time comes."

That's essentially what happened. Do not mistake his travels for ineffectiveness. Breslow pitched 570⅔ innings at an ERA+ of 122. He was particularly brilliant for the 2013 Boston Red Sox. With a 1.81 ERA, he was a critical part of a bullpen that won the World Series. He struggled with command early in his career. Back in 2008 he was 13th among lefty relievers. Now he's third.

4. Richard Bleier

Bats Left, Throws Left
New York Yankees, 2016
Baltimore Orioles, 2017–2020
Miami Marlins, 2020–present

He is a late bloomer, but Richard Bleier is putting together a career that could make him the finest left-handed reliever in Jewish baseball history when he's finished playing.

Bleier, son of Lawrence and Kathleen and pride of Plantation, Florida, stayed in state and played at Florida Gulf Coast University, where he was a teammate of Boston Red Sox hurler Chris Sale. The Texas Rangers selected him in the sixth round of the 2008 Major League Baseball draft, but his low strikeout rates kept him from drawing much attention, while leading to a fluctuation of his ERAs thanks to the vagaries of balls in play luck.

Here's how the great John Sickels graded Bleier, as a C prospect, in *The Baseball Prospect Book 2010*: "A strike-throwing ground ball machine, he hits his spots within the zone with an 88-90 MPH sinker...He also has a decent slider and change-up...watch for any improvement in his K/IP. If he handles [Double A], he could be a number four starter."

Over three-plus years with the Double A Frisco Roughriders, his K/9 never reached 5.0. He ran into similar patterns after the Toronto Blue Jays selected him in the minor league portion of the Rule 5 draft and then when he moved to the Washington Nationals system in 2015. His control kept him in pro ball—his lack of swing-and-miss pitches led to him languishing.

He signed with the New York Yankees in 2016, hoping a new organization—and one that valued analytics—might view his outlier control differently. And they did—calling him up to the majors finally in 2016, where Bleier was very much himself. Pitching out of the bullpen, however, his 1.96 ERA and 5.1 K/9 reflected an ability to convert his fastball, which averaged 90.9 MPH, without losing any of his absurdly good command.

He did much the same thing for three seasons with the Baltimore Orioles, posting a pair of seasons with ERAs below 2.00 in 2017 and 2018 and walking just 25 in 151⅓ innings from 2017 to 2019.

The Miami Marlins brought him home to Florida in 2020, and though his ERA rose a bit in 2021 to a still-strong 3.05, he also managed to increase his K/9 to 6.8, suggesting he is getting better, and in a sustainable way, even in what is his age-34 season, typically a period of decline in a player's career. A cutter that's turned into his put-away pitch is key. Nor has his improved swing-and-miss come at the expense of his control—in 58 innings Bleier has walked *six* hitters.

Bleier pitched for Team Israel in the 2013 World Baseball Classic but not in 2017 or the 2021 Olympics, since MLB players can't participate. "It was really appealing to me to do it again," Bleier said in 2017. "I wanted to represent Israel in the Classic. But I feel like I have such a small window at this point in my career. I didn't get to the big leagues until I was 29. I felt I should do whatever I could to get as much big league time as I can with what little time I have left."

Heading into 2022, it doesn't seem like that time is short after all. FanGraph's Dan Szymborski ZIPS projects him to pitch to a 3.74 ERA in 2022, but even that may reflect comps who had a different path and career arc than Bleier's unconventional one. He's also accumulated 5.4 WAR, trailing Harry Eisenstat's 6.6, Scott Radinsky's 6.5, and Craig Breslow's 6.0 but blowing them out of the water on ERA+—148 to Breslow's 122, Radinsky's 118, and Eisenstat's 116. Now that he's here in MLB, a career that takes him into his late-30s at his current level of success or close to it will make him the clear leader among Jewish lefty relievers.

5. Scott Schoeneweis

Bats Left, Throws Left
Anaheim Angels, 1999–2003
Chicago White Sox, 2003–2004
Toronto Blue Jays, 2005–2006
Cincinnati Reds, 2006
New York Mets, 2007–2008
Arizona Diamondbacks, 2009
Boston Red Sox, 2010

Coincidentally, Scott Schoeneweis, like Scott Radinsky, is a left-handed relief pitcher that has survived both cancer and Tommy John surgery to become an outstanding major leaguer. In essence, the difference between Radinsky and Schoeneweis is that while both were devastating against lefties, Radinsky handled righties nearly as well, while Schoeneweis struggled mightily against them.

Schoeneweis grew up in South Jersey as I did, even played for Lenape High School in Medford, which is a conference rival of my own high school. Going on to Duke, he had a sensational freshman year followed by a diagnosis of testicular cancer that spread to his lymph nodes. Through aggressive chemotherapy—he told the *New York Post* on October 18, 2002, that he "took six months of chemotherapy in three months"—he was able to return to the baseball team the following year—where he promptly blew out his elbow, requiring Tommy John surgery.

Either of these problems could have ended another person's career—and the cancer could have done much worse than that. But Schoeneweis instead returned to form his senior year, graduated with a degree in history, and was drafted in the third round of the 1996 draft by the Anaheim Angels, four picks ahead of Washington Nationals first baseman Nick Johnson and 19 picks ahead of Bishop Eustace High School's Blaine Neal of Marlton, New Jersey. (It was a good draft for South Jersey pitchers.)

It isn't quite clear why it took the Angels so long to make Schoeneweis into a reliever—he didn't have a tremendous amount of success as a starter in the minors. After he went 7–10 with a 5.45 ERA in 2000 as a starter for the Angels, they promptly tabbed him as Opening Day starter in 2001. He started well in 2001 with a 3.04 ERA in his first eight starts before allowing 11 runs in start No. 9, the first Angels starter ever to allow that many runs in one outing. "At least I'll be in the record books for something," he told reporters after it was over.

He went 10–11 with a 5.08 ERA in 2001 and 6–6 with a 5.38 ERA as a starter in 2002 before being moved to the bullpen—where he pitched to a 3.25 ERA as the Angels won a World Series.

Schoeneweis' Achilles heel was right-handed batters. His line against lefties stood at .229/.304/.309, while against righties he was at .294/.368/.470. Years after teams had discovered this, his 2007 manager, Willie Randolph, used him repeatedly against righties, subjecting him to unjust booing from the Shea Stadium crowd, even as he put up his customary .204/.308/.247 line against left-handed batters.

Schoeneweis has a terrific sense of humor and was one of the more enjoyable interviews in the New York Mets clubhouse. When I talked to him early in 2008, he claimed he didn't hear cheers, but the absence of boos at the start of what was a far more effective year for the Mets was "kind of eerie. You get used to it, I guess. It's like people who live in the city and move to the country, how they can't sleep nights."

As usual, there is truth behind every joke. Schoeneweis' difficult hand dealt to him by life continued in 2009, when his wife, Gabrielle, died of a drug overdose at 39. Schoeneweis retired in 2010, largely to be a full-time single dad to his three children. Schoeneweis, as effective as a lefty specialist as he's ever been, has weathered far worse than an angry Shea crowd.

6. John Grabow
Bats Left, Throws Left
Pittsburgh Pirates, 2003–2009
Chicago Cubs, 2009–2011

If Terry Bradshaw is the favorite son of Pittsburgh, then John Grabow certainly holds the title for the Pittsburgh suburb of Squirrel Hill, which is host to 16 Jewish congregations and nearly half-Jewish, according to a September 12, 2007, article in the *Pittsburgh Tribune-Review*.

Grabow told Jonathan Mayo of JewishSports.com in 2004 that he welcomes the attention of the Jewish community and even his appearance in the Jewish Major Leaguers Baseball card set. "That would be something that would be cool," Grabow said. "My grandmother would really like that. And she'll get a kick out of the card."

Grabow was drafted in the third round of the 1997 draft ahead of Eric Byrnes, Chone Figgins, and Xavier Nady. He spent five fitful years in the minors, however, before the Pittsburgh Pirates realized he was a reliever in 2002. By 2003 he'd reached the big leagues to stay.

Grabow was a fixture in the Pirates' bullpen for six seasons and over that time posted an ERA+ of 105. But he was more valuable than that would suggest. For one thing, he is reasonably effective against both lefties and righties with an OPS below .800 against both. That matters for matchup reasons, even though Grabow's career ended a decade before the minimum three batter rule was instituted. A plus change-up helped keep righties honest in the manner of John Franco's career.

For another, though he has a fine strikeout and walk rate, he does pitch to contact a good bit in front of what have been poor defensive teams year after year. Errors alone do not account for the lack of range exhibited by many Pirates fielders during Grabow's tenure. On a better team, Grabow's ERA+ would certainly have been better.

7. Ryan Sherriff

Bats Left, Throws Left
St. Louis Cardinals, 2017–2018
Tampa Bay Rays, 2020–2021

Ryan Sherriff grew up in Culver City, California, with maternal grandparents who'd survived the Holocaust. The St. Louis Cardinals grabbed him in the 28th round of the 2011 draft, where he put up intermittently solid results but never all that impressive until he decided to drop his arm angle in 2016. By 2017 he'd reached Busch Stadium and struck out better than a batter per inning with a 3.14 ERA in his first shot at the major leagues.

Unfortunately, Tommy John surgery followed an elbow injury that ended his 2018 season in May, and the Cardinals released him. Tampa Bay, a place for many wayward pitching projects, signed him. And since joining the Rays, he's managed to cobble together a sinker/slider arsenal into an effective approach, especially against lefties. He got a number of key outs in the 2020 World Series, pitching against his late father's favorite team, the Los Angeles Dodgers.

He's also battled mental health issues and even stepped away from the game briefly in 2021. He pitched on a talent-laden Triple A Durham Bulls team in 2021, then returned to the Rays in August, helping them win an American League East title. That he did it while living honestly and fully in the public eye makes him so easy to root for. He's 31, and Dan Szymborski's FanGraphs ZIPS projects him to have a 4.64 ERA in 2022, so stardom is likely elusive. But those aren't the stakes, really. And Sheriff knows it. "I also want people to know this: understand that athletes are people, too," he told *Sports Illustrated* in 2021. "And please treat people with decency. That's a good place to start."

8. Steve Rosenberg

Bats Left, Throws Left
Chicago White Sox, 1988–1990
San Diego Padres, 1991

Steve Rosenberg, pride of Coral Springs High School in Florida—where he starred in football as a quarterback, basketball as a point guard, and baseball as a center fielder—moonlit as a reliever in his sophomore year at Broward County Community College. That earned him a scholarship from University of Florida to pitch, which turned him into a fourth-round pick by the New York Yankees in the 1986 draft.

He made quick work of his stop in Low A Oneonta with a 1.00 ERA in 10 innings and earned a promotion to New York's High A team: Fort Lauderdale of the Florida State League.

That meant living at home, eating his mother's cooking. "Okay, this is my career now, but I still think of it as a game, where I go out there, play, and have fun," Rosenberg told Sharon Robb of the *Fort Lauderdale News* in July 1986. "The only difference now is I'm getting paid for something I love to do. How lucky can you get?"

The Yankees tried to leap him over Double A entirely, sending him to Triple A Columbus, but after middling results there, they sent him down to Albany-Colonie of the Double A Eastern League, where he pitched to a 2.25 ERA. This being the 1980s Yankees, no developmental failure would be complete without a rushing of prospect followed by a trading of prospect for a player whose best days were behind him, and so Rosenberg was on his way to the Chicago White Sox in a five-player deal that sent Richard Dotson to New York.

By the spring of 1988, national baseball reporter Peter Pascarelli had two White Sox prospects listed as "Players to Watch" in his season preview: Jack McDowell, who went on to win 127 games and the 1993 AL Cy Young, and Rosenberg. The White Sox gave him a clear shot at a bullpen role, but he faltered in spring training and got sent down to Triple A, finally debuting in June.

Rosenberg performed moderately well as a classic middle reliever for Jim Fregosi, pitching to a 4.30 ERA in 46 innings for an ERA+ of 93. Fregosi was replaced after the 1988 season by Jeff Torborg, who elected to move Rosenberg into his starting rotation in late May 1989, filling big shoes: Jerry Reuss, winner of 220 career games, was sent to the bullpen to make room for Rosenberg. By the end of his second start, he'd impressed Torborg. "He pitched super," Torborg told the *Chicago Tribune*

Overall, the numbers did not bear out Torborg's early optimism: a 4–13 record, 4.94 ERA on the season. By 1990 he was back in the bullpen, primarily for Triple A Vancouver. He finished his career with the San Diego Padres, who acquired him in a deal for Joey Cora, then in the New York Mets' system. He threw 209⅔ innings of 4.94 ERA baseball in his career.

We nearly had a second member of his family here—the St. Louis Cardinals signed his son, Dante, as an undrafted free agent in 2014. Alas, he topped out at High A Palm Beach, though like his dad, he had a chance to play less than an hour away from his Coral Springs home.

9. Marv Rotblatt

Bats Both, Throws Left
Chicago White Sox, 1948, 1950–1951

In today's era Marv Rotblatt probably never would have gotten the chance to pitch at the major league level due simply to his height. Baseball-Reference.com lists him at 5'7"; an April 25, 1951, profile of Rotblatt in *The Sporting News* lists him at 5'8".

The diminutive Rotblatt was remarkable for his time, but there were other exceptions to the tall pitcher rule, such as Bobby Shantz, who stood just 5'4". But by the 2021 season, just one pitcher, Marcus Stroman, was listed at 5'7". No one else is shorter than 5'10", among those with at least 50 innings pitched in 2021, and only 17 more hurlers are 5'10" or 5'11". Every other major league pitcher is 6'0" or taller.

But Rotblatt's change-up, called "the best I've ever seen" by then-manager Paul Richards, was his ticket to the big leagues. Rotblatt was, like Augie March, Chicago-born; he then earned a degree in journalism at University of Illinois. He had brief stops in the majors in both 1948 and 1950, throwing a combined 27 innings—he seemed to put the minors in his rear-view mirror in 1950, when he posted a 22–9, 2.67 ERA with Memphis of the Double A Southern Association. "Best advice about pitching success I ever heard came from Hugh Mulcahy while I was at Memphis," Rotblatt said in that same *TSN* profile. "Be able to get your breaking stuff over the plate when you're behind and you'll be a winning pitcher."

The problem with Mulcahy providing advice on being a "winning pitcher," of course, is that his nickname was Hugh "Losing Pitcher" Mulcahy, and his career record was 45–89. Rotblatt posted a 3.40 ERA in 47⅔ innings for an ERA+ of 120 but never reached the majors again, with limited success in minor league seasons at outposts like Memphis, Atlanta, Allentown, and Topeka.

Rotblatt's legacy has outlived him—he died in 2013—with an annual softball game named in his honor played at Carleton College in Minnesota. Rotblatt received this recognition for obscure reasons—a student there had a baseball card of his—but Rotblatt accepted an invitation to come play in the event and even homered. Considering his willingness to play along, it is a shame it appears the episode Rotblatt appeared on *You Bet Your Life*, the great Groucho Marx game show, has been lost to history.

10. Syd Cohen

Bats Both, Throws Left

Washington Senators, 1934, 1936–1937

Syd Cohen, brother of Andy, was a man of changing identities. He began his professional career as an outfielder but became a pitcher. He started his collegiate career as a member of the Crimson Tide but became a Southern Methodist Mustang. Playing in the United States, he was Syd Cohen; when he played in Mexico, he changed his name to Pablo Garcia.

Cohen pitched parts of three seasons in the major leagues, posting ERA+ marks of 59, 91, and 144. But despite the improvement and a career ERA+ mark of 100 in 109 innings, he never saw major league action after the age of 31. He did pitch in the minors until age 49, even returning to Mexico 19 years after he appeared as an outfielder and once again under the name Pablo Garcia.

By any name, Syd has a legacy: he was the final American League pitcher to strike out Babe Ruth and owned Lou Gehrig—the great New York Yankees first baseman struck out three times in 17 plate appearances against Syd.

11. Aaron Poreda

Bats Left, Throws Left

Chicago White Sox, 2009

San Diego Padres, 2009

Texas Rangers, 2014

Boy, it looked for a minute there like Aaron Poreda was going to be the next great Jewish lefty. Son of John and Barbara and pride of Moraga, California, Poreda is an intimidating 6'6" on the mound and touched triple digits with his fastball when the Chicago White Sox selected him 25th overall in the 2007 Major League Baseball Draft.

He immediately jumped into the top three on most Chicago prospect lists and was 63rd in all of baseball by 2009, according to *Baseball America*: "Poreda finished his first full season in Double A and then displayed one of the most impressive arms in the Arizona Fall League. General manager Kenny Williams refused to give him up when the Rockies wanted him in a proposed Brian Fuentes trade—a high compliment given Williams' willingness to deal prospects. Poreda's calling card is his fastball, which generally parks in the mid-90s and has touched 100 mph. White Sox coaches have helped him develop a power slider, and while it isn't a plus pitch, it does keep hitters from sitting on his fastball. He throws strikes easily and is built for durability. Poreda still is refining his slider, and he doesn't have a lot of trust in his rudimentary change-up. His fastball straightens out at times, making him hittable. To succeed against big leaguers, he'll have to learn how to change speeds and possibly develop a cut fastball, a weapon favored by White Sox pitching coach Don Cooper. Poreda's AFL performance was so good that he forced himself into consideration for Chicago's 2009 staff."

Williams did get around to trading him, though, making him the centerpiece of a 2009 trade deadline deal for Jake Peavy. Poreda, pitching for both Chicago and the San Diego Padres, showed off his raw talent—12 strikeouts, but 13 walks, in 13⅓ innings.

But the command got worse, deserting him to the tune of 64 walks in 54 innings, first in Triple A, then after a demotion to Double A. By the end of 2011, he'd been left off the 40-man roster by San Diego, and the Pittsburgh Pirates tried to pick him up and salvage his career. He then blew out his elbow, had Tommy John surgery, and missed a year.

Despite all of this, his evident talent was so clear that he got another chance with the Texas Rangers in 2014, who sent him to Triple A Round Rock. His command had returned, so on April 19, nearly five years after his last big league appearance, he turned up in relief for the Rangers. Poreda pitched to a 3.20 ERA through July 3, but four straight outings in a week allowing runs after that ended his big league career, and the Rangers optioned Poreda to Triple A.

He elected to sign with the Yomiuri Giants of Japan in 2015 and finished his career with two solid seasons in the Nippon Professional Baseball league.

12. Tony Cogan

Bats Left, Throws Left
Kansas City Royals, 2001

Tony Cogan did not give up. He first reached the major leagues in 2001 but kept on fighting to get back until retiring in February 2010. Much of his late-career heroics came with the Gary South Shore Rail Cats of the independent Northern League, which sent a number of players to the major leagues. He posted a 2.77 ERA and 25 saves in 2007 as Gary's closer and pitched effectively in 2008 as a starter for the Rail Cats. Even in 2009, his final active season, he won eight games, pitched to a 3.60 ERA, and tossed his first career shutout.

Ironically, he reached the major leagues on an expedited timetable—a strong spring in 2001 earned him a big league job with the Kansas city Royals, though he'd thrown only a handful of innings above Class A. "To tell you the truth, I came into camp confident that I could do well," Cogan told *The Kansas City Star* in March 2001. "My goal was to make the team."

He did as a swingman. Alas, Cogan did not impress in his 24 big league innings with Kansas City, posting a 5.84 ERA in 24⅔ innings with 13 walks and 17 strikeouts. His ERA+ was 83, and even for a pitching-starved team like the Royals, that wasn't enough to get it done.

Weep not for Tony Cogan, however: the Stanford grad with an economics degree is now a wealth manager for William Blair.

13. Andrew Lorraine

Bats Left, Throws Left
California Angels, 1994
Chicago White Sox, 1995
Oakland Athletics, 1997
Seattle Mariners, 1998
Chicago Cubs, 1999–2000
Cleveland Indians, 2000
Milwaukee Brewers, 2001

Andrew Lorraine, like Tony Cogan, is a product of Stanford University who struggled to find regular major league work. Lorraine's last major league outing came in 2001, but he kept at it through the end of the decade, throwing 24 innings for the 2009 Orange County Flyers of the Golden Baseball League, playing for manager Phil Nevin and alongside major leaguers like Robert Fick, Damian Jackson, and Brian Lawrence.

Still, Lorraine made his mark along the way, pitching a complete-game shutout for the Chicago Cubs on August 6, 1999, the first Jewish pitcher to do so since Steve Stone on June 21, 1980.

As for his distinctive name, it was Levin, according to a September 22, 1999, article in the Jewish World Review. But his paternal grandfather, serving in the Alsace-Lorraine section of France during World War II, liked Lorraine so much he changed his surname.

By any name, his career ERA of 6.53 in 175 major league innings did not live up to the billing he enjoyed as a fourth-round pick by the California Angels in 1993 ahead of guys like Paul Bako, Scott Spezio, and Mark Loretta.

Lorraine did find a large measure of success in the minor leagues, however—his career line is 104–80 with a 4.21 ERA, and with the lion's share of those innings coming in the hitter-friendly Pacific Coast League, that is even more impressive than it sounds.

14. Ed Mayer

Bats Left, Throws Left
Chicago Cubs, 1957–1959

It took Ed Mayer five years to reach the big leagues—and shortly after he did, his arm gave out. But he's far from bitter about this. Mayer, a Cal-Berkeley product who grew up in San Francisco, chased his major league dream from 1952 to 1957 in San Jose, California; Yuma, Arizona; Greensboro, North Carolina; Montgomery, Alabama; Omaha, Nebraska; Rochester, New York; and Fort Worth, Texas. Along the way, he said he faced anti-Semitism everywhere from the fraternities at Cal to comments about his religion from teammates and opponents alike. But Chicago Cubs manager Bob Scheffing loved another minority group he belonged to—lefties.

After Mayer's mediocre start and two solid relief appearances in 1957, the Cubs converted him into a full-time reliever in 1958, and he made the club out of spring training. On April 17, 1958, he converted his only save opportunity, pitching one-and-two-thirds scoreless innings to help Chicago edge the St. Louis Cardinals 4–3. "Mayer forced pinch-batter Hal Smith to hit into a double play in the eighth inning and pitched himself out of a jam in the ninth," the *Chicago Tribune* reported the next day.

But by June in three of his final six appearances, he failed to retire a batter, and the Cubs sent him down. "I pitched to the June cutdown date," Mayer said. "By then my arm was starting to be not so good. The Cubs noticed it. Fortunately, they sent me to Portland, and that was the end of my big league career."

Mayer claimed that he took a test in college that concluded he didn't want to be anything professionally, but he managed just fine after his baseball career ended. Not only did he teach in middle school for 25 years, but his crossword puzzles have appeared in *Games* magazine. Still, the brief, shining major league moments for Mayer were captured on his vanity license plate: "OLD CUB."

15. Matt Ford

Bats Both, Throws Left
Milwaukee Brewers, 2003

Matt Ford was a victim of his own success. After a successful high school career in Coral Springs—at Taravella, though, not Steve Rosenberg's alma mater, Coral Springs High—he was a third-round pick in the 1999 draft by the Toronto Blue Jays, two picks ahead of Hank Blalock, two picks after Josh Bard. Ford was slowly making his way up the Toronto organization's ladder, winning an ERA title for Dunedin of the high A Florida State League with a 2.37 ERA in 118 innings. That attracted the attention of the Milwaukee Brewers, who drafted Ford in the Rule 5 draft.

The Rule 5 draft allows major league teams to select anyone not on another team's 40-man roster—with the proviso that the team must keep the player on the major league team all season or offer the player back to his original team. So Ford, rather than continuing his development, found himself making the jump from A ball to the major leagues. Ford quickly impressed his general manager—"Ford has shown he can pitch," Doug Melvin told reporters that spring—and pitched pretty well, particularly considering the circumstances of his debut. In 43⅔ innings, Ford put up a 4.33 ERA for an ERA+ of 100, league average. For context Johan Santana, who made a similar jump after becoming a Rule 5 selection by the Minnesota Twins, pitched 86 innings with a 6.49 ERA for an ERA+ of 80.

But Ford was not able to find his way back to the major leagues. Despite a solid 3.94 ERA with Double A Huntsville of the Southern League in 2004, the Brewers released Ford. He pitched to a 2.61 ERA with Triple A Omaha after signing with the Kansas City Royals, and Kansas City let him go. After his numbers dipped to a 4.50 ERA in 2006 with Triple A Rochester of Minnesota's system, Ford couldn't get a position in affiliated baseball and pitched in the underrated independent Atlantic League for the Bridgeport Bluefish, then the Schaumburg Flyers of the Northern League, to no avail.

16. Bob Tufts

Bats Left, Throws Left
San Francisco Giants, 1981
Kansas City Royals, 1982–1983

Like Craig Breslow, Bob Tufts is another Jewish player with an Ivy League pedigree with an undergraduate degree from Princeton and MBA from Columbia. Here is what the Jewish Ivy League team would look like:

C Moe Berg (Princeton)

P Craig Breslow (Yale)

P Bob Tufts (Princeton)

P Leo Fishel (Columbia)

P Bob Davis (Yale)

So you'd need a lot of strikeouts. But you'd have the pitching depth to do it.

Tufts is a member of a number of select groups. He is also one of the Jewish players who converted to Judaism, finding inspiration in his study of the Holocaust while at Princeton.

We lost him too soon—I had the privilege of getting to know him a bit, and he was a delightfully funny character in person and on Twitter alike. Sadly, he suffered from multiple myeloma and died in 2019 at just 63.

Tufts' ERA also fails to do him justice. Although he posted an ERA of 4.71 in 42 major league frames for an ERA+ of just 84, he struck out 28 in those 42 innings and walked just 14. It was his batting average against of .328 that kept him from major league success. Strangely enough, his batting average against when facing righties was .328, and when facing lefties, it was...328. That doesn't seem coincidental, that must be the work of...a witch!

And it was. Tufts told Murray Chass of *The New York Times* on September 21, 2005, that "I have a relative [Elizabeth Morse] who was the first woman tried and convicted of witchcraft in Essex County [Newbury, Massachusetts, in 1680]."

Fortunately, Tufts embraced Judaism more than witchcraft (as far as we know), even traveling to Israel in 2006 to teach the game of baseball, along with fellow Jewish convert Elliott Maddox, according to April 19, 2007 edition of the *New Jersey Jewish News*. Let's just hope nobody got the wrong idea when they saw him floating in the Dead Sea.

17. Roger Samuels

Bats Left, Throws Left
San Francisco Giants, 1988
Pittsburgh Pirates, 1989

If Roger Samuels had come along 20 years later, he'd have been a favorite of statheads everywhere. His strikeout rate, combined with his lack of major league chances, would have made him a cause celebre. There'd be Free Roger Samuels websites, he'd be mentioned by any stat-savvy fan of a team that needed bullpen help, and his failure to find major league work would be roundly cited as proof that major league teams had no concept of how to put together a bullpen.

In 692⅓ minor league innings, Samuels struck out 536 for a relatively good strikeout rate of 7.0 per nine. But through age 26, that was even higher at 7.08 per nine innings. He stood out among his peers, too. For Triple A Phoenix in the PCL, a hitter's haven, he pitched to an ERA under 3.00, while no teammate of his pitched to an ERA below 5.00.

That earned him a trial with the San Francisco Giants when Mike LaCoss got hurt in July 1988, and he showed he belonged immediately with two hitless innings in his debut. By season's end, Samuels struck out 22 in 23⅓ innings, walking just seven. His ERA was a respectable 3.47 for an ERA+ of 96, and the Pittsburgh Pirates saw enough to deal veteran infielder Ken Oberkfell for Samuels.

But Samuels got just five games and three-and-two-thirds innings to prove himself in Pittsburgh and he pitched to a 9.82 ERA for the Pirates. He returned to the minor leagues, where he posted good strikeout rates and even reduced his walk rate considerably, which had been the one factor holding him back. Samuels put up a 2.83 ERA for Triple A Tidewater in the New York Mets' system in 1990, then left the game. Apparently, there was no room for a strikeout pitcher with improving control who stood 6'5".

If only he'd come along even a bit later, he might have revived his prospects in the independent league scene that emerged in the mid-1990s. He'd get inspirational emails from numbers crunchers, and some team might have taken another shot on him. Instead, Samuels fell short of what might well have been a solid major league career. By all indications, far lesser relievers have spent far more time in the major leagues.

18. Moe Savransky

Bats Left, Throws Left
Cincinnati Reds, 1954

Moe Savransky could have been a classmate of Ronald Patimkin, the older brother of Brenda in Philip Roth's *Goodbye, Columbus*. Savransky played baseball and basketball at Ohio State from 1948 to 1953. Considering that Brenda was an undergraduate in the story, Ronald was her older brother, and the book was released in 1959, Roth was writing it in the period of 1956–1958. That places Ronald right in the middle of Savransky's time there. Of course, the fact that Patimkin is fictional makes it unlikely that their paths crossed.

But it gives you an idea of what it meant for Savransky to be the star of Ohio State's baseball team, leading the Buckeyes to the College World Series in 1951. I like to think somewhere there is a record with Bill Stern's voiceover extolling the virtues of Savransky.

Professional players could do both at that time, so even as he starred for Ohio State, he was winning 11 games with a 2.92 ERA for Triple A Buffalo. Stardom loomed—Savransky threw a mid-90s fastball, along with a classic 12-to-6 curve.

But while Roth himself missed the Korean War, serving in 1955–56, Savransky's development time was interrupted by the Forgotten War in 1952–1953. There is no question he came back from the service as a different pitcher. In 1951 for Buffalo of the International League, Savransky pitched 185 innings with a 2.92 ERA. To put that in perspective, Tom Acker, who went on to pitch four league-average seasons in the big leagues, was at 3.69.

When Savransky returned, he spent 1954 with the Cincinnati Reds, posting a 4.88 ERA in 24 big league innings. The Reds sent him to Triple A Charleston in 1955—he put up a 5.44 ERA in 134 innings. Picked up by Seattle of the Pacific Coast League near the end of 1955, he declined further—6.14 ERA in 14⅔ innings—even with a Jewish batterymate in Joe Ginsberg.

It's no surprise—given how a surgeon botched his arm and, eventually, his career. "I had bone chips in my left elbow because my manager...when I was in the minor [leagues]...got me to throw a screwball and I threw it and threw it and I got bone chips," Savransky said, according to his SABR bio. "They were bad, they were hurting me, so I finally had them operate on it. It's a simple operation, they go in there, cut the fat away, take the chips out. He took my... tendon and he pinched it from both sides and cut it down the middle."

Wonderfully, Savransky is still with us at the age of 92, as this book goes to press, and follows the modern game closely. With proper medical care, it would have been fun to see what would have come of his career.

19. Mike Milchin

Bats Left, Throws Left
Minnesota Twins, 1996
Baltimore Orioles, 1996

Mike Milchin, a hard-throwing lefty, was drafted in the second round of the 1989 draft by the St. Louis Cardinals, 33 picks ahead of Tim Salmon, 43 ahead of John Olerud, and 74 picks ahead of Jeff Bagwell. And had Milchin stayed healthy, the preceding sentence might not have seemed so crazy.

Milchin helped the U.S. Olympic Team to a gold medal in 1988 with a 4–1 record, two saves, and a 1.93 ERA. His strikeout rate at Clemson rose to 11.54 his senior year—and in his rookie season with Hamilton of the New York-Penn League, it stood at 10.02.

But it came steadily down as he faced more and more injuries. He broke a toe, his shoulder gave him problems, his knee required surgery—his career was like asking your Great Uncle Sidney, "So what's new?"

By the time he got to the major leagues, his ability to strike out hitters was still there—29 in 32 innings—but his command disappeared, as he allowed six home runs, 28 runs, 44 hits, and 17 walks in those innings with the Minnesota Twins and Baltimore Orioles.

Milchin is now an agent with ISE Baseball, an agency that represents some of the premier talents in baseball, such as Justin Verlander, Miguel Cabrera, and Jose Abreu. With some luck on the injury front, Milchin could have been on that list, too.

20. Gus "Happy" Foreman

Bats Left, Throws Left
Chicago White Sox, 1924
Boston Red Sox, 1926

A strong argument can be made that players in the old days enjoyed playing more than they do today. I cite not increasing salaries or simple nostalgia, but the undeniable fact: 16 players had "Happy" as a part or all of their nicknames in major league history, and not one of them played after 1952.

Among the Happys, Foreman ranks around the middle of the pack—far behind Happy Jack Chesbro, who made the Hall of Fame, and standouts like Happy Felsch, Happy Al Milnar, Happy Archer McKain, Happy Townsend, and, of course, the Happy Rabbit, Stan Rojek, known informally as The Last of the Happys.

But Foreman's 11⅓ major league innings at an ERA+ of 137 puts him ahead of Happys, ranging from Happy Pat Hartnett to Happy Iott, who was also known as Biddo. Strangely, while Happys have fallen off, there has not been a corresponding rise in Grumpys—zero in major league history, at least officially. (Hard to understand how Barry Bonds avoided that tag.) The age of the Sleepys came much earlier—of the four sleepys, Sleepy Bill Burns was the most modern and he last played in 1912.

Bashfuls and Sneezys have never made the major leagues either, which is predictable—Bashful would probably take too many pitches, while Sneezy is asking for trouble, picking a profession primarily played on grass (and during spring and fall allergy season!) And the absence of Dopeys, in such a cerebral game, is certainly for the best.

And, as should surprise no one who saw the leadership role he provided to the Seven Dwarfs, there have been 85 Docs, stretched across seemingly every era of Major League Baseball. Roy Halladay had the nickname Doc most recently, while All-Stars ranging from Dwight Gooden to Doc Cramer have the honorary medical title.

Anyhow, Happy Foreman, son of Sam and Tillie, Russian Jewish immigrants both, pitched to a strong 2.63 ERA in his pro debut with the Clarksdale Cubs of the Class-D Mississippi State League. The year 1922 found him showing up in various semipro games from Bastrop to Monroe, Louisiana, the former an eventual home for Black Sox like Joe Jackson and Eddie Cicotte, and the latter was where he won a Labor Day doubleheader, pitching both games.

"Happy Foreman was beyond the shadow of a doubt the star of the game," *The Monroe News-Star* wrote after one such performance.

Foreman won 14 games in 1923 for the Decatur Commodores and prepared to do even better the following year, writing to the sports editor of *The Shreveport Times* in January 1924 on the occasion of signing his contract with the Gassers that he was in Hot Springs, Arkansas, "taking baths and climbing mountains, getting ready to give battle for my position."

The waters worked: he won another 16 between Shreveport and Beaumont in 1924. Reportedly, Shreveport gave him up when he wanted to start more games, and he returned to beat his old team, a local reporter putting it thus: "If it gives Gus Foreman a feeling of great exaltation to chastise the Gassers, his goblet of happiness ought to be brimfull." Foreman hit .366 as well, part of a lifetime of capable batting.

After drinking deeply from his goblet, he joined the Chicago White Sox in September of the 1924 season but only pitched four garbage-time innings. He did, however, travel with the White Sox for an exhibition game against the Giants in London and met the future King George VI.

Despite struggling to a 5.85 ERA in 1925 with the Fort Worth Cats of the Class A Texas League, the pitching-starved Boston Red Sox signed him in 1926, and he pitched to a 3.68 ERA over seven-and-one-third innings. Foreman continued in minor league ball for the remainder of the decade in outposts like Bloomington, El Dorado, and Peoria.

21. Bud Swartz

Bats Left, Throws Left
St. Louis Browns, 1947

Imagine being 18-year-old Bud Swartz, high school pitching phenom from Los Angeles, so young when the St. Louis Browns bid and won his services in July 1947 that he had to make the trip with his mother. The Browns won the bidding in part because Swartz's father, Arthur, was a scout for them and in part because St. Louis allowed him to come to the big leagues immediately, a mixed blessing for sure.

Arthur was also known as Bud, leading to Don Larsen noting he was signed by one Bud Swartz (the father) and played alongside another Bud Swartz (the son).

Sure, in raw numerical terms, Bud Swartz's major league career, in which he allowed four earned runs and seven walks in five-and-one-third innings, was not a success. In fairness to Swartz, he was just 18 when he got his only big league shot. At a more age-appropriate stop the following year—the Class B Springfield Browns of the Three-I League—Swartz pitched to a 3.71 ERA in 114 innings.

However, Swartz is one of only 351 major leaguers to post a career batting average of 1.000 with one hit in one at-bat. The undefeated batting record didn't carry over into his minor league career, where he hit just .164. After his baseball career ended, Bud The Younger went on to run grocery stores, restaurants, and even dabbled in real estate back home in California.

22. Herb Karpel

Bats Left, Throws Left
New York Yankees, 1946

In the midst of an impressive minor league career that saw Herb Karpel win 120 games as a starting pitcher—seven times reaching double figures in victories and three times posting full-season ERAs at 2.53 or below—Karpel was summoned to New York to pitch for the Yankees in April 1946. His first appearance was an unqualified success: summoned by manager Joe McCarthy (no, not that one) with the bases loaded in the eighth inning of a game against the Washington Senators, he induced Buddy Lewis to pop up to Joe Gordon, ending the threat.

Asked to do the same thing the next day, this time a bases-loaded jam in the seventh inning, it...did not go as well. Mickey Vernon doubled in two runs. Lewis got his revenge, tripling. Stan Spence hit a sac fly, Cecil Travis hit an RBI single, and Karpel's ERA was 10.80. The Yankees sold him outright to Newark, and though he posted a 14–8 record, 2.41 ERA, winning the International League's ERA title, it wasn't enough to bring him back.

Let's just take a moment and look at what it meant to win the International League's ERA title in 1946. Jackie Robinson of the Montreal Royals played in the IL. So did Eddie Joost of Rochester, Hank Sauer of Syracuse—such a fearsome slugger, there's a gate named after Sauer at the stadium where the Syracuse Mets play. Future All-Star Eddie Robinson hit 34 home runs with a .983 OPS in the IL that year. And Karpel needed to outpitch hurlers like Billy Pierce and Art Houteman to win this award—it was not purely a hitter's league.

That he never pitched in the big leagues again is not a reflection on Karpel nearly as much as it is the extremely small margin for error any pitcher had in a time of no guaranteed contracts, permanent ownership by one team due to the reserve clause, and 16 small pitching staffs.

In today's game, Karpel, after six seasons in the minor leagues, would become a free agent and likely would draw interest from teams short a starting pitcher, which is basically everybody. But instead, Karpel resumed his stellar minor league career, and the major leagues never heard from him again—he finished out his career in the PCL with Seattle, then Hollywood. By 1952 he was in Bellingham, Washington, playing semipro ball.

23. Rob Kaminsky

Bats Right, Throws Left
St. Louis Cardinals, 2020

I'm not sure it's possible for me to express how exciting a prospect Rob Kaminsky was for me specifically. Kaminsky grew up in Englewood Cliffs, New Jersey, son of Donna and Alan, and he pitched at St. Joseph's Regional High School in Montvale—all a stone's throw from my house. He was simply dominant. Most of his senior season in 2013 was devoted to figuring out whether—and this is not hyperbole—he'd give up a run. I thought maybe I'd been misremembering, but no! "Struck out a season-high 16 against Wayne Hills on Saturday," *The Bergen Record* reported in April 2013. "Improved to 4–0 with that 4–1 win, still has a 0.00 ERA, and has 54 strikeouts in 26 innings."

He was the Shohei Ohtani of Bergen County, too: that same paper notes he was 9-for-13 at the plate that week.

Kaminsky was obviously a major disappointment his senior season. A late dip raised his ERA all the way up to…0.10. It had been 0.20 his junior season, a season *The Record* said, "North Jersey baseball junkies will be talking about… for a long, long time." Somehow his senior season was better! The St. Louis Cardinals convinced him to forego the full ride to North Carolina by selecting him in the first round of the 2013 draft, so a future loomed where he'd even get to hit with the National League playing by the correct, no-DH rules.

Kaminsky got his first taste of pro ball with the Gulf Coast League Cardinals and pitched to a 3.68 ERA, but that dropped to 1.88 in Class A Peoria in 2014. I was working on a book about the Cardinals at the time, and the thought that I could feature a Jewish lefty from New Jersey who'd celebrated a baseball-themed Bar Mitzvah and whose hero was Sandy Koufax was almost too exciting to contemplate. This is a man with a blog post titled "What New Jersey Means To Me" on his personal website. This is my guy, I don't know how else to put it.

Kaminsky had a 2.09 ERA with high A Palm Beach in 2015, when at the trade deadline, the Cardinals sent him to Cleveland for Brandon Moss, needing an extra power bat for their stretch run. "For my first couple of years as a minor leaguer, I was part of one organization; then one night around midnight, I got a phone call and just like that I was officially with a second organization heading toward an entirely different part of the country," Kaminsky said in a 2017 piece he wrote about life as a minor leaguer. "It's a tough pill to swallow so suddenly. And while that is certainly part of the job, I'd be lying if I said it doesn't take its toll. But, yes, we did sign up for it and we do get to enjoy the perks along the way—so what we learn to do is to swallow that pill as quickly as we can and refrain from whining. After all, this game goes on with or without you. Figure it out."

It was disappointing, but Kaminsky continued his steady rise, conquering Double A in 2016 in Akron, pitching to a 3.28 ERA with a three-pitch arsenal highlighted by his curveball that has looked big league ready back in high school. But when injuries cost him much of 2017, and his first brush with

Triple A led to a 5.11 ERA in 2019, it began to seem like Kaminsky might not even be in this book.

All of which made his minor league free agency, signing with the Cardinals, and their decision to promote him to the big leagues in 2020 such a contrast with...essentially everything else that happened in 2020, given, you know, the Plague. It was, in fact, a COVID outbreak that led to Kaminsky getting a roster spot in St. Louis. He pitched four-and-two-thirds innings with a 1.93 ERA, so he certainly did well with his opportunity.

But after a brief stint in Lehigh Valley, the Philadelphia Phillies' Triple A team, he was placed on the injured list, then let go in August 2021. I don't know, you guys. He's 26 years old as this book goes to press with a 2.81 career minor league ERA. He's a lefty who throws 90+ with three pitches. Dan Szymborski's FanGraphs ZIPS has him pitching to a 5.05 ERA next season with 38 strike-outs in 41 innings pitched. Scott Kazmir made a comeback this year at 37. If Kaminsky wants, he should keep trying. I think he's still got a chance to be a special major leaguer.

24. Brian Bark

Bats Left, Throws Left
Boston Red Sox, 1995

In the midst of a solid 1995 season for Triple A Pawtucket, Brian Bark received the reward many organizational soldiers receive: a call-up to the Boston Red Sox in July, getting the call after returning to his apartment in Pawtucket late one summer evening. "I was really surprised but very happy and excited," he told *The Boston Globe*.

He pitched three games with the Red Sox, allowed two hits and a walk, no strikeouts but also no runs. His last pitch in the major leagues came September 8, 1995, against the New York Yankees with two men on and Don Mattingly at the plate. Bark induced an inning-ending double play to get out of the inning. Not a bad way to go out.

25. Ed Wineapple

Bats Left, Throws Left
Washington Senators, 1929

Big Ed Wineapple could do it all. He was an excellent basketball player, an All-American for Providence College in 1929 after transferring from Syracuse, 50 years before the formation of the Big East. He crushed minor league pitching, too. He was a .288 hitter in 104 minor league at-bats, and seven of his 30 hits went for extra bases, including four home runs.

While the Washington Senators fell to the Detroit Tigers 16–2 on September 15, 1929, no one can claim that Ed Wineapple was the primary culprit among the Senators pitchers. Wineapple gave up just a pair of earned runs over four innings, walking three and striking out one. It was promising enough that a *Record-Journal* story on Washington's 1930 prospects included the phrase, "Maybe this new southpaw, Ed Wineapple, is just the man they need!"

Washington disagreed, sending Wineapple to Chattanooga as part of a 1930 odyssey that landed him in four cities—he never pitched in a regular season game for Chattanooga, then went on to New Haven, over to Harrisburg, and then finally to Elmira, where he played for fellow Jew Jake Pitler and the Colonels in 1931 as well.

12

Right-Handed Relievers

The talent level of Jewish right-handed relievers, as a whole, is not that deep. More than a score of Jewish righty relievers have pitched in the big leagues—just three of them have logged as many as 300 innings. But just as clearly, the finest of any Jewish reliever, regardless of throwing hand, is Larry Sherry.

Sherry was a hard-throwing rookie that became the dominant relief pitcher in the latter part of the 1959 season, a similar path to Francisco Rodriguez of the Anaheim Angels in 2002. Sherry got the chance to pitch in the World Series at the end of his rookie year and took home a World Series MVP award in the process.

Sherry's dominance and varied repertoire led many to think his future was as a starter. Ultimately, Sherry proved to be a far better reliever than starter with just a 4.44 ERA in games he began, 3.55 in games he entered in the middle of the action. And while that split is within range for the expected ERA split

Al Levine

between starter and reliever, early in his career, when he was in both roles, the numbers are stark. In 1959 Sherry posted a 3.10 ERA as a starter, 0.74 as a reliever. In 1960 he was at 5.56 as a starter, 3.46 as a reliever. And in 1961 he had a 3.40 ERA as a reliever—in his one start, he allowed six runs over two innings for an ERA of 27.00.

Al Levine is the other righty with a strong case—he posted six seasons with an ERA+ of 100 or better, as Sherry did, and Levine's career ERA of 3.96, once adjusted for park and era, puts him at an ERA+ of 118. Sherry's career ERA+ was at 102. But Sherry pitched 799⅓ innings, while Levine logged just 575⅓ or roughly 30 percent fewer innings. Sherry's ERA+ also suffers for his time pitching half his games in Dodger Stadium, but his numbers were no stadium mirage—he actually fared better away from home in his career (3.54 ERA) than at home (3.79 ERA).

Sherry's numbers also suffer from his 16 starts, and though the two pitchers pitched in an identical number of games—416—Sherry provided more value to his teams in those games with his additional workload. Add in his value as measured by his contemporaries—not only the World Series MVP in 1959, but Sherry also received a pair of MVP votes for his versatile 1960 season—and the edge goes to Sherry.

1. Larry Sherry

Bats Right, Throws Right
Los Angeles Dodgers, 1958–1963
Detroit Tigers, 1964–1967
Houston Astros, 1967
California Angels, 1968

In the Dodgers' defense, it is easy to see why it appeared that Larry Sherry had a chance to be a very fine major league starter. In 1957 Sherry led the Texas League in strikeouts as a starter and earned manager Walter Alston's praise in the spring of 1958. "Stan Williams may be faster, but Sherry's fastball has more life," Alston said in the March 26, 1958, issue of *The Sporting News*. "He showed me some pretty good stuff and he's come up with a fine change-up—something Williams doesn't have at all."

Considering that Williams went on to post a 3.56 ERA in 208 career starts, that Sherry was ahead of him developmentally says a lot. Even Sherry's relief outings showed starter potential. His August 15, 1959, performance earned him prominent mention in *TSN*'s August 26, 1959 "Hats Off" column. Replacing an ineffective Johnny Podres with one out in the first, Sherry pitched eight-and-two-thirds innings of scoreless relief for Los Angeles.

By the 1959 series, Sherry's "backup slider" was being praised by Dodgers coach and former manager Charlie Dressen. And while his relief work in the 1959 World Series earned him, according to *TSN*, "the Ed Sullivan show...two days later was on the Pat Boone Show," the Dodgers still tried to make him a starter.

Three other important notes about Sherry. He is a fine example of scouts over stats. In the minor leagues, his season as strikeout king in the Texas League was his only season with an ERA under 4.39. But the Dodgers clearly saw something in him that got him promoted after posting a 7.82 ERA in C ball, a 4.90 ERA in B ball, a 4.39 ERA in A ball, and even a 4.91 ERA in Triple A.

Sherry was a teammate of Barry Latman for Fairfax High School, which also produced Jewish catcher and Sherry's brother Norm Sherry. It is noteworthy that Sherry was one of the first Dodgers therefore to pitch in Los Angeles. He logged 20⅔ innings for Brooklyn's Triple A farm team in Los Angeles during Brooklyn's last season with the Dodgers.

Sherry went on to coach as well both for the minor league Seattle Rainiers and Major League Baseball stops in Pittsburgh and Anaheim.

One of my favorite aspects to Sherry's career is that he was born with club feet, but overcame this—did you know that Kristi Yamaguchi and Mia Hamm did as well? Clearly, we live in amazing medical times. But his father, who *The Sporting News* says was "a studio worker in the Hollywood film industry," described an emotional moment for him, a race Sherry ran in at age 10. "I had tears in my eyes as he ran the best he could to finish third," Sherry's father told *TSN*.

By high school he was a multi-sport star. Just an incredible story.

2. Al Levine

Bats Left, Throws Right
Chicago White Sox, 1996–1997
Texas Rangers, 1998
Anaheim Angels, 1999–2002
Tampa Bay Devil Rays, 2003
Kansas City Royals, 2003
Detroit Tigers, 2004
San Francisco Giants, 2005

There would have been a time when Al Levine's signing by the 2008 Newark Bears would have been hailed by a huge, vibrant Jewish community in the city. But the city, which once held 70,000 Jews and 50 different shuls, now has just one synagogue with a population of 300.

Still, between the Levine signing and the opening of The Jewish Museum of New Jersey in December 2007, it was a big year for Jewish Newark—Levine, in what proved to be his final active season, pitched to a 1.59 ERA. Levine had been out of baseball for two years before returning in 2008 and has a career line worthy of praise.

Al Levine is not only a Jew, but he is also a Saluki—the Chicago White Sox selected him in the 11th round of the 1991 Major League Baseball Draft out of Southern Illinois. Interestingly, even in college, he was already a reliever—his destiny was understood early on, though the White Sox tried to make him a starter for several years at stops like the Utica Blue Sox and Birmingham Barons, where he was a teammate of Michael Jordan's in 1994. But M.J.'s destiny was basketball, and Levine's the bullpen, as both realized by 1995.

The astounding thing about Levine's success is that he did it with an obscenely low strikeout rate. For his career, Levine struck out 4.4 batters per nine innings, which is among the lowest rates among modern relievers with his level of success. Nor did his walk rate stay extremely low—3.7 is above average. And even his batting average against wasn't particularly impressive—.270 is good but not great.

But that batting average against drops to .256 with runners in scoring position. With two outs and runners in scoring position, Levine's BAA falls to .220. If there was such a thing as a purely clutch pitcher, Levine would be it. Coming through with runners on base is what propelled him to an ERA+ of 118.

3. Jose Bautista

Bats Right, Throws Right
Baltimore Orioles, 1988–1991
Chicago Cubs, 1993–1994
San Francisco Giants, 1995–1996
Detroit Tigers, 1997
St. Louis Cardinals, 1997

And the winner of the most unlikely moniker for a Jewish player is...Jose Bautista! He narrowly edges Ruben Amaro Jr. No conversion here either—the product of a Dominican father and Jewish mother posted some sensational minor league seasons, along with a pair of terrific major league years in relief and another seven that ranged from competent to less so.

Bautista was signed by the New York Mets in 1981 at the age of 16. The Mets brought him along slowly and were rewarded for it, as Bautista put up a solid season in A ball, going 13–4 with a 3.13 ERA in 135 innings with Columbia in 1984. He followed it by going 15–8 with a 2.34 ERA for high A Lynchburg. The Mets then chose to make him repeat Lynchburg, and his ERA rose to 3.94. But by 1987 he posted a 10–5, 3.24 ERA season in the all-important jump to Double

A Jackson. His K-rate showed he wasn't yet ready for the majors—95 in 169 innings pitched—but at 22, he was a solid prospect.

The Mets at that time were so overstuffed with young pitching that they could not protect Bautista on the 40-man roster, so the Baltimore Orioles plucked him away in the Rule 5 draft. The 1988 Orioles, of course, had no reason to avoid wasting a roster spot on Bautista—the team started 0–21, meaning they were out of contention by Tax Day. But Bautista was put to work and acquitted himself well. The 6–15 record is indicative of little other than that Baltimore was terrible. He posted an ERA of 4.30, good for an ERA+ of 91—not bad for a rookie making the jump from Double A. As his manager, Frank Robinson, told *The Baltimore Sun*, "We're going to have to give him more runs." By April 1989 he was being talked about as a future star. "We had good luck with Bautista last year," Orioles general Roland Hemond said on the occasion of the following year's Rule 5 draft. Bautista, in other words, was a success story.

Bautista spent the next three years on the Triple A-MLB shuttle, gradually improving his walk rate at Triple A Rochester and pitching decently for the Orioles as a fill-in starter and reliever. He did not accept it calmly. Upon Bautista's demotion in June 1989, then-Orioles beat reporter Tim Kurkijan captured Bautista firing his hat into his locker in anger. Asked if he was upset about the decision, he replied: "What do you think?"

After two more years in Baltimore, he signed with Kansas City in 1992 but failed to make the big league club. But in 1993 the Chicago Cubs signed him, and he turned in one of the finest relief seasons any Jewish pitcher ever had. As a swingman he pitched 111⅔ innings of 2.82 ERA baseball for an ERA+ of 140. Though he struck out just 63, he was extremely stingy with walks, allowing just 27.

Bautista was good in 1994, though not as excellent as in 1993, posting a 4–5 record and 3.89 ERA. The performance earned him a two-year contract with the San Francisco Giants. By the bay, his performance suffered mightily in

1995—his ERA ballooned to 6.44—but recovered in 1996, as he posted a 3.36 ERA for a 121 ERA+.

Sadly, this turned out to be his last hurrah in the major leagues. After struggling in 1997 for both the Detroit Tigers (6.69 ERA) and St. Louis Cardinals (6.57 ERA), Bautista finished his playing career with two nondescript seasons in the minors.

Overall, Bautista's career totals—a 4.62 ERA in 685⅔ innings for an ERA+ of 87—don't really tell the tale. Bautista was often much better than that. Unfortunately for him, just as often, he was much worse. After he pitched in the minor leagues through the end of the 1990s, though, Bautista has passed along his wisdom in minor league coaching stops, including 13 years as pitching coach for the Kannapolis Intimidators in the Chicago White Sox system.

4. Sam Nahem

Bats Right, Throws Right
Brooklyn Dodgers, 1938
St. Louis Cardinals, 1941
Philadelphia Phillies, 1942, 1948

While Moe Berg gets the most attention among baseball's well-known intellectuals, attention should also be paid to Sam Nahem, who fit a major league career into a life filled with political and legal accomplishments.

Make no mistake about it: Nahem's politics did not help him to reach Moe Berg level fame. Nahem was a Communist, and at no point in his life could that have made life in America easy for him. It didn't stop him from serving ably in World War II and it didn't keep him from sustained major league success—walking too many batters did—although perhaps this was simply Nahem's way of sharing the wealth.

Nahem was a Brooklyn kid and signed with the Brooklyn Dodgers after completing his degree at Brooklyn College. By the time he was dealt to the St. Louis Cardinals in a trade that brought Ducky Medwick in return, Nahem had secured a pennant for the Class A Nashville Volunteers with a clutch performance in the Southern Association playoffs and he had passed the New York Bar. But Nahem, like Berg, did not have the inclination to practice law. "Time enough for the law," Nahem told *The Sporting News* on May 22, 1941, "after I make good in the big leagues." He went on to post a 2.98 ERA in 81⅔ innings for the Cardinals, though he walked 38 and struck out just 31. But the Cards dealt him to the Philadelphia Phillies. A year later, after posting a 4.94 ERA for the Phillies, Nahem entered the service and didn't reappear in the major leagues until 1948, where he closed out his career in Philadelphia. However, Nahem spent much of his service time playing baseball to entertain the troops in Europe and helped integrate the baseball teams that did so—insisting on Willard Brown and Leon Day, two Negro League stars, be part of his Overseas Invasion Service Expedition (OISE) All-Stars.

Nahem's life was only 32 years old when he last pitched in the big leagues, and he had miles to go before he slept. He was not an observant Jew—in Nahem's *San Francisco Chronicle* obituary, his son, Andrew, referred to Nahem and his brother as atheists: "My father rebelled against Hebrew school when he was 13."

But culturally Jewish, Nahem lived the ideal life of the politically progressive Jew. He married an art student, had three children, and the family moved to Berkeley, California, in 1964. He worked for Chevron Chemical, becoming a labor leader for the Oil, Chemical and Atomic Workers of America. According to his son Ivan, he said of Chevron, "We're all a bunch of intellectual Jews here and we're supposed to be proletarians." Little wonder Nahem and his family loved the Marx Brothers.

In his retirement, he still volunteered at the University Art Museum, and his companion described his cooking in complimentary terms. He may not have been the best pitcher in Jewish baseball history. Biblically speaking, perhaps he wasn't even the best Jew. But it is hard to imagine a better dinner companion in Jewish baseball history than Sam Nahem.

5. Lloyd Allen

Bats Right, Throws Right
California Angels, 1969–1973
Texas Rangers, 1973–1974
Chicago White Sox, 1974–1975

The 1968 draft was top-heavy on Jews—both Dick Sharon and Lloyd Allen were among the first 12 picks. Unfortunately, neither lived up to first-round billing, particularly Allen, who put up some good minor league seasons but pitched to a 4.69 career ERA in 297 innings—an ERA+ of just 71.

Allen went 12th overall in 1968. Just five picks later, the San Francisco Giants grabbed Gary Matthews. Thirteen picks after Allen, the Los Angeles Dodgers selected Bill Buckner. And 116 picks later, the Boston Red Sox nabbed Cecil Cooper.

Allen had some stellar performances en route to the big leagues. In 1969 he pitched to a 2.27 ERA with 126 strikeouts in 127 innings for San Jose of the Class A California League. That earned him a brief call-up in 1969, a slightly longer one in 1970, and he arrived in the majors for real in 1971. And his first full season was extremely successful—94 innings at 2.49 ERA for an ERA+ of 130. He struck out 72, walked 40. His 15 saves ranked seventh in the American League. "I decided he and Mel Queen would be my power right-handed pitchers in the bullpen," Angels manager Lefty Phillips told the *Los Angeles Times.* "If we were going to win this year, I felt I had to have Lloyd Allen."

But the drop-off in Allen's performance in 1972 and afterward seems like it has to be at least partially due to injury. His ERA jumped to 3.48, which meant an ERA+ of 84. He walked more batters than he struck out—and he only fanned 53 in 85⅓ innings. And his 1973 was far worse—a 9.42 ERA, 40 ERA+, 44 walks in 49⅔ innings, just 29 strikeouts, and a trade to the Texas Rangers.

Nothing changed in Texas or after being picked up by the Chicago White Sox either. He seemed to recover some of his form in 1976 with Double A Tulsa, winning 11 games and pitching to a 2.81 ERA with the walks down to just 56 in 154 innings. But he didn't get another major league shot. He pitched another three minor league seasons—in 1977–1978, a total of just 24 innings. So it appears an injury eventually caught up with him.

As always, it is impossible to predict the future of pitching prospects. Few examples are starker than Lloyd Allen, who started so bright and finished with a career ERA+ of 71.

6. Mike Koplove
Bats Right, Throws Right
Arizona Diamondbacks, 2001–2006
Cleveland Indians, 2007

A tremendously effective sidearmer, Mike Koplove, pride of Philadelphia, son of Steve and Joni, grew up a Philadelphia Phillies fan. He was at Veterans Stadium in 1990 when Terry Mulholland threw a no-hitter. He's Philly through and through.

He tried to make the Phillies in the spring of 2009 but wasn't quite able to make the cut. But his legacy was already secure by then from his six seasons of 122 ERA+ pitching with the Arizona Diamondbacks to a gold medal with USA Baseball at the 2008 Olympics. He didn't put the medal in the safe deposit box, he told the *Tucson Citizen* in 2002, because "Every now and then I just like to look at it."

Koplove only collected two saves in his major league career, but he didn't mind: "I love setting up," he said. "I'll actually get more innings as the set-up guy. I've set up more than I've closed and I'm pretty comfortable with that role."

Koplove concluded his career just over the Delaware River with the Camden Riversharks. Koplove is back home, scouting for the Phillies, tweeting at his favorite Philadelphia sports teams, and in 2019 was inducted into the Philadelphia Jewish Sports Hall of Fame.

7. Al Schacht

Bats Right, Throws Right
Washington Senators, 1919–1921

There have been 25 right-handed relief pitchers who were Jewish. But Al Schacht belongs to a more exclusive club—he is one of only three Clown Princes of Baseball recognized by the Baseball Hall of Fame.

Ralph Berger described Schacht's act in a SABR Biography Project: "He would come in with his battered top hat and ragged tails, blowing mightily on a tuba. Maybe he'd wield a catcher's mitt that weighed 25 pounds into which one could fit an entire meal. In fact, this zany guy once ate a meal off home plate." I have nothing to add to this.

Schacht is listed by Baseball-Reference.com at 5'11", 142 pouns, both of which appear to be generous, and still places Schacht as the 10th lightest pitcher since 1901. But on pure will, Schacht battled his way through the minors and put up a season that no one would be ashamed of in 1919 for Jersey City of the Double A International League—19–17, 1.95 ERA in 318 innings. The success finally got him a chance to play big league baseball with the Washington Senators.

In all, his three seasons were fairly successful. Though a collision at second base midway through the 1920 season supposedly ruined his arm, he still managed to put up successful lines in a pair of minor league seasons after leaving the major leagues. He finished with a 4.48 ERA in 197 major league innings with Washington, walking 61, and striking out 38. (Keep in mind that in 1921, only 10 pitchers had as many as 101 strikeouts.)

But Schacht became a performer for decades. During World War II, Schacht, according to Berger, did "159 stage shows, visited 72 hospitals and 230 wards, and traveled over 40,000 miles" in a two-month period. Then it was on to the Pacific theater. He performed at 25 World Series and wrote four books on the subject, including *Clowning Through Baseball*.

For all his clowning, this clown is recognized as a Clown Prince of Baseball by the Baseball Hall of Fame. But only Max Patkin (a Jewish minor league pitcher, by the way) of the Clown Princes of Baseball has been so honored by the International Clown Hall of Fame. Certainly, no fair-minded Clown Hall voter can claim with a straight face that Buttons the Clown, T.J. Tatters, and Bumpsy Anthony are all Clown of Famers, but Al Schacht isn't.

But at 6'7", what did Buttons have to do to prepare for the Big Red Shoe Review, other than show up in his normal footwear? Why should Patkin get the edge because he appeared in *Bull Durham*, while Schacht had passed away? Surely, there must be room in that Hall of Fame for this fine clown. When it comes to clowns, I'm not a small Hall guy. I want those doors to open and for honorees to come out, one after another, in an endless parade. To deny Schacht admission is a shot of seltzer to the face of every clown-minded individual in America.

8. Robert Stock

Bats Left, Throws Right
San Diego Padres, 2018–2019
Boston Red Sox, 2020
Chicago Cubs, 2021
New York Mets, 2021

Robert Stock was selected as a catcher with a strong arm in the second round of the 2009 Major League Baseball Draft by the Jeff Luhnow-led St. Louis Cardinals, but by 2012 it was clear he wouldn't hit enough to reach the big leagues as an everyday player, and St. Louis converted him to pitcher.

Stock, who incidentally is a plus-plus follow on Twitter, has spent much of the decade bouncing back and forth between affiliated and independent ball. He's never managed to bring down the walks sufficiently to take advantage of a solid ability to miss bats, but his heat is still sufficient to lead to cameos in each of the past four seasons.

Stock had a real opportunity, though, when he got called up by the New York Mets in July 2021 at a time when many other New York hurlers were injured. Unfortunately, he joined them, tearing his hamstring in his July 20 start, ending his season.

Stock will be 32 in 2022, and Dan Szymborski's FanGraphs ZIPS projects him to pitch to a 4.58 ERA with 46 strikeouts in 39⅔ innings. That's useful. His chances of shooting way up this list are still very much in play.

9. Wayne Rosenthal
Bats Right, Throws Right
Texas Rangers, 1991–1992

A big Brooklyn-born right-hander out of South Shore High School in Brooklyn, then to Queens for college at St. John's, Wayne Rosenthal was drafted in the 24th round by the Texas Rangers in 1986 and needed to prove himself. He had a big slider and a fastball but no expectation of dominance.

He did at every level—striking out more than a batter an inning at three different levels, including Triple A. He put up full-season ERAs of 0.73, 1.70, 2.05, and partial season marks of 2.22 and 2.40. On June 26, 1991, that led to a chance in the major leagues. His first hitter to face? Jose Canseco. "I didn't know what to feel—pumped up or scared," Rosenthal told Roxanne Mozes of *Newsday* later that year. "I walked him on four pitches."

But he came back to strike out future Hall of Famer Harold Baines, got Mark McGwire to fly out to right, and ultimately escaped the inning scoreless.

It sadly was not an omen. Rosenthal did not find that success in the major leagues. He put up a 1991 season with the Rangers of a 5.25 ERA in 70⅓ innings. His strikeout rate was good—7.8 per nine innings—but his walk rate was too high at 4.6 per nine. And after a rough start in 1992, he was dispatched to Triple A, where he posted a 5.69 ERA and was released. After posting a 4.80 ERA with Duluth-Superior of the independent Northern League, Rosenthal called it a career.

Rosenthal clearly had the ability to make hitters swing and miss and he's knowledgeable enough about pitching to have served as Miami Marlins pitching coach for several years, currently holding the position of minor league pitching coordinator. Given the current crop of young pitchers in Miami, that's some impressive work.

10. Alan Koch

Bats Right, Throws Right
Detroit Tigers, 1963–1964
Washington Senators, 1964

Alan Koch, pride of Demopolis, Alabama, and son of Hazel and Jacob, visited his parents in March 1963 after spending six months in military service. Then? "He left Sunday for Lakeland Florida to train with the Detroit Tigers," *The Demopolis Times* reported.

The home visit worked—he was assigned to Syracuse, won his first nine starts, and was 11–2 when the Tigers called him up in late June. He struggled in his brief time there, however, with a 10.80 ERA in 10 innings pitched, and after the Washington Senators purchased him in May 1964, things didn't improve much. Koch posted a 5.41 ERA over 128 career innings for an ERA+ of 70.

By the spring of 1965, Koch was part of the "New Breed" of baseball player, according to the March 13, 1965, issue of *The Sporting News*. Koch graduated from Auburn University, then returned during offseason to earn a master's degree in American history from Alabama. The column goes on to note that not only does fellow Washington pitcher Jim Hannan have a master's degree in business administration, but "The Senators could rank as the most intellectual club in the majors because coach Eddie Yost also has a master's degree in physical education."

Even this article sells the Senators short. Manager Gil Hodges was known as one of the smartest managers of his time. Second baseman John Kennedy won a Pulitzer Prize for the landmark book *Profiles in Courage* and guided us through the Cuban Missile Crisis. And nobody can approach the size of infielder Don Zimmer's head. So how did the smartest team in baseball finish? Ninth place, 62–100. A little Nuke LaLoosh might have helped.

Koch chose to return home to Decatur over a 1965 assignment to the Hawaiian Islanders of the Pacific Coast League and became an attorney. So that education certainly paid off.

11. Hy Cohen

Bats Right, Throws Right
Chicago Cubs, 1955

Hy Cohen's military service presented a different kind of challenge for his pitching development. Cohen posted a solid 16–10, 2.86 ERA season for Des Moines of the Class A Western League in 1951. But he missed 1952 and 1953 while serving in the military.

When he returned, clearly his pitching prowess returned as well. Cohen won the Western League ERA title for Des Moines in 1954, pitching to a 1.88 ERA to go along with his 16–6 record. He walked 53, struck out 100, and in the mind of Don Newcombe, who had served with him, Cohen was ready for stardom. "He's got more stuff than most major league pitchers right now," Newcombe said in the November 20, 1954, edition of *The Sporting News*. "His fastball is wicked, his curveball breaks very sharp and he has a more effective slider than most major leaguers. I'll be surprised if he isn't a consistent winner for the Cubs in 1955."

But to Newcombe's surprise, Cohen wasn't a consistent winner, though in his defense, he only got one start and six relief appearances before being sent down in June. His totals were uninspiring, however—17 innings of 7.94 ERA pitching, 10 walks, and just four strikeouts. And after being sent to Los Angeles of the Pacific Coast League, he was just 5–10 with a 3.60 ERA.

Now part of this may be the jump from A ball to the majors, and even the PCL was Triple A. But after a two-year layoff, Cohen threw a lot of innings in 1954—a jump to nearly 200 innings from zero. That jump may well have affected his pitching. At the very least, 1955 was likely the worst season for Cohen to make an impression on the heels of his 1954 total.

Cohen pitched several more seasons in the minor leagues, including a 1957 that saw him go 15–7, 2.72 ERA in the Double A Southern Association for the Memphis Chicasaws. But despite some brutal Chicago Cubs teams, Cohen never got a second chance.

Cohen went on to coach baseball at Birmingham High School in Los Angeles, winning a pair of city titles. Sadly, we lost him in 2021, a few months after he contracted COVID-19.

12. Keith Glauber
Bats Right, Throws Right
Cincinnati Reds, 1998, 2000

Keith Glauber was a 42nd-round draft pick. He exceeded expectations by even making it to the major leagues. Only two of the 42nd-round picks logged big league time in 1994—only once in the decade of the '90s did more than two 42nd rounders make it, and five times in the decade, none of the 42nd rounders reached the promised land.

A pair of shoulder surgeries ended his professional baseball career. He's a self-described "husband, father, and coach" now, and the latter two come together with his son Andrew, an excellent pitcher at Red Bank High School in New Jersey who is heading to Belmont Abbey College.

But the elder Glauber was more than just a 42nd-round draft pick prior to his injuries. Over eight minor league seasons, Glauber posted an ERA of 3.93, a strikeout rate of 7.25, and a walk rate of just 3.22. He allowed .66 home runs per nine innings. And in a pair of call-ups, he took his game to another level.

In 15 major league innings, Glauber posted a 3.00 ERA, striking out eight and walking just three. He did not allow a home run, and his ERA+ for his major league tenure was 158. It isn't clear what else the Cincinnati Reds could have expected from him or why he didn't receive more of a chance for Reds clubs that ranked tenth in the National League in ERA in 1998 and fifth in 2000. Unfortunately for Glauber, his performance suffered in 2001, when the Reds, 14th overall in the National League in ERA, almost certainly would have called upon him.

Maybe Andrew will do what Keith didn't and have a long major league career. I think Keith should've had a chance to enjoy one, too.

13. Justin Wayne

Bats Right, Throws Right
Florida Marlins, 2002–2004

Justin Wayne presented me with a terrific dilemma when he made his major league debut on September 3, 2002. Lured by the single-admission double-header as well as the promise of history, I was in the stands at Shea Stadium. With a loss in the first game, the New York Mets had a chance to set the National League record for most consecutive home losses. It would be on my conscience forever if someday my grandchildren asked about that moment, and I told them I was elsewhere.

But after the record was set, the Mets faced Jewish pitcher Justin Wayne in the nightcap. And so my loyalties were set against one another—was I more of a Mets fan or more of a Jew?

Ultimately, perhaps my wardrobe decided for me—I had on my Mike Piazza jersey but no tefillin. I decided on a rooting strategy that was, strictly speaking, a *shande* for the *goyim*. My reasoning was that Wayne, a top draft pick by the Florida Marlins, had a bright future ahead of him. So when the Mets knocked him out after four innings on the strength of home runs by Raul Gonzalez and Roberto Alomar, I decided to simply enjoy what was a rare positive offensive performance by my favorite team.

Unfortunately, the start was symptomatic of Wayne's difficulties in the major leagues. It should have been a red flag that if late-career Alomar could hit him, anybody could hit him. In 61⅓ major league innings, Wayne posted a 6.13 ERA with 36 walks and 37 strikeouts. He got hit hard as a starter (6.62 ERA) and as a reliever (5.53 ERA).

And oddly, even in the minor leagues, Wayne never approached his dominant strikeout numbers from his time at Stanford University. His strikeout ranged from 8.63 to 10.3 per nine innings as an undergrad against top competition but fell to 5.92 in his 547 minor league innings.

Wayne's post-baseball had a sad coda. He was sentenced to 40 months in prison in 2018 for committing insurance fraud.

14. Ed Corey
Bats Right, Throws Right
Chicago White Sox, 1918

Like Roy Hobbs in *The Natural*, Ed Corey made it to the big leagues as a pitcher, pitched very briefly, then years later surfaced as a minor league outfielder. Also like Hobbs, Corey was a successful minor league pitcher with a 2.68 ERA in 57 innings for the Double A Louisville Colonels in 1919—though he did pitch to a mediocre 4.50 ERA in two big league innings. A broken leg ended his 1918 season, however, and he never returned to the major leagues.

But unlike Hobbs, Corey didn't get to play outfield in the major leagues, topping out at Double A. He failed to literally tear the cover off the ball with a hit and, as far as I can tell, he didn't get shot by some crazy lady in black.

15. Ryan Sadowski
Bats Right, Throws Right
San Francisco Giants, 2009

The pride of Davie, Florida, and son of Elaine and Arnold, Ryan Sadowski got off to a roaring start with the San Francisco Giants after the team selected his contract from Triple A Fresno in June 2009, tossing six shutout innings to beat Ryan Braun and the Milwaukee Brewers 7–0.

By his second start, he was getting advice from Giants teammate Randy Johnson, according to the *South Florida Sun-Sentinel*, en route to another shutout performance. "Man, I'm playing with four All-Star pitchers," was all Sadowski could think as the Big Unit talked about ignoring the score.

Sadowski went to University of Florida before the Giants picked him in the 12th round of the 2003 draft. But it was a slow build to his big league cameo filled with barriers that would have ended other careers—arm surgeries, a subdural hematoma that led to brain surgery—all from a pro career that only happened after Elaine called all 30 teams to drum up interest in a tryout after Sadowski got buried on the depth chart at University of Florida. "They would laugh at me when I called, so I figured if my mom called, they'd be intrigued," Sadowski told Harvey Fialkov of the *South Florida Sun-Sentinel* in 2009.

Unfortunately, Sadowski struggled in his four starts after that and got sent to the minors by August. That winter, he headed to the Korean Baseball Organization, where he pitched three seasons for the Lotte Giants and found his next career, too: as an international scout for the Kia Tigers.

16. Harry Shuman

Bats Right, Throws Right
Pittsburgh Pirates, 1942–1943
Philadelphia Phillies, 1944

There is a story in *The Encyclopedia of Jews in Sports*, likely apocryphal, that Harry Shuman was signed to a contract after pitching batting practice as a lark for the Philadelphia Athletics while a Temple University law student. His throwing apparently impressed Connie Mack, who signed him to a minor league deal.

The story doesn't hold up, as Shuman actually pitched for Temple and came to Shibe Park in the summer of 1935 to get some work in. So he was clearly a pitcher already by the time Mr. Mack saw him. By the following spring, *The Philadelphia Inquirer* referred to him as "a redhead giant 20 years old," which sure sounds like someone more inclined toward top pitching prospect and less an unassuming law student.

However he got started, Shuman took a few years to figure out how to pitch, but something changed for him between 1938, when he posted a 3–6 record and 6.24 ERA for the Class B Richmond Colts of the Piedmont League, and 1939, when his record for Richmond improved to 17–12. Two seasons later, an 18–6, 2.24 ERA campaign with the Class B Harrisburg Senators earned him a shot with the Pittsburgh Pirates in 1942.

Even in the talent-diluted World War II majors, Shuman didn't have much success in the major leagues. In 50⅔ innings his ERA was just 4.44, and he walked 20 while striking out just 10.

Still, the Philadelphia product got the chance to pitch for his hometown Phillies in 1944. But when the Phillies sold him to Los Angeles of the Pacific Coast League, he decided to stay in his hometown. "We just had a baby, and he was making about $700 a month," said his wife of 57 years, Phyllis Rendelman Shuman, in *The Inquirer* obit on him in October 27, 1996. "He was a very, very good family man."

Shuman went on to work in a number of city jobs, including supervisor of sales tax collection for the Department of Revenue, which is probably the only person who gets booed in Philadelphia more than the team's players.

17. Izzy Goldstein

Bats Both, Throws Right
Detroit Tigers, 1932

When Hank Greenberg posted a monster 1932 season for the Beaumont Explorers of the Texas League, winning the circuit's MVP award, a Jewish star in the Texas town was old hat, thanks to Izzy Goldstein.

Goldstein, one of the three players in the Odessa-to-major league pipeline, had been the star of the 1931 Beaumont team. Goldstein led the team in wins with 16, put up a solid 3.58 ERA, and even contributed seven doubles and three triples at the plate.

Considering that Beaumont's home run leader just two years earlier had been a man named Easterling and a teammate of Goldstein's was named Christian, Goldstein likely stood out on that team, to say nothing of Beaumont's reputation for a small number of Jews. W.T. Block wrote in an article entitled, "A Brief History of the Early Beaumont Jewish Community: "Except for itinerant wagon peddlers, no other Jews are known to have arrived in Beaumont until 1878, when Morris J. Loeb moved his family here and opened a cigar store. Wolf Bluestein and J. Solinsky settled in Orange in 1876."

So when Greenberg explained that many fans in Beaumont told him that they'd never before seen a Jew, this wasn't hyperbole. Sounds like with Goldstein and Greenberg, they were still short of a *minyan*.

Unfortunately, Goldstein did not make the transition to Detroit as well as Greenberg. Given a chance to both start and relieve for the Detroit Tigers in 1932, Goldstein pitched to a 4.47 ERA in 56⅓ innings, which was good for a solid 106 ERA+ in the hitting-heavy 1932 American League. But he walked 41 in 56⅓ innings and struck out just 14. He continued to dominate in Beaumont, however, with a 1.58 ERA in 57 innings—he split his season between the two teams.

Goldstein pitched for the Toronto Maple Leafs of the International League in 1933, but his 9–7, 4.17 ERA season did not bring about a second major league trial.

Rob Edelman had a terrific line about Goldstein in an August 20, 2004 article on Jewish baseball players. A one-sentence summation of the life of Izzy Goldstein reflects the 20th century American-Jewish experience: "He was born in 1908 in Odessa, pitched in 16 games for the 1932 Detroit Tigers, and died in 1993 in Delray Beach, Florida."

18. Scott Effross
Bats Right, Throws Right
Chicago Cubs, 2021–present

19. Josh Zeid
Bats Right, Throws Right
Houston Astros, 2013–2015

This is a story really of how the Jewish baseball network helps players thrive. Josh Zeid had a brief career that included parts of two seasons with the Houston Astros. But he continued on as a pitcher for Team Israel, appearing in both the 2017 World Baseball Classic and the 2021 Olympics.

His day job is pitching coordinator for the Chicago Cubs, and that allowed him to be the point person when it was suggested to Scott Effross that he learn to throw sidearm. "I was in minor league camp and got into a couple of [big league spring] games and threw pretty well," Effross told Sahadev Sharma of The Athletic in September 2021. "That gave me more confidence before everything got shut down. I then just stayed at home and threw a ton of live BPs. I lived in Pittsburgh, and we had a really good group of guys, pro guys and college guys. I basically spent the whole summer twice a week throwing live BPs."

Of course, once COVID hit, he kept in touch with the Chicago assistant general manager and vice president of pitching on his progress: Craig Breslow.

It is a small but promising sample out of Effross. In 14⅔ innings he walked just two hitters and struck out 18, pitching to a 3.68 ERA. With early studies about the three-batter rule indicating that it isn't leading to a reduction in specialists, Effross may find himself with a career akin to someone like Joe Smith, a right-handed sidearmer who broke in during the 2007 season and was as effective as ever for the Seattle Mariners in 2021.

It's also a heartwarming reminder that not only are there Jews in baseball here in 2021, but they are also helping one another get better.

20. Sid Schacht

Bats Right, Throws Right
St. Louis Browns, 1950–1951
Boston Braves, 1951

Sid Schacht, who got a late start in professional baseball—due in part to World War II, followed by an extended illness of his mother's—was a tremendous minor league pitcher who struggled in his brief major league travels.

Schacht began his minor league career at age 29 with the Stamford Bombers of the Class B Colonial League—he'd pitched as Sergeant Sid Schacht for teams like the Aloe Field Snipers during the war—and immediately had huge success. Schacht went 18–7 with a 2.94 ERA in 190 innings. Repeating the level in 1948, Schacht improved to a 2.09 ERA. Moved up to the Eastern League in 1949, he had his best season, 19–5, a 2.44 ERA, and just 59 walks in 181 innings.

A fine spring earned him a spot on the 1950 St. Louis Browns roster, and this write-up in the March 29, 1950 issue of *The Sporting News* under the headline, "Another Chucking Schacht:" "He doesn't fit the pitchers' physical tape measure and he lacks the blow-'em-down fastball baseball men like to see, but rookie righthander Sidney Schacht stands a strong chance to make the Browns' hill staff on his strong spring showing. Poise and control, seldom seen in a young hurler, have caught the experienced eye of manager Zach Taylor." The article details such spring feats as striking out Ralph Kiner on three pitches.

Unfortunately, as spring turned to summer, Schacht's strikeouts turned to walks. He posted a 16.03 ERA over eight games, including a start, and was soon dispatched to Kansas City Blues of the American Association for more seasoning. Of course, he was already 32.

Returning in 1951, Schacht still couldn't get anybody out as a Brown, posting a 21.00 ERA. He was better for Boston after the Braves grabbed him off of waivers on May 13, but despite a 1.93 ERA in four-and-two-thirds innings, he accumulated two losses. Sent back to Milwaukee of the American Association, he finished 4–1, 4.09 and called it a career.

Schacht's career major league totals are ugly—21⅔ innings, 21 walks, 12 strikeouts, a 14.34 ERA for an ERA+ of 33. In the minors it is a different story: 55–29 career record, 2.84 ERA. That disparity, and the small sample size, leads me to believe Schacht with more time would have had more big league success. He was doing more important things, however, before his career began.

20. Moxie Manuel
Bats Right, Throws Both
Washington Senators, 1905
Chicago White Sox, 1908

Of the four baseball Moxies, he was the only Jewish Moxie, and I only hope it was said with affection, as in, "You have some moxie, kid, as a Jew playing the lion's share of your career in the turn-of-the-century South!"

Incredibly, Moxie Manuel, though I have him listed in the right-handed section, was in fact ambidextrous. A fan of his recalled in 1946 for *The Charlotte Observer*: "He was one of the leading pitchers of his day and he could pitch with either hand. He was one of the very best left-handers in the Southern [Association] and the very best right-hander. Often pitched doubleheaders, one with his left hand and the second with his right hand. In 1907 versus Memphis he pitched two 1–0 games, one each way." As someone who has covered the career of Pat Venditte closely, it brings me no small joy that a Jewish hurler helped pave the way for Venditte a century earlier.

Manuel made his professional debut in 1903 at age 22 for the Class D Vicksburg Hill Billies (no, seriously) of the Cotton States League. He went 14–12 and returned in 1904, improving to 21–11. Promoted to the Class A Southern Association, he went just 6–8 for New Orleans in 1905 but earned his first shot at major league time that September anyway. But he pitched to a 5.40 ERA in 10 innings for the Washington Senators, walking three and striking out three. In a depressed offensive year, that meant an ERA+ of 52.

But his name wasn't Give Up Easily Manuel. It wasn't Sigh of Resignation Manuel. So, he returned to New Orleans in 1906 and improved his record to 17–15. He jumped to 20–11 in 1907, and according to *The Big Book of Jewish Baseball*, even pitched to some left-handed batters with his left hand. An ambidextrous pitcher—*what moxie!* And that was good enough to get him another big league shot—this time with the Chicago White Sox.

Manuel was the primary reliever for the White Sox in 1908. But on a team with 107 complete games, this doesn't provide as much work as one might expect 100 years later. Manuel even threw three complete games himself and yet totaled just 18 games and 60⅓ innings. He pitched to a 3.28 ERA, which sounds very good, but in 1908 offensive terms—league average ERA was 2.31—it puts his ERA+ at 71. He walked 25 and struck out 25.

Clearly not sufficiently impressed, the Sox let Manuel head to Birmingham of the Southern Association. And though he went just 11–18 in 1909, Moxie Manuel didn't throw in the towel. He wasn't called Easily Surrenderable Manuel—somewhat because "surrenderable" isn't a word—but mostly because he had moxie.

So in 1910 Manuel went 18–14. And though he went 1–4 in 1911, he didn't get another major league call. And there is no record of Manuel pitching in professional baseball after that. Sometimes, you need more than moxie. You need a team that values moxie. In 1912, the Cleveland Indians needed some—they signed Moxie Meixell. They needed moxie. But they also needed an outfielder.

21. Steve Wapnick

Bats Right, Throws Right
Detroit Tigers, 1990
Chicago White Sox, 1991

Steve Wapnick, it must be said, played *Let's Make a Deal* with the Major League Baseball draft—and lost badly. He started with the car and ended up with the bag of popcorn.

He was selected in the second round of the January 1985 draft (the draft was divided into January and June phases then) by the San Diego Padres—but didn't sign. He was then drafted in the fifth round of the June 1985 draft by the Oakland Athletics—but didn't sign. In 1987 he was drafted in the 30th round by the Toronto Blue Jays and signed at last. I'd have cut my losses, too.

The sad thing is that the Blue Jays had a real steal in Wapnick, but an arm injury ruined what should have been a solid career as a major league reliever. Wapnick dominated at every level, putting up ERAs of 3.02, 2.05, and 2.24 in his first three minor league seasons to go with strikeout rates of 8.63, 10.29, and 8.05. Promoted to Double A, he posted an ERA of 0.49. Sent to Triple A, his ERA jumped—to 0.69. "I was sitting in the bullpen last night, and they were talking about how to pitch to Pedro Guerrero," Wapnick told Tim Brown of *the Los Angeles Times* in August 1989. "I thought, 'God, I'm only one step away.'"

But the Blue Jays hadn't put Wapnick on the 40-man roster, and the Detroit Tigers tried to stash him on the major league roster for a year, choosing him in the Rule 5 Draft. Wapnick's control deserted him there in 1990, and after seven innings, six strikeouts, but 10 walks—leading to a 6.43 ERA—along with the diagnosis of a heart murmur, Wapnick was returned to the Toronto system.

He had a solid 1991 season for Triple A Syracuse with a 2.76 ERA and 58 strikeouts in 71⅔ innings against just 25 walks. That led to the Chicago White Sox asking for him in a trade for Cory Snyder. In five late-1991 innings for the Sox, Wapnick's control abandoned him again—he had four walks in those five innings—but entering his age-26 season, his future appeared bright.

Sadly, injury seems to have curtailed his career. He didn't make the 1992 White Sox and put up subpar numbers at Triple A—in 71⅔ innings he walked 48 hitters, striking out 59, and had a 4.42 ERA. Signed by the Seattle Mariners, he put up worse numbers for Triple A Calgary—his walks dropped, his strikeouts dropped more, and the ERA rose to 4.96. At that point, Wapnick called it a career, though he did win Calgary's team award for most community involvement.

22. Conrad Cardinal

Bats Right, Throws Right
Houston Colt .45s, 1963

23. Larry Yellen

Bats Right, Throws Right
Houston Colt .45s, 1963-1964

Expansion teams take different approaches. The New York Mets, born in 1962, decided to bring back as many familiar New York names as possible with Gil Hodges, Duke Snider, Don Zimmer, and others on the roster during the team's first few seasons. The Houston Colt .45s, meanwhile, seemed to come up with a different plan, one that included this: let's stockpile young, untested Jewish arms. Larry Yellen and Conrad Cardinal were the fruits of this approach.

It's hard to say either approach was a success. The Mets lost 100 or more games each of the team's first four years. The Astros never lost 100 games but failed to win the National League West until 1980.

Cardinal and Yellen were both Brooklyn-born—Cardinal in March 1942, Yellen in January 1943. Cardinal was grabbed by Houston first after a solid first professional season with Jamestown of the New York-Penn League. Cardinal went 14–7 with a 3.74 ERA—in Class D ball. Houston signed him, and by April 21, 1963, he was making a start for Houston.

Needless to say, the jump from Class D to the majors didn't go well. Cardinal did not make it out of the first inning in his only major league start and gave up runs in five of his six major league appearances. This is unfair to put on him, however—no organization should promote a kid from Class D to the majors. In 13⅓ innings his ERA was 6.08 for an ERA+ of 52, and he matched his seven strikeouts with seven walks.

Cardinal returned to the Texas League, which still represented a huge jump—D ball to Double A ball. He held his own with a 4.26 ERA for San

Antonio to go with a 9–9 record. Sent down to A ball with likely a complete lack of confidence, he pitched poorly and by 1965 was out of baseball.

Buoyed by this success, the Colt .45s decided when they signed Yellen to have him essentially skip the minor leagues altogether. With just 99 innings with San Antonio under his belt—good ones at a 2.82 ERA, 74 strikeouts—Yellen got a September 26, 1963, start. He pitched pretty well, too—five solid innings, two earned runs, one walk, three strikeouts—against a Pittsburgh lineup that featured Roberto Clemente, Willie Stargell, and Donn Clendenon.

Suitably impressed, Houston decided to keep him with the big club in 1964. But Yellen just wasn't ready. In 21 innings he walked 10, struck out just nine, and posted a 6.86 ERA for an ERA+ of 51. Sent to the Oklahoma City 89ers of the Pacific Coast League, then to Amarillo of the Texas League, Yellen never again found the form that led the Colt .45s to originally rush him. By 1965 Yellen, too, had thrown his last pitch.

Any team that decides to stock the roster with Jews is okay by me. What the Colt .45s hoped to gain from this is unclear. Their rushing of young position players—which included Jewish third baseman Steve Hertz—did not prevent players like Joe Morgan, Rusty Staub, and Jerry Grote from extended major league success. But pitchers, as the stories in this text and everywhere else will make clear, need to be handled carefully. It is worth wondering what Yellen and Cardinal could have been with a slow, steady developmental process.

24. Steve Ratzer

Bats Right, Throws Right
Montreal Expos, 1980–1981

Steve Ratzer was a pitcher with fantastic control that saw his career minor league numbers, and quite possibly his best shots at the major leagues, compromised by playing the majority of his time in the thin air of Denver.

After playing at St. John's University, Ratzer, the pride of Paterson, New Jersey, signed with the Montreal Expos in 1975 as an undrafted free agent. He quickly made good use of his ticket to professional baseball, climbing from rookie ball to Double A in the span of two years. His numbers were stellar at each level, including 73 innings of 1.48 ERA pitching with Double A Quebec City of the Eastern League.

Then Ratzer met Denver, where Montreal had its Triple A farm team. In 1978 Ratzer posted a 7–10 record, 5.00 ERA in the Rocky Mountains. But let's put those numbers in context. Bryn Smith, who went on to a solid major league career, put up a 6.83 ERA in 1978 for Denver. Scott Sanderson, another solid major league pitcher, came in at 6.06. Need more? All but one regular in the Denver lineup had an OPS of .778 or better—and so did four bench players.

Ratzer spent three full years in Denver, improving each season, before he got a chance to pitch for Montreal. The key was his walk rate or lack thereof. He was at 1.96 walks per nine innings in his minor league career—but he dropped that number to 1.64 in his time with Denver. By 1980 he posted a 15–4 record with a 3.59 ERA.

But Ratzer, whose time in the major leagues lasted from October 1980 to May 1981, did not bring that walk rate up with him. In his 21⅓ career innings with the Expos, Ratzer walked nine, struck out just four, and had a lifetime ERA of 7.17 for an ERA+ of 51. Sent back to Denver, he continued to keep the walks down. But with a surplus of pitchers, Montreal traded Ratzer to the New York Mets for infielder Frank Taveras.

How Ratzer didn't get a shot with the 1982 Mets is utterly beyond me. While he posted an 11–7, 3.08 ERA season for Triple A Tidewater, the big club lost 97 games thanks mostly to a brutal pitching staff that ranked 11th in the National League in ERA.

Picked up by the Chicago White Sox for 1983, he was assigned to Triple A...which meant a trip back to Denver! His walk rate was again terrific—just 16 in 61⅔ innings—but his home run rate shot way up, and he posted a 6.75 ERA. How much of that was luck? Probably a lot. But it turned out to be his last season in baseball. Home after a long road trip, his two-year-old daughter,

Lauren, didn't recognize him. Ratzer decided that was enough time on the road.

Instead, he went into the restaurant business. At age 42 in 1996, he became a self-described "bagel guy" who owned his own shop.

25. Duke Markell

Bats Right, Throws Right
St. Louis Browns, 1951

Second only to Henry Bostick among the best gentile conversions of Jewish names is Duke Markell, born Harry Markowsky. But his middle name was Duquesne, and he came by the French honestly. Born in Paris, France, he was one of eight major leaguers from the City of Lights.

As a result, Markell could never be president of the United States, but he filled plenty of other roles. Markell was an International League ace, a police officer, and union agitator—which can't have helped his cause as he tried to get regular major league work.

Markell began his career with the Class D Hickory Rebels, posting a 5–2, 2.63 ERA season in 1945 over 82 innings. He broke out with a 19–9 record, 3.51 ERA in 1947 for Seaford of the Class D Eastern Shore League, but despite his solid efforts, he could get no higher than the Class A Utica Blue Sox for the remainder of the decade. Finally, after another 19-win season for the Class B Portsmouth Cubs, Markell got a chance to pitch for the Double A Texas League Oklahoma City Indians. His 13–19 record obscured a 2.77 ERA, and the pitching-starved Browns picked Markell up near the end of the 1951 season.

Markell got into five games, including two starts for the Browns. But like Sid Schacht earlier in the 1951 season, Markell did not come through on behalf of the Jews for the Browns. In 21⅓ innings, Markell walked 20, struck out 10, and pitched to a 6.33 ERA for an ERA+ of 71.

So Markell returned to the minor leagues and in his first exposure to Triple A in 1952 he won 14 games for the Toronto Maple Leafs and led the

International League in strikeouts with 120. Markell went on to post ERAs under 4.00 in four of the five years he spent in the International League, winning 56 games in those five years.

But along the way, he got another chance. The Philadelphia Phillies signed him for the 1954 season and gave him a chance to make the starting staff in the spring. "I am sure I can win for the Phillies," Markell said in the December 30, 1953, issue of *The Sporting News*. "Maybe it sounds like boasting, but I feel I can take my place behind Robin Roberts and Curt Simmons and win my share of games."

Instead, the fifth starter spot went to the forgettable Bob Miller. How forgettable? You know the Bob Millers on the 1962 New York Mets? Bob "Lefty" Miller and Bob "Righty" Miller? This Bob Miller wasn't either of those Bob Millers.

But Markell's lack of fear is unsurprising since in the offseason he patrolled the Bronx as a police officer. Markell didn't mind speaking up. As he told *TSN* in the January 13, 1954, issue, "If I don't make it with the Phillies, I'm going to hang up my glove and quit baseball."

Instead, he kept on pitching and logged his third no-hitter by 1955. But by 1957 with his skills waning, Markell spoke out publicly about the fact that minor league players had no pension system. "We realize it might be tougher for us to get pension money than it was for the big leaguers," Markell said in the May 8, 1957, issue of *The Sporting News*. "But we're convinced it could be done. Naturally, we don't expect to get as much as the major leaguers do."

Markell did not accomplish this—minor leaguers still don't have a pension—but his willingness to speak out was remarkable. And Markel won 144 minor league games. That should have entitled him to some financial peace of mind.

26. Hal Schacker

Bats Right, Throws Right

Boston Braves, 1945

On the strength of an 18–7, 2.97 ERA season for Class A Hartford of the Eastern League in 1944, Hal Schacker, son of Rebecca and Samuel, got the chance to pitch for the 1945 Boston Braves. But even in the diluted wartime National League, things did not go well for Schacker. In 15⅓ innings Schacker walked nine, struck out six, and pitched to a 5.28 ERA for an ERA+ of 75.

But Schacker was just 20 and probably figured he'd get another chance once he paid his dues. Unfortunately, he never did. In September of 1946, *The Nashua Telegraph* reported Schacker would be the scheduled pitcher for Pawtucket— where he carried a 0.84 ERA—"if the latter isn't a member of the United States Army by gametime." Schacker had already gone through preinduction ceremonies and ultimately missed the entire 1947 season serving his country.

But back in civilian life, on the strength of a 20–7, 2.93 ERA season in 1948 for St. Petersburg of the Class C Florida International League, he was mentioned in *The Sporting News* as a possible Philadelphia A's prospect for 1949: "Connie [Mack], who took Schacker on the recommendation of [scout] Lou Finney, was impressed with his new pitcher's physique. Schacker, who pitched last winter in the Panama League, stands six feet, weighs 195 pounds, and is only 23 years old."

But Schacker didn't stick with the A's. Returning to the Florida International League, he posted a 2.75 ERA in 177 innings in 1949, but his record dropped to 9–9, which probably hurt his chances to advance. He pitched 1950 in the Class C Provincial League, splitting his time between St. Hyacinthe and Sherbrooke. After a dispute with management of the Savannah Indians of the Class A South Atlantic League, Schacker found himself pitching semipro ball in Canada by that summer. Soon enough, he secured a job with the U.S. Post Office in Florida, where he worked until retirement. By his death in 2015, this child of the Depression was an avid Tampa Bay Rays fan.

27. Cy Malis

Bats Right, Throws Right
Philadelphia Phillies, 1934

Cy Malis, pride of Philadelphia, son of Frank and Anna, learned the game of baseball playing on the hypercompetitive sandlots of the city. He was an accomplished player in this world when he got his lone shot with the Philadelphia Phillies. He allowed two runs in three-and-two-thirds innings in relief on August 17, 1934. He walked two and struck out one. The Phils lost to Paul Dean and the St. Louis Cardinals 12–2.

Thanks to the wonderful research of Gary Cieradkowski, we know that he then made his way out west, pitching for the Los Angeles Angels of the Pacific Coast League. That helped him meet the Hollywood connections who helped him find semipro work once his tenure in the PCL ended.

But there was so much more to his life. Malis played Major League Baseball. He served in World War II, sustaining wounds that led to a morphine addiction. His doctors gave him alcohol to help him off of the morphine. Guess what he got addicted to next?

He appeared in 37 movies and television shows and went on to found Narcotics Anonymous, helping many others after him fight addiction. It is hard to overstate how groundbreaking this was at a time when drug addiction was seldom even talked about.

And he even was a stand-in for a Stooge! According to Stoogeworld.com, it was for Larry.

Top 10 Cy Malis Films (as voted by IMDB.com users):

1. *Night Editor*
2. *Somebody Up There Likes Me*
3. *Destination Tokyo*
4. *The Undercover Man*

5. *Framed*

6. *Johnny O'Clock*

7. *Dangerous Business*

8. *The Court-Martial of Billy Marshall*

9. *The Fuller Brush Girl*

10. *Around the World in 80 Days*

28. Brad Goldberg

Bats Right, Throws Right

Chicago White Sox, 2017

Brad, son of Marla and Brian, is Ohio through and through. He grew up in Beachwood, where he was Bar Mitzvah'd, and returned to Ohio State University following a brief collegiate detour to Coastal Carolina. At those two colleges, he excelled to the point the Chicago White Sox selected him in the 10th round of the 2013 draft.

Goldberg made quick work of three levels in 2013, pitching to a 1.54 ERA with 49 strikeouts against nine walks in his first 35 professional innings. Chicago thought it had a future star. "He's a little older, so I think people shied away from him just because of his age, but we like his arm," White Sox assistant general manager Buddy Bell told MLB.com about Goldberg in February 2014. "He's got some sink, big, [Curt] Schilling-type looking body."

Goldberg continued to post impressive results with a three-pitch arsenal led by his sinker and by 2017 he'd reached the big leagues.

It didn't go well—an 8.25 ERA in 11 games, 14 walks against three strike-outs—but a strong track record in the minors made a better case for him returning than that small sample. He also recorded a pair of saves for Team Israel in World Baseball Classic qualifiers. He looked to be on the cusp of becoming a Jewish Jeff Reardon for our times.

It didn't happen, though. His walk rate kept climbing in two stops in 2018—first with the Double A Birmingham Barons, then in Jackson, Tennessee, once the Arizona Diamondbacks acquired him mid-year. That would be his final season in pro ball. He took a job instead as pitching coach for Ohio State. Maybe that's just where he performs best. After three years at OSU, he announced in December 2021 that he'd been hired as pitching coach of the Cleveland Guardians.

29. Zack Weiss

Bats Right, Throws Right
Cincinnati Reds, 2018

It's getting late for Zack Weiss, who is 29 and three years removed from his lone major league appearance with the Cincinnati Reds in 2018, though he did get back into affiliated ball when the Seattle Mariners signed him this past season. In Triple A Tacoma, he pitched to a reasonable 4.31 ERA with 56 strikeouts in just 39⅓ innings. Another chance is possible.

I hope he gets it. The one he received, on April 12, 2018, after overcoming nearly two years missed due to arm injuries, did not go according to plan. Entering a game against the St. Louis Cardinals with the Reds trailing 5–4, Weiss gave up a home run to Jose Martinez, then another to Yadier Molina. He walked Paul DeJong and Kolten Wong. He was replaced by Tanner Rainey, who fared no better, allowing both DeJong and Wong to score. The failure to record an out means Weiss' career ERA is...infinity. No one in Major League Baseball history—by definition—has a higher mark.

Weiss is not a pitcher who deserves an infinity ERA. He also allowed the game-winning runs on Jose Bautista's single in the 2021 Tokyo Olympics, ending Israel's run in a loss to the Dominican Republic. A win would have carried Israel into a showdown against the United States. It's not too late. A pitcher with Weiss' ability deserves some better peak memories out of what's been a baseball career of almosts.

The All-Time Jewish Team: Unbeatable

Starting Lineup

C Harry Danning 1939

1B Hank Greenberg 1938

2B Ian Kinsler 2011

3B Alex Bregman 2019

SS Lou Boudreau 1948

LF Ryan Braun 2011

CF Goody Rosen 1945

RF Shawn Green 2001

Bench

C Mike Lieberthal 1999

1B Kevin Youkilis 2009

IF/OF Danny Valencia 2011

3B Al Rosen 1953

OF Art Shamsky 1969
OF Sid Gordon 1948

Starting Pitchers

Sandy Koufax 1966
Barney Pelty 1906
Ken Holtzman 1970
Max Fried 2020
Steve Stone 1980

Relief Pitchers

Dave Roberts 1971
Saul Rogovin 1951
Jose Bautista 1993
Al Levine 2001
Scott Radinsky 1996
Larry Sherry 1959
Erskine Mayer 1914

According to the baseball statistician Konstantin Medvedovsky, this team in a 2021 National League environment would score 1,094 runs and allow just 496. What does this mean? It means the Jewish All-Stars would absolutely dominate in any league.

Let's start with offensive prowess. The 1,094 runs would exceed the 1931 New York Yankees for the highest run total for any team since 1900. That team was one of just seven teams since 1900 to score 1,000 runs, including: the 1930 St. Louis Cardinals, 1930 Yankees, 1931 Yankees, 1932 Yankees, 1936 Yankees, 1950 Boston Red Sox, and 1999 Cleveland Indians. Only the 1930 and 1931 Yankees failed to make the playoffs due to two extremely strong years by the Philadelphia Athletics—but the Yankees won 94 and 86 games in those seasons.

What kept these two New York teams from succeeding? Pitching. In 1931 the Yankees allowed 760 runs, which translated to a 4.20 ERA—third in the American League. The Athletics allowed 626 runs, which translated to a 3.47 ERA. In 1930 the Yankees' staff was flat-out mediocre—allowing 898 runs, sixth in the American League, and posting a 4.88 ERA.

Keep in mind also that these teams played in some of the most favorable run environments, while the Jewish team would score 1,094 runs in a what has been a pitching-tilted campaign. Hence, the most similar offensive team would be the 1950 Red Sox, who posted 1,027 runs in a less-than-ideal offensive environment era-wise, though Fenway Park played as a huge hitters' park. That team got a career year from Walt Dropo at first base (.322/.378/.583). Bobby Doerr had 27 home runs and 120 RBIs at second base. Johnny Pesky's on-base percentage at third base was .437. Vern Stephens at shortstop was an obscene .295/.361/.511. Even lesser offensive players like Dom DiMaggio (.328/.414/.452), Birdie Tebbetts (.310/.377/.444), and Al Zarilla (.325/.423/.493) were forces. Oh, and the other offensive starter was some guy named Ted Williams, who actually was well below his career numbers at a paltry .317/.452/.647.

The Jewish team outscored that Boston team by 67 runs.

Now let's compare the Jewish team's pitching performance to the best of all time. The Jewish team allowed 496 runs. That is an absurdly low number. To find competitors one has to look to teams in some of the most run-depressed eras. Let's go to 1968, which is informally known as the Year of the Pitcher. Bob Gibson posted a 1.12 ERA, and Denny McLain won 31 games. The Baltimore Orioles allowed 497 runs, and the Detroit Tigers allowed 492. The two teams finished 1-2 in the 1968 American League race, and the Tigers won it all. The difference between these two and the Jewish team? Detroit, the champion, scored 671 runs, and Baltimore checked in at 579. In other words, the two teams *combined* scored just 156 more runs than the Jewish team alone.

And it is no different in comparison to the other great pitching staffs. In a strike-shortened season, the Atlanta Braves in 1995 allowed 540 runs. The 1986 New York Mets allowed 578 runs. The 1954 Indians checked in at 504 runs.

Even the 1966 Brooklyn Dodgers, who got the full advantage of the same Sandy Koufax career season the Jewish All-Star team has, allowed 490 runs.

So what does this mean? Based on the Pythagorean win/loss record, which converts runs scored and runs allowed into a likely record, the Jewish team would post a 134–28 record—an .827 winning percentage. This would be easily the finest season in baseball history. The 1906 Chicago Cubs were 116–36 for a .763 winning percentage. They'd have finished far behind the Jewish team. Ditto the 1998 Yankees (114–48), the 1954 Indians (111–43), the 1986 Mets (108–54), and any other outfit in baseball history.

Make no mistake—this team would have been by far the greatest in baseball history.

Overall Top 10
1. Hank Greenberg
2. Sandy Koufax
3. Lou Boudreau
4. Ian Kinsler
5. Shawn Green
6. Ryan Braun
7. Alex Bregman
8. Al Rosen
9. Sid Gordon
10. Ken Holtzman

Fearless Prediction: Top Ten, 2035
1. Hank Greenberg
2. Sandy Koufax
3. Alex Bregman
4. Lou Boudreau
5. Ian Kinsler
6. Shawn Green

7. Ryan Braun

8. Max Fried

9. Al Rosen

10. Sid Gordon

2022's Top Jewish Baseball Prospects

1. Hunter Bishop, OF, Giants

2. Zach Gelof, 3B, Oakland A's

3. Jared Shuster, P, Atlanta Braves

4. Sam Delaplane, P, San Francisco Giants

5. Jacob Steinmetz, P, Arizona Diamondbacks

6. Andy Yerzy, C/1B, Diamondbacks

7. Jake Suddleson, OF, A's

8. Simon Rosenblum-Larson, P, Tampa Bay Rays

9. Evan Kravetz, P, Cincinnati Reds

10. Josh Wolf, P, Cleveland Guardians

11. Kenny Rosenberg, P, Rays

12. Shawn Gossenberg, SS, Chicago White Sox

13. Ryan Gold, C, Toronto Blue Jays

14. Ben Gross, P, Minnesota Twins

15. Tyler Uberstine, P, Boston Red Sox

16. Jake Miednik, P, Guardians

17. Mike Rothenberg, C, Detroit Tigers

18. Mike Lazar, P, Milwaukee Brewers

Acknowledgments

I received so much help and support in the writing of this book. Thank you to Noah Amstadter and Jeff Fedotin for believing in this project at Triumph.

A huge thank you to Adam Darowski at Baseball-Reference.com, who was incredibly generous with his time and research and, of course, Sean Foreman, creator of Baseball-Reference.com. Someday, you'll be in the Hall of Fame, Sean.

Thank you to Greg Casterioto of the Philadelphia Phillies and Liam Davis of the Baltimore Orioles for connecting me with vital Jewish figures past and present. Thank you to Eve Rosenbaum of the Orioles for indulging even my silliest questions. Thank you, Konstantin Medvedovsky and Dan Szymborski, for running my Jewish frames through their statistical windows.

Huge shoutout to the Society for American Baseball Research and to the great work of that organization personified in Jacob Pomrenke and John Thorn. Thank you to Bob Wechsler and Martin Abramowitz for their help tracking down obscure Jewish baseball questions and all their research in this field. Thank you to the countless journalists whose work I encountered

304 THE BASEBALL TALMUD

and relied upon through the Newspapers.com archive for telling the stories of Jewish baseball for over a century.

Thank you to my editorial team at *The Next* women's basketball newsroom—Jenn Hatfield, Bailey Johnson, Penny Guevara, and Jackie Powell—for always inspiring me and covering extra work that allowed me to complete this manuscript on time.

Thank you to my in-laws, Hilary and Jason, for always providing childcare when I work on my projects and bragging about my work like a blood relative would.

Thank you to my mom for always believing in the path I see and giving me the confidence to pursue it and to my dad for giving me the sense of historical curiosity and specific joys of baseball and Judaism that led me to this project. I am quite clearly the result of your emotions and intellects and I never lose sight of that.